W9-BGL-513

Issues in Native American Cultural Identity

Critic of Institutions

Roberta Kevelson
General Editor

Vol. 2

PETER LANG
New York • Washington, D.C./Baltimore • San Francisco
Bern • Frankfurt am Main • Berlin • Vienna • Paris

Issues in Native American Cultural Identity

Edited by

Michael K. Green

PETER LANG
New York • Washington, D.C./Baltimore • San Francisco
Bern • Frankfurt am Main • Berlin • Vienna • Paris

Library of Congress Cataloging-in-Publication Data

Issues in Native American cultural identity / edited by Michael K. Green.
p. cm. — (Critic of institutions; vol. 2)
Includes bibliographical references and index.
1. Indians of North America—Ethnic identity. 2. Indians of North America—Civil rights. 3. Indians of North America—Social conditions. I. Green, Michael K. II. Kevelson, Roberta. III. Series.
E98.E85I77 305.897—dc20 94-44264
ISBN 0-8204-2593-1 CIP
ISSN 1068-4689

Die Deutsche Bibliothek-CIP-Einheitsaufnahme

Issues in native American cultural identity / ed. by Michael K. Green - New York; Washington, D.C./Baltimore; San Francisco; Bern; Frankfurt am Main; Berlin; Vienna; Paris: Lang.
(Critic of institutions; vol. 2)
ISBN 0-8204-2593-1
NE: Green, Michael K. [Hrsg.]; GT

Cover design by Nona Reuter.

The paper in this book meets the guidelines for permanence and durability of the Committee on Production Guidelines for Book Longevity of the Council on Library Resources.

Printed in the United States of America.

ACKNOWLEDGEMENTS

I would like to acknowledge the support of the Philosophy Department at the State College of New York at Oneonta and of Dr. Achim Köddermann, whose comments and suggestions were always most helpful. I would also like to acknowledge the encouragement and support of my wife, Margaret, and my daughter, Megan. Finally, thinks to Marge, Andrea, Patty, and Rhonda for helping to bring it all together in good form.

Table of Contents

Table of Contents

CULTURAL IDENTITIES: CHALLENGES FOR THE TWENTY-FIRST CENTURY

*Michael K. Green

I. Toward the Twenty-First Century

With the demise of imperialism and external colonization, the twentieth century has seen the end of a five hundred year process of expansion of the European powers. During this phase of colonial expansion, Europe conceived itself as leading humanity out of a dark state of ignorance and into the light of day as it brought civilization to the many non-Europeans of the world. It claimed to possess the universal perspective of humanity in general in contrast to the more limited and particularistic perspectives of the other peoples of the world. From this universal perspective, all particularities were destined to disappear into the melting pot of a cosmopolitan civilization in which each person would give up his/her own particular cultural identity and take his/her place as a member of a new world order in which all cultural differences would disappear.

However, the civilizing mission of the Europeans was not embraced with open arms. These local cultures proved to be very resilient. In 1917 a Russia that felt its culture under siege by outside forces underwent a cultural revitalization under Marxism and attempted to opt out of the global system while attempting to create its own universal system that it thought better administered to the needs of mankind. This century has seen the rise and fall of the Russian empire. China also underwent a cultural renewal and sought out its own path independently of the emerging world order, and it too is undergoing a fundamental re-orientation. More recently, various Islamic nations have gone through cultural renewals in which "fundamentalists" have seized power and attempted to set their nations upon their own paths of development.

Stirrings of cultural renewal can be heard from other peoples and nations throughout the world. Within the British Commonwealth, there are ethnic stirrings in Cornwall, the Isle of Man, Orkneys, Scotland, Shetland and Wales—not to mention Northern Ireland.[1] In France, there are such rumblings among the Alsatians, Bretons, Corsicans, and Occitanians.[2] Spain is facing similar challenges from movements among the Basque, Catalan, Galician, Andalusian, and Canaries.[3] Holland has ethnic stirrings among the Frisians, and Belgium has the Flemish-Walloon linguistic problem.[4] Switzerland must contend with the Jurassiens,[5] and Italy with the emergence of the Lega Lombard, Lega Venetia, Sicilians, and Tyroleans.[6] In Romania and Bulgaria, there are conflicts with the Hungarian and Turkish minorities.[7] Czechoslovakia has split along ethnic lines. There are also ethnic splits between the Danish and the Inuits in Greenland.[8]

These awakenings of ethnic consciousness are found not just in Europe, but on virtually every continent on the earth. In Asia, India has three hundred and fifty groups of indigenous peoples, and many of these groups desire to be self-determining.[9] In the Middle East, Turkey, Iran, and Iraq must contend with the Kurds and the Armenians.[10] The relations between the Bakonjo and Baamba peoples in Uganda are typical of numerous such problems in Africa as are the recent conflicts in Rwanda.[11] The recent uprising of indigenous people in Mexico is symptomatic of a multitude of ethnic tensions throughout central and south America.[12] Chile has to contend with the Mapuches;[13] Brazil with over two hundred different peoples within its borders.[14] Finally, the United States has over four hundred indigenous nations within its borders.[15] Stirrings of cultural renewal can be found among them as well as among the African-Americans and the Hispanics within its borders. Many of the differences that were supposed to disappear with the advent of the era of cosmopolitianism are reasserting themselves.

Within this historical context, a volume that examines issues in the cultural identity of the Native Americans is so important. The world seems to be entering a new era in which plurality is and will become more prevalent. The tension between those who supposedly tend to the universal interests of humanity and those who are concerned with the particular interests of a specific culture are becoming greater and greater. A whole host of questions are posed by this pluralistic world. Is there a universal human nature? How real and basic are the differences that divide humanity? What is cultural identity, and how important is cultural identity for human existence? These are just some of the basic questions that call for a re-examination as the world moves into a new millennium. As an introduction to a collection of articles that in one way or another discusses issues of cultural identity in the Native American context, it is appropriate that this article begin with some reflections upon the concept of cultural identity and of its importance for the new era into which the world is moving.

II. Cultural Identity: Theoretical Issues

Two issues need to be examined—one arising from the identity aspect, the other form the cultural aspect of the concept of cultural identity. One of the first modern philosophical treatments of social identity can be found in Rousseau, who states: "[i]t is what these interests hold in common that forms the social bond."[16] These interests are the ties that bind the individuals together with a collective sense of community. They are, in Rousseau's words, the "heart,"[17] the "spirit,"[18] or the "mainspring"[19] of the group. Here three distinct concepts need to be distinguished. A group of individuals either have no significant commonalities, or they have some such commonalities. If the latter, either these commonalities are not consciously recognized as such, or they are.[20] A random aggregate of individuals is different from a group of individuals who have organized themselves so as to self-consciously give expression to their conceptions of their distinctiveness. Both of these, in turn, are different from a group with common traits whose members are unaware of their common identity. The first is typically referred to as a population, while the second is described as a nation. When it has a territory and has evolved its own mechanism of sovereign self-government, it is referred to as a nation-state. However, between the two extremes, there is the case of a group of individuals who share common traits and yet are unaware of themselves as having a common identity. These can be termed a people. Both Rousseau and Hegel dealt with the development of self-conscious nation-states out of peoples through a process in which commonalities came to be recognized and then served as the core around which the group self-consciously organized itself. Both were analyzing a process that has had special significance over the last two hundred years. Social scientists have validated many of the ideas of Rousseau and Hegel. They have found that a cultural group that constitutes itself as a nation-state goes through a typical set of stages. Initially, there is a people with a common culture. Through conflict with other decidedly different cultural groups, these people become aware of their cultural similarity. They receive consensual validation from their fellow group members and conflictual validation from the members of the other culture.[21] Once this self-consciousness has arisen, steps are taken to institute some form of political institutions by which the group can government itself and thus constitute itself as a nation-state.[22]

The notion of identity, then, has both an external and an internal component so that the question of identity unfolds on two levels. On the external level of institutions and actions, individuals have the same cultural identity when they share the same culture (a concept shortly to be analyzed). Through education certain values and traditions, which constitute a certain way of life, are passed from generation to generation. As the distinction between populations, people, and nations indicate, the fullest sense of identity, though, requires consciousness of identity. On the level of consciousness, individuals share an identity when they self-consciously recognize themselves as sharing the same culture. Thus, a culture identity arises through the exercise of powers of self-determination by a group which defines itself. Identity in the fullest sense is internally constituted by a group, and thus is an act of self-definition on the part of that group.[23] In this process of self-definition, philosophy and religion have a special role to play. Both are manifestations of a group's consciousness and conception of itself. They identify the shared values and core conceptions of people, society, and nature that are constitutive of the culture.

If it is true that individuals share the same cultural identity when they self-consciously share the same culture, then the question arises, what is a culture?[24] The concept of culture can be taken in four different senses. In one sense, culture is contrasted with that which is outside or beyond culture, i.e., with non-culture. In making this distinction, the question is, where is the line drawn between entities capable of having a culture and those that are entirely incapable of having a culture? Are all different groups of individuals, who are human beings in the biological sense, capable of having a culture, or are there some groups who are human beings in the biological sense but lack the ability to have a culture? How does one draw the distinction between those who are capable of having some kind of culture and those who are incapable of having any culture? In a second sense, the culture of one group is contrasted with the culture of another. In making this distinction, the question is, how is the culture of one group similar to or different from the culture of another? The last two senses of "culture" are used within a group of individuals with a culture in the previous sense. In a third sense, culture is taken in a relational sense in which the cultural is contrasted with the social, the economic, and the political. In this sense, culture refers to the more creative and intellectual aspects of a group's way of life. Culture in this sense refers to the art, philosophy, and religion of the group. Finally, in the last sense, a cultured individual is contrasted with an uncultured one, i.e., with one who has failed to conform to acceptable cultural styles or norms. This is an evaluative use of "culture" relative to the norms and cultural styles of a particular way of life.[25]

The Europeans collasped the first and second sense of "culture." They thought that no one else had a culture. They then identified European High Culture (the fourth sense of "culture") with the norms of acceptable cultural styles as the epitome of culture in the normative sense. The basis for this view was the premise that there were some groups of individuals, namely all non-Europeans, who had no culture. They were poor Caliphans existing beyond the reach of humanizing culture. The Europeans had the mission of bringing culture and civilization to these non-Europeans, who were considered to be uncultured savages—merely animals that looked like human beings. Savages were defined as cultureless animals. Several characteristics were supposed to be true of savages because of their culturelessness.[26] They were not processed or refined. They lacked development. Instead, they existed in a raw state. This rawness and lack of culture permeated all aspects of their existence.[27]

As savages, they were naked. This in turn was a sign of their amorality and lack of self-consciousness. Supposedly, Adam and Eve donned clothing only after they had eaten the apple in the Garden of Eden and, as a result, became self-conscious. Even when the savages were thought of as clothed, this clothing reflected their undeveloped and raw state. Savages wore raw hides, animal skins, feathers, or some other manner of dress that made them look like animals. Savages lacked the rules and directions of civilization. As a result, they had no inhibitions and no limitations as to object or circumstances on the exercise of their sexual appetites. Economically, savages were typically thought of as hunters and gatherers. As the latter, they ate uncooked or raw foods, and, as the former, they probably even practiced cannibalism. Savages had a total disregard for life and thus practiced various forms of self-torture and self-mutilation. They had no settled social, political, or economic organization and no concept of private property. Neither did they understand how to use resources efficiently.[28] Savages were thought to be born thieves as well as to be lazy and incompetent individuals because it was thought that they didn't respect the rules of property ownership. Their language, if they were thought to have one, consisted of one-syllable words and guttural and simplistic utterances.[29] Physically, since they were like wild animals, savages were well-developed. Their natural life was conducive to the development of highly developed senses of smell and sight. The core of Native American stereotyping consists of this concept of the cultureless savage.[30] Initially, the Native Americans were conceptualized in accordance with the medieval image of the wild man, who was supposedly a hairy creature living apart from civilized society.[31] According to the Puritans, the natives were unstructured and lawless. Contacts between the two groups could cause the Puritans to "grow wild."[32] Differences in types of cultural existence were equated with differences between those with and those without culture, so that the Native Americans were considered only marginally human.[33] Native Americans were thought of as being outside the bounds of civilization, devoid of culture, and "deficient in intellect, accomplishment, and culture."[34] They were "the zero point of human society."[35] The savage, being uncultured, could best be understood in terms of animal and animal behavior. Savages were often compared to animals–they were considered to be like dogs. Indeed, early pictures of Native Americans portrayed them as dog-headed natives.[36]

Instead of recognizing that non-Europeans had a different culture, the assumption was made by the Europeans that they had no culture and thus were living no better than an animal existence. They were savages and barbarians. In this, they were relying upon a mode of conceptualization that is a part of many culture's conception of the world–the distinction between the insider and the outsider. Outsiders were thought of as part of the undifferentiated chaos of the outside. Thus, they came to be seen as living a disorganized, chaotic, and lawless mode of existence because they did not conform to the cultural styles of Europe to which the Europeans were accustomed and in terms of which they organized their relations with the world and with others. Thus, there was a confusion between having a different order and having no order.

This is the background from which so much of the thought of non-European peoples must begin. They must demonstrate that they are not cultureless animals but human beings with culture. Thus, individuals with cultures have settled ways of acting and established procedures for dealing with problems. Uncultured individuals respond to problems in terms of immediate instinctive actions. Although such instinctive actions may have a natural order to them, they do not have a cultural one because they are not developed by human beings by themselves and for themselves. Thus, a culture consists of the total configuration of the patterned styles and themes of a people which have been developed over long periods of time. These are transmitted from generation to generation, worked and reworked by each generation, and provide the ways in which individuals relate to the world and to each other as well as the ways in which they understand and expressively re-create these relations. Culture can be distinguished into external culture, which consists of the economic, social, political, and technological styles of a people, and internal culture, which consists of the religious, philosophical, artistic, and scientific styles of a people. It is by means of these styles in these different areas that human beings develop structure and meaning in their lives.

By providing a set of settled pathways upon which individuals can develop their own variations, a culture provides a shared framework of expectations that allow them to work together. A cultural identity gives the individuals a sense of a common past and of a shared destiny. It unifies and integrates the individuals, gives them a sense of belonging, and a sense of their own uniqueness as a people. Further, a culture provides the individuals within that culture with a way of life that is constitutive of what it is to be a human being. It provides a framework in terms of which individuals can work out for themselves their own identities with their own styles, which are variations upon and a creative synthesis of the cultural styles of life available in their cultures. It is in terms of these that an individual finds meaning in life. Deculturation can lead to severe psychological disorientation, such as, dissolution of the self, a sense of meaninglessness, aimlessness, and depression. This creates a painful situation, which the individual then may attempt to escape by the use of alcohol or drugs or by self-stupefication through pleasures. In contrast to the European view which held that there was only one system of human meaning, it must be recognized that there are several such systems.

Cultural identity on the minimal level arises when a group of individuals share the same or closely similar styles in all or many of the above areas. They have similar styles in technology as well as in economic, social, and political systems. They have similar religious, philosophical, artistic, and scientific styles or themes. The groups with cultural identity on this level can be seen to be developing variations on similar themes. In the fullest sense, though, individuals have a cultural identity when they are self-consciously aware of these similarities in these areas, and when they consciously work within the same traditions and with the same themes.

The Europeans assumed that there was only one possible pathway, the European's, of developing. A cultural theme that was strongly developed in the Europeans was the organization of social institutions along hierarchical lines. This was mirrored in their conceptions of the world in that they organized the world into a hierarchy of existence. Thus, they posited a hierarchical and teleological organization of the human race in which the non-Europeans were at the beginning and the Europeans were at the farthest end of this path of development. Hegel probably developed this point of view most fully. However, once it is recognized that non-Europeans have cultures too, then, contrary to Hegel, it becomes evident that human beings have long ago passed from the uncultured to the cultured stage. There is no reason to think, though, that there is only one path to cultural development nor that there is only one way of being human.

The example of the Europeans show that cultural identities can not only be internally developed but also externally assigned. Cultural stereotypes are of the latter kind. Individuals act toward each other in accordance with their conceptions of the other person's identity. Individuals who are conceptualized as sharing one's own cultural identity are treated according to the background assumptions as to how individuals in the same moral community are to be treated. However, if the individual is not thought of as one who shares one's own cultural identity, then one typically may be uncertain as to how to treat that individual. Debates might arise as to whether the members of this group are or are not to be allowed admittance into the moral community and hence considered members of the group.

Throughout this collection of articles, the distinction between internally derived and externally assigned identities is central to an understanding of the problems faced by groups who have been the victims of cultural disruption but are attempting to reconstitute their culture. One of the first tasks such a group faces is to overcome the identities assigned to them by the disrupting culture in order that they might assert their own conceptions of themselves. This can be a very difficult and painful process as the externally assigned identities can be internalized by many members of the subordinate culture and thus can estrange them from their own cultural heritage.

The identity assigned to "the other," i.e., the cultureless savages of the world, by the Europeans and the Americans developed in three directions. By some, the Native Americans were assigned the identity of "civilizable savages." Under this conception, the savage can and should go from his state of uncultured animality to a state of civilization and culture under the tutelage of an educator or guardian. From this point of view, the Native Americans were thought of as childlike and as being dependent on the paternalistic care of the dominant culture. They can be tamed—raised out of their wild state—and as a result become assimilated to the dominant culture.

Another identity assigned to the Native Americans arose out of the conflict between the European and the Native cultures. They came to be seen as "Bloodthirsty Savages"—predatory animals that kill aimlessly and wantonly, that probably practices cannibalism, and that rape, pillage, and plunder for no other reason than the pure joy of destruction. From this perspective, the Native American is portrayed as the ultimate killing machine. He comes decorated with war paint, he carries a tomahawk, and he is always ready to scalp, torture, murder, and menace innocent individuals. It is this image that plays such a part in the sports world in which Native Americans often serve as emblems of bloodthirstiness.[37] As the threat of the Native Americans to the dominant culture decreased as a result of their extermination and/or assimilation into the dominant culture, this image of the bloodthirsty savage was transformed into the image of the noble, tragic warrior. Such an individual was doomed to defeat at the hands of a stronger power, but he/she met his/her fate with Stoic resistance and firm resolve. The Native Americans became the symbol of heroic resistance and tragic defeat.

A third conception of the savage can also develop out of this interplay between two cultures. Probably, every culture has some individuals who are disaffected and alienated. Modern civilization, which is an amalgamation of several cultures and which for many lacks any intrinsic unity, probably has even more such individuals, including some of their most prominent thinkers.[38] Among such individuals, an idealized image of "the other" can serve a critical function relative to the culture within which they find themselves. In this manner the image of the Noble Savage is born—an idealized image that typically reflects more the yearnings and dissatisfactions of those who created the image than the actual situation of the individuals upon whom the image is projected. In this vein, the Native Americans became children of nature living simple, innocent lives.

In these ways the relations between the two cultures is played out in terms of four types of Savages—the Bloodthirsty one, the Tragic one, the Civilizable one, and the Noble one. All of these images are the result of the dynamics of cultural encounter outlined above and thus have very little to do with the real life situation of the people that the image is supposed to portray. They reveal more about the culture doing the portraying than the individuals supposedly being portrayed. In addition, they prevent any real understanding from developing between the two cultures.

Thomas C. Fiddick in "Noble Savages, Savage Nobles: Revolutionary Implications of European Images of Amerindians" argues that some of the identities externally assigned to Native Americans by Europeans functioned to awaken revolutionary impulses among the European masses and to mobilize them to throw off the yoke of feudalism. Contact with the cultures of the Americas increased the range of what was thought possible among the general European population. Some Europeans thought that the natives of America were agents of Satan and that the natural state of humanity was a war of each against all. However, others thought that the natives were living as Adam and Eve did in the Garden of Eden. It was this identity that had revolutionary significance in Europe. Individuals at that beginning of time were thought to live in a sinless state of harmonious equality and freedom, and they were thought to exhibit charity and compassion toward one another. They were free from human greed and vices. Once Native Americans were conceptualized in these terms, as Noble Savages living in a state of innocence, individuals began to believe that it should be possible to return to this state of nature and to recapture these natural relationships among individuals again. This state of natural equality and freedom contrasted sharply with the feudal system in which there was inequality and a lack of freedom as well as a lack of charity and compassion on the part of the upper classes toward the lower ones. The nonhierarchical systems of the Natives thus helped give impetus to the revolutionary movement that destroyed feudalism.

III. Civilizing Processes and Externally Assigned Identities

Once the centrality of cultural identity is recognized, then it can be asked, is it possible to transcend cultural identities and develop a perspective from the point of view of the whole human race? This tension between universalism and particularism will continue to be a major problem for the forseeable future. It has too often and too easily been assumed that universalism is good and desirable. This question is beyond the scope of this paper. However, a more limited question isn't. Looking back on the past, it can be asked, did the Europeans succeed in expressing a universal point of view for all humanity, or were the points of view developed during Europe's various civilizing missions merely expressions of their own cultural styles and themes? As we enter the twenty-first century, it seems clear that neither in theory nor in practice did the Europeans succeed in developing a universal point of view. The European nations themselves were built up largely as a result of a process of internal colonization in which a supposed trans-ethnic and trans-cultural nation was created by the extinction and/or assimilation of other cultural groups. Thus, with regard to France, Safran states:

> It is increasingly admitted that the unity of the French state was the result of a long process of conquests, annexations, and treaty violations; that the peripheral regions that became components of France sometimes ended up with less freedom and democracy than they had possessed before; and that the impoverishment of Corsicans, Bretons, and Occitans that followed that incorporation was a form of "internal colonization."[39]

This centralizing tendency was exported to Germany by Napoleon and so with respect to Germany, Halfmann states:

> The foundation of the "Deutsche Reich" resembled more the extension of Prussia over a large territory than the bringing together of independent states.[40]

With regard to Italy, Noether states:

> Deluded by their own idealism, intellectuals recoiled from the real Italy. Through the struggles of the *Risorgimento*, caught in their own national euphoria, they had forgotten that Italy existed only in the minds of a very small minority. The vast majority, illiterate and speaking a medley of tongues that in some instances bore little resemblance to Italian, understood little and cared less about the new nation.[41]

These processes of internal colonization were often not followed to completion since, as discussed above, many of these groups still exist and are discontented with their subordinated status within their respective nations. External colonization was often a continuation of this process of internal colonization. Native Americans faced two such civilizing processes that arose from the Europeans.

The Latin Civilizing Process. The Classical communities of the Greeks and Romans were natural ones and, thus, admittance was initially by birth only. The Roman cultural complex within which Christianity matured was also a very hierarchically organized one. The Christian community, though, was one into which a person could gain admittance through a rite of initiation. This supposedly allowed the development of a broader based community than was possible under the tribal or city-state assumptions of a natural community. Thus, Baptism became the central part of a group of rites of initiation into the hierarchically ordered Christian community.[42] A person as a catechumen prepared for baptism through instruction into the ways and the Gospels of the church. In early Christianity, extensive studies were involved before Baptism. Through this rite, one participated in the death and resurrection of the Messiah, cleansed one's soul from past sins, and was thereby born into the Faith. Baptism was conceived in terms of creation by authorization. Thus, Christians had two births—one in the flesh and another in the spirit.

Since God was seen as the Father and Christ was His Son, the faithful could, through Jesus, become adopted children of God. The church itself was thought of as the Mother (*mater ecclesia*),[43] who gave spiritual birth to these sons and daughters through Baptism. Each bishop was father to his congregation. The abbot was the father to his monks. The English word "pope" comes from the word "papa," meaning father. Baptismal sponsorship and corresponding spiritual kinship relations came to be recognized. Thus, the baptizee, the baptizer, the sponsor, and the child's parent were linked in a spiritual kinship, "so holy as to take precedence over other bonds of kinship."[44] Thus, those who sponsored the person being baptized and were responsible for his spiritual development became his God-parents. The one who performed the baptism became his *Pater spiritualis*. A co-parents relation between the sponsors and the natural parents was also recognized. New opportunities for sponsorship were allowed by the church, so that spiritual parents for pre- and post-baptismal rites were added.

By the High Middle Ages, the hierarchical conception of the universe underlying the Classical civilization was elaborated into a metaphysics by Aquinas.[45] God became not only the head shepherd tending his flock but also an all-powerful authorizing father, who, by His authorizations, created the world. The whole system of kinship terms with which the hierarchical control of the children by the father was conceptualized was used to formulate Aquinas' great metaphysical system and the world became populated with Natural Law that circumscribed the authorized sphere of each thing. Each thing was given a vocation, i.e., an authorized sphere of influence and activity. Metaphysically, this view was developed in terms of the distinction between being and essence. Essence, which specifies what something is, signifies merely a possibility and not something that exists. Instead, existence must be added to essence in terms of the act of being (*esse*). This comes from God as He, through creation, pours Himself into the essences. By so doing, He gives each the amount of existence that its essence can hold.[46] In order to create the most diversity with the greatest order, He must arrange these essences in a hierarchical system in which He holds the highest place. By giving *esse* to an essence, He thereby authorizes it to exist. He withholds such authorization from others and so they remain mere possibilities. In a similar manner, Baptism authorizes one's admittance into the Faith and thereby gives one a spiritual birth or existence and admittance into the hierarchical chain of being. Catholicism initially had a strong Roman core and developed by the conversion of others and thus their assimilation into the one and only proper order. As it developed, it also came to have a strong Frankish core as the Franks became closely allied with Rome and vigorous promoters of the Faith.

With the discovery of the "New World," the question became, what was the status of the indigenous people, i.e., how did they fit into the hierarchy of being? Were they human beings or not? If so, then what steps should be taken to convert them, and what steps should be taken if they refuse to be converted? In 1537 Paul III declared Native people to be rational, and thus human, beings. Thus, they were capable of being converted. The question then became, should they be converted by forceful or by peaceful means, and, if the latter, whether with or without an understanding of the Faith? The Spanish explorers were mainly aristocratic individuals who were accustomed to hierarchical cultural styles. They also had a dislike of manual labor and little interest in becoming farmers or miners. Thus, civilization had taken the form of importing feudalism to the Americas. However, on April 16, 1550 Charles V suspended all conquest until it could be determined whether the Natives were being treated properly. Thus, a famous debate between Las Casas and Sepúlveda occurred. The latter argued that just wars could be waged against the natives for four reasons—first, because they engaged in idolatry and sins against nature; second, because the naturally inferior is made by God to serve the naturally superior; third, because the Spanish have the divine mission of spreading the Faith; and fourth, because the weak among the natives need to be protected from those who were stronger. The natives were inferior for many of the reasons already discussed. They were war-like, simple-minded, and had no private property, law, letters, or capacity for political institutions. They needed to be taught by their conquerors. Las Casas argued that conversion should occur peacefully.

The Natives were like fertile soil that should be cultivated so that they can be integrated into the Christian world in accordance with their God-given vocation.[47]

The Christians set themselves the task of converting the world because they possessed the universal point of view, i.e., the point of view of mankind. What seems more likely is that this point of view is a culturally constructed one that is valid only upon a limited set of assumptions about human beings and society, assumptions which may be true in one cultural context but not in another. In its New World version, the Latin civilizing mission had a strong Spanish ethnic core that was used to suppress other ethnic and cultural groups. Far from being a universal point of view, it was a limited and particularistic point of view claiming to be a universal one.

The Anglo/Saxon Civilizing Mission. The north European cultural complex out of which the code of private property and individual rights developed was distinctively different from that out of which the Latin code of Natural Law arose. The warrior ethos was very highly developed, and the group consisted of the armed warriors who came to the assembly (the Thing) armed to decide issues of concern to its members. The basic unity of the society was the *comitatus*, a group of warriors who competed with each other and with other groups of warriors for primacy of place within the group or society. The social order was based on conflict and alliance. The civilizing mission for such a cultural complex came to be conceived of as the subjecting of this conflict and competition to rules. This required individuals to move from a state of nature in which there were no rules to govern this conflict to the state of civil society in which there was a code that protected the individual rights of the competitors and distinguished between legitimate and illegitimate forms of conflict and competition. This too was a seemingly universalistic solution to the problem of human existence since it gave everyone the opportunity to enter into an agreement with others so as to form a political society and thus to have his/her basic rights protected from the predatory behavior of others. Individual rights were like social fortresses or defenses that were erected around the individual so as to keep him/her from suffering harm at the hands of others, who were always willing to inflict it. Thus, the natural state of physical violence and destruction was to be exchanged for a humanized one of a civil society based on individual rights and political, social, and economic competition, all sublimated forms of warfare.

This became the basis for the Anglo/Saxon's civilizing mission. Great Britain started with the invasions of the Anglo/Saxons, who took over the agricultural low lands and either exterminated the various Celtic people or pushed them onto marginal lands. This development was interrupted by the invasions of the Normans, who had superior military technology in the form of the armed knight and who by a process of external colonization established lateral ethnic ties and ushered in feudalism. With the further development of military equipment, the suppressed Anglo/Saxon culture, which was based on the family homestead and private ownership of land, was able to reassert itself. In pursuit of land to make the realization of this cultural style possible, the British then colonized America and other parts of the world. Far from having a universal point of view, this is the development of a nation out of a dominant ethnic core, which provides the cultural styles and themes in terms of which the non-Anglo/Saxons were to be civilized.

This background provides the framework in terms of which the civilization of the natives was to occur. This was strongly developed by John Locke. According to him, there were initially few people and much land. People were hunters and gathers. Being "natural" people, they ate "natural" foods, like, acorns, fruits, and venison, and they wore natural clothes made from skins, leaves, or moss. Thus, the hunters and gathers could own the fruits of the land, but not the land itself. The earth was held in common. Property arose when someone labored so as to appropriate a natural object in order to preserve his existence. Such appropriation was legitimate as long as it left sufficient quantity of goods of appropriate quality so that others could preserve their existence. No one was justified in wasting the goods of nature by appropriating them but not using them so that they spoiled and no one gained any benefits from them. However, under these conditions life was hard, because unassisted nature was so barren that it was difficult for an individual to wrestle a comfortable existence from its materials.[48] At this stage of human development, political institutions were based upon paternal power, since each small family group or clan subsisted by itself.

For Locke, history belongs to the industrious and the rational. Presumably, it was such individuals who invented agriculture. With agriculture came the notion of land ownership. By laboring on the land, the agriculturalist appropriated the land from the common store and converted it to private property.[49] The agriculturalist must take land from its crude, natural state and make it capable of being cultivated and bearing crops. He/she must clear the land, plant crops on it, fence it in, and kill animals (such as deer) that eat his/her crops. He/she chops down the trees that bear the acorns for the hunters and gathers. He/she removes the trees and bushes that provides them with fruits and berries. He/she kills the deer (or buffalo) upon which these people depend for clothing and shelter. Land becomes the principle type of property.[50] The conditions of labor also change. Under agricultural conditions, to labor is to subdue nature by wrenching it from its naturally crude and undeveloped state.[51] Indeed, these people were carrying out God's command to be fruitful, multiply, and to replenish the earth.[52] By so doing, the industrious and the rational contribute to the public good by increasing the total wealth available to mankind and thus making it possible for humanity to live under better conditions.[53] However, at this stage the productive forces were still very poorly developed, since no one had an incentive to produce more than he/she and his/her family could use. Thus, individuals lived in peace with one another, since there were natural limits to their acquisition. With the invention of money, the industrious and rational were able to further subdue and develop nature so as to use it for the benefit of humanity by further increasing the wealth of nations and making it possible for the arts and sciences to flourish.

According to Locke, the hunters and gathers required large tracts of land to move across in order to support a small population. Thus, they left a large part of nature untouched and unimproved. Land that was productive but not used was being wasted, and thus, a hunting and gathering economy was a very wasteful one.[54] Once agriculture was invented, hunting and gathering violated one of the basic laws of nature; it tied up resources in such a way that others could not deprive benefits from them. This in itself gives just cause for war against the native peoples. When the natives resisted this appropriation, a second justification was provided for waging a just war against them. Agricultural appropriation was legitimate, since it converted wasted into useful land. Thus, the hunters and gathers who resisted this appropriation were waging an unjust war and thus could be met with force. Only recently has the doctrine of vacant lands been repudiated as a principle of international law.[55]

The United States developed as an extension of this orientation. Through a process of internal colonization, indigenous peoples and nations were exterminated, displaced, and/or assimilated into the predominant Anglo/Saxon orientation. The United States imposed laws on the Native people and nations, removed and exploited their resources, suppressed their religion and culture, and placed restrictions on the conduct of their own internal and external affairs. The United States was involved in forty wars against the Natives, and it has been estimated that approximately a quarter million Native individuals were killed by the various government and government-sanctioned actions.[56] At the same time, through a series of cases beginning with *Fletcher v. Peck* (1810) and going through *Johnson v. McIntosh* (1823), *Cherokee Nation v. Georgia* (1931), *Worcester v. Georgia* (1832), *United States v. Kagama* (1886), *Cherokee Nation v. Hitchcock* (1902) and *Lone Wolf v. Hitchock* (1903), the lands of the Natives were declared open to development and the Native people were reduced to "domestic dependent nations." In 1885 the United States passed the Major Crimes Act, which extended the jurisdiction of federal power over the internal affairs of the indigenous nations. Then the General Allotment Act of 1887 was passed. This further opened Native lands for development by forcing the privatization of land and opening up the excess for settlement. In 1924 the Indian Citizenship Act imposed citizenship on all Natives. The Termination Act of 1953 dissolved one hundred and nine indigenous nations, and the 1956 Relocation Act attempted to force individuals off reservations.

As was the case with the Spanish civilizing mission, the individual rights point of view is a culturally constructed one based upon certain assumptions about human beings (namely, that they are competitive individualists) and society that are not true for all humanity. Again, we find particularity masquerading as universality. As with the Spanish, it could become the universal point of view only by destroying all other alternative points of view and converting individuals into the type of people upon whom the system is predicated by breaking down their cultures and assimilating them to the dominant culture. This process has been resisted not only by the indigenous people of North America but by other significant cultural groups around the world. The French, the German, and the Japanese have developed their own distinctive market economies that are decidedly different from the Anglo/Saxon model and which fit within their own respective cultural configurations.

Stephen Osborne in "The Voice of Law: John Marshall and Indian Land Rights" contrasts two conceptions of law. Law in so far as it claims to speak with the voice of civilization claims to be disinterested, universal, and grounded in a transcendent source. It claims to speak with the voice of reason itself. By these laws, hunters and gatherers, who leave land in an unused and wasted state, should give way to agriculturalists. The Native Americans are identified as civilizable savages who will move from being uncivilized to be civilized under the direction of American law.

However, if one moves beyond the form in which the law is presented and examine the content of the law itself, one finds that far from being the voice of reason law is a cultural practice based upon culturally-bound assumptions. Osborne details John Marshall's ambivalence as he move from one of these points of view to the other. In *Johnson v. MacIntosh*, Marshall spoke with an authoritative voice, while asserting that his decision was not based on natural justice but upon the necessity of preserving the assumptions of the system upon which the law was based. Thus, if that system was based on the assumption that discovery bestowed title and that conquest granted legitimacy, then the Court had no choice but to uphold these assumptions. In *Cherokee Nation*, Marshall appealed to the Founding Fathers and Constitution in order to discover a decision while writing into law the cultural narrative of Manifest Destiny and laying the basis for considering the Native nations to be domestic dependent nations who were in a state of pupilage to the American nation. Even when Marshall did finally acknowledge Native sovereignty in *Worcester v. Georgia*, the law was not able to be implemented because it was contrary to the cultural and historical context within which the law was supposed to exist.

Wilkins in "Judicial 'Masks': Their Role in Defining and Redefining the Tribal/Congressional Relationship 1870-1924" distinguishes three kinds of judicial consciousnesses. Each of these conceptions of law and the legal process posits a different identity for the Native Americans. There is the Constitutional/Treaty approach to law in which the justices of the Supreme Court conceive of themselves as merely interpreting and applying existing law as given in the Constitution and the various treaties into which the United States government has entered. The justices conceive of themselves as administers of impartial justice. From this point of view, the Natives are recognized as being members of independent sovereign nations. Another mode of judicial consciousness is manifest in the Civilizing/Paternalistic conception of law. According to this mode of consciousness, law is the best way of civilizing the culturally inferior savages. From this point of view, a distinction must be made between those who have been civilized and those who haven't. Thus, the Court posits two possible identities for Native Americans. One's treatment depends on how one is identified, because members of uncivilized groups are given a distinctively different legal treatment than members of civilized ones. The uncivilized natives are identified as hunters and pagans who follow "heathenish" rules and engage in practices that are "repugnant to morality and decency." Law has to be used to civilize these individuals, and this is done by replacing indigenous institutions with Western ones. Sometimes the Court seems to conceptualize all native Americans as uncivilized. Other times it seems to make a distinction between civilized and uncivilized natives. Sometimes it seems to recognize that some groups have become civilized by discarding their indigenous institutions and adopting Western ones. Nevertheless, even civilized groups have to be protected by the government since they need to be protected from themselves and from outside influences that could corrupt them. Thus, all Native Americans are conceptualized as child-like and dependent. However, some are more dependent than others. A third type of judicial consciousness is given in the Nationalism/Federalism approach to law. From this point of view, law is a mechanism for creating an American national identity. The function of law is to integrate the territories of the United States into a single nation-state by assimilating elements that have not been Americanized. From this point of view, all indigenous institutions have to be destroyed so that all peoples within the borders of the United States can become members of one nation-state. Native Americans are identified as non-Americans who need to be Americanized. Only the first type of consciousness recognizes the possibility of native self-determination or sovereignty. The other two treat natives as dependents of the government and provide the legal basis for the development of the notion that native peoples are "wards" of the federal government and members of "domestic dependent nations."

III. Revitalization Processes and the Self-Constitution of Internal Cultural Identities

These civilizing processes of the Europeans provided the conflictual validation that propelled many peoples of the world to become aware of their cultural identities and to unite to resist these processes of civilization. During times of rapid social change or among marginal individuals, i.e., individuals excluded from the social structure, societies can undergo revitalization processes. As a social structure breaks down and individuals can no longer maintain a sense of worth and dignity within that social system, an individual or group can formulate a new, utopian image of society. Often, these codes are formulated as a result of a prophetic or mystical experience. The individual undergoes what Wallace calls a mazeway resynthesis in which after a period of extreme stress the person's whole complex of values and beliefs are swept aside and replaced by new ones. The existing culture is thought of as corrupt and hence of needing to be destroyed and replaced by another. The new code is presented as offering salvation for the individual and society. It offers a way for individuals to recapture their self-respect and sense of self-worth. By means of hysterical conversion large masses of people can be converted to the movement. The heightened sense of mutual concern present in such movements provides a foretaste of the liberation to be achieved after the dismantling of the existing social relations. After the extermination of all evil, there would be a return to the lost, usually anarcho-communistic, order that existed at the beginning of time. There would be no human authorities, taxes, rents, or dues. Such movements tend to conceive of the community as a homogeneous, unstructured unity that transcends the differentiations and contradictions of the established social order.[57] They emphasize universal human values such as peace, harmony, fertility of the mind and body, universal justice, and the equality and brotherhood of all.

What has been hidden by the tendency to see history as a unilinear process cumulating in a world system based upon European models is the extent to which history has been driven by cultural factors. Indeed, history can probably be seen as driven more by cultural conflict and resistance than by class conflicts. Christianity initially arose as a movement among a marginalized people who were attempting to resist the Romanization of their culture. The Protestant Reformation was itself a movement by which the Germanic peoples of northern Europe threw off the yoke of Latin culture and its civilizing process. It was the beginning of a process of cultural self-awareness and the construction of internal cultural identities among various ethnic groups within Europe. The French and English revolutions can also be seen as cultural revitalization movements. The first involved an uprising of the Roman/Gallic culture against the Frankish culture that had imposed feudalism upon them. The second involved an uprising of the Anglo/Saxon culture against the Norman one that had imposed feudalism upon it.

The nineteenth century was full of indigenous revitalization movements in the United States. William Pencak in "Placing Native Americans at the Center: Indian Prophetic Revolts and Cultural Identity" examines the creative responses of Native Americans to their encounter with the European cultures. Far from being passive recipients of culture, the natives were engaged in process of creative synthesis and reformulation as they reconstituted their traditional identities in ways to strengthen them in the face of the challenges presented by the colonization of the Europeans. Cultures that are disrupted in fundamental ways so that they develop identities that no longer provide meaning to many of the individuals in those cultures typically undergo revitalization movements. During such processes, new identities are created after traumatic contact with another culture. Such movements are characterized by nativism, revivalism, vitalism, millennarianism, and messianism. As a result of these movements, a new cultural identity can be created. This new identity can take one of three courses. It can allow individuals to assimilate into the other culture, it can reject all influences from that other culture in order to maintain cultural purity, or it can combine in a creative manner attributes from both of these cultures. Pencak then goes on to discuss the problematic nature of cultural identity among other groups in the United States and to show how tenuous cultural identity has been for many peoples within the United States.

The twentieth century has also seen a plethora of revitalization movements as various cultures attempt to shake off the Anglo/Saxon and the Latin civilizing processes. Probably, the most significant for the early and middle twentieth century were the various communist liberation movements. Marxism served as the intellectual justification for a host of nationalistic cultural revitalization movements and the rise of a third cultural system claiming to represent the universal interests of mankind—communism.

Modern communism can trace its origins back to Joachim of Fiore in the thirteenth century. He influenced several of the Radical Protestant movements, who in turn influenced modern communistic movements. This can be seen at Frankenhausen in former East Germany where there is a fifty by five hundred foot painting honoring Thomas Müntzer. Marx undertook to secularize this tradition. In his version, those that were marginal in the current order, the proletarians, were going to rise up and destroy the whole capitalistic order. All its laws and legal institutions are based upon private property, and, since this was the source of the oppression of the proletariat, this must be destroyed. The Revolutionary Spirit would take possession of the masses and lead them to the New Jerusalem. Modern communist parties blend Weber's conceptions of charismatic and bureaucratic forms of authority so as to engender a charismatic bureaucracy in which revolutionary spirit, doctrinal purity, and dedication to the cause become criteria for advancement.[58] The Revolution becomes the only justification for everything that one does. Private property, the family, the state, the division of labor, scarcity, competition, exchange, nationality, class struggle, money, and cultural identity will all be transcended in the final stages of communism through the creation of an era of abundance.[59] In the religious version, God provided this abundance, while in the secular, technology and social production provided it. Finally, a true community based on the unconditional and all-round development of the individual will be formed and complete freedom, equality, and brotherhood will reign. When the objective conditions for egoistic individuality are overcome, then this selfish type of individual will disappear and be replaced by a new type of human being in which the social feelings are present in a pure and full form. Marx aims to create the objective conditions in which such social feelings are unbounded in extensity and maximal in intensity, purity, and duration. According to Marx, ethnic nationalism and even racial differences were to be ultimately transcended by communism. Marx thought that Africans were a degenerate form of humanity and that Jewish cultural identity, the sensuous nature of the individuals in the Latin and Irish cultures, and the whole Slavic race would disappear with the coming of the communist era.[60]

Marxism became tinged with a Russian ethnic core as it developed in the Soviet Union. The Russians were suffering from a type of ethnic occupation due to the fact that the upper classes were thoroughly Westernized, and they had a rather dismal opinion of the indigenous Russian culture. This allowed Marxism with its glorification of the lower classes to serve as the basis for the overthrow of the Westernized upper class and for a nationalistic revival of Russian culture. The Bolsheviks were able to garner the support of other ethnic groups with its pledge to respect their cultural autonomy. The Russian constitution recognized a right of ethnic nations to self-determination and to succession. However, as the Soviet Union developed, it became increasingly centered around a Russian ethnic core, since it was the Russian-centered Communist Party that could determine whether a people were a nation or not. Russian achievements in every field were highly praised and the state borders were closely monitored.[61] Also, ethnic groups were repressed and relocated. For example, the Crimean Tartars were first granted an autonomous republic. However, under Stalin, Russians were encouraged to move into the Crimea and then from 1928 to 1939 Stalinist purges destroyed the indigenous leadership. In 1944 Stalin consolidated Russian control of the territory, deported all the Crimean Tartars, systematically destroyed all their cultural monuments within their former territory, and placed them on reservations. With the collapse of the Soviet Union, ethnic tensions involving, Abkazians, Armenians, Azerbaijians, Chechens, Ingush, North Ossetians, South Ossetians, and various Siberian people are on the rise.[62]

Again, another system claiming to represent the interests of mankind turned out to represent fundamentally the interests of a specific ethnic group. Similar analyses can be made of other communist movements. Chinese communists were able to co-opt a nationalist movement by promising ethnic self-determination. It turned into a Han domination of these ethic groups.[63] Yugoslavia turned into a Serbian suppression of other ethnic groups,[64] and in Ethiopia there was an Abyssinian core that suppressed the Oromos and other groups.[65] Similar patterns can be found in Czechoslovakia and in Vietnam.[66] As in the cases of the Latin and the Anglo/Saxon civilizing mission, the communist civilizing mission operates upon certain assumptions about what a human being is. However, it turns out that these assumptions are not true about human beings as such, but only of humans within a particular cultural and historical context, and they can claim universality only by destroying alternative conceptions of humanity and other cultures and assimilating these other people to its conception of humanity. It can become universal only by eliminating other alternatives and thus recreating the world in its own image.

Marxism shares with the Latin and the Anglo/Saxon civilizing process the same assumption that all culture identities will disappear as a new supposedly cosmopolitan world-society forms. As people become enlightened, they will abandon their old ways and adopt the new ones. Thus, Marxism has, along with the other theories and processes of civilization, served to mask the extent to which cultural conflict drives history. Much of what has been considered class conflict is actually cultural conflict. There is also evidence that ways are usually found of moderating class conflicts that occur within a single ethnic or cultural group. All members of such a group conceive of themselves as having a common history and a common destiny. As a result, they typically develop ways to keep the group together, and thus they find ways to decrease class conflicts. All individuals are thought of as belonging to the same moral community and thus as having claims upon the community. One way in which class conflict within an ethnic group is moderated is through external colonization in which the ethnic group can expand by eliminating other ethnic groups. However, when class conflict occurs between different ethnic or cultural groups, there is no such assumption that all the involved individuals are part of the same moral community. Thus, the lower classes in such a situation typically are not conceived of as having a moral claim upon the community. Thus, they can be subject to very exploitative treatment.

Donald Grinde, Jr. in "Human Rights, Identity, and the History of

Indigenous Peoples: A Semiotic and Native American Perspective" analyzes the ethnocidal tendencies in the three civilizing ideologies that have made a claim to universal validity. These are the ideologies of colonialism, capitalism, and Marxism. Each employs strategies of genocide, segregation, and/or assimilation to break down and destroy other cultures. Nation-states posit a centralized political structure and a common history. Thus, in creating a nation out of diverse cultural groups, the dominant group must create a history that makes it seems as if the people in that "nation" did have a common history. Historians employ several strategies in order to achieve this end. The Natives may be obliterated from history in that there is no mention of them. No role is history is assigned to them. Thus, the Natives are given no identity. Alternatively, historians may impose identities on the Natives that makes it seem as if they disappear. Again, several strategies can be employed to accomplish this aim. One is to identify Native Americans as culturally inferior and hence destined to disappear in the course of history. Another is to identify those who don't assimilate as suffering from a moral deficiency (e.g. alcoholism), thereby denying them any historical significance. A third strategy is to portray all people as if they were the same because they are all human beings. However, since the historians conception of humanity is culturally and historically conditioned, by asserting that everyone is the same, the historian is asserting that everyone is like the individuals in the dominant culture. To counter these narratives that construct a common history for the United States which in fact doesn't have a common history, there is the need for perspectives on history to be developed from an indigenous point of view. Because it is through its view of history that a people constructs for itself its own identity and because there are many nations within the United States, it follows that pluralistic perspectives on history are needed in order to capture the aspirations of all the peoples within it's borders.

Laurie Anne Whitt, in her article "Indigenous Peoples and the Cultural Politics of Knowledge," develops this perspective further by examining the knowledge system of the dominant culture and determining how it legitimizes illegitimate forms of cultural appropriation. Such actions are made possible, she argues, because of two assumptions of the dominant knowledge system. The dominant knowledge system has been positivism and its lingering philosophic offsprings. By assuming that scientific knowledge in the Western sense is the only legitimate form of epistemological relation to the world, it in essence denies any validity to indigenous perspectives on the world. By assuming that knowledge acquisition is a value neutral process, it denies that any of the objections raised to the acquisition of knowledge about indigenous cultures could serve to put restraints on the acquisition of scientific knowledge on indigenous people by examining them and their culture. By these two steps, positivism denies any intrinsic meaning to indigenous perspectives and then mutes any moral objections raised about the treatment of indigenous culture as long as that treatment is done in the pursuit of scientific truth. Whitt finds both of these assumptions false. Indigenous cultures, she argues, have their own epistemology, which emphasizes the transformation of the knower so as to get him/her to fit into an ordered whole instead of the acquisition of facts and which places respect at the center of its epistemological theory. Also, positivists have not been able to consistently maintain their value-neutrality stance.

Positivists have had a fundamental problem developing a reasonable approach to the study of culture. In the hey-day of positivism, it was proposed:

> that in order to study a ritual dance in a primitive society we should not do what anthropologists have always done, that is, carefully inquire of the participants as to the acts and their meanings. Rather . . . we should project upon the stage a three-dimensional grid and with a stopwatch, plot the physical movements in space and time.[67]

As Collingwood correctly argued, positivism reduces all to mere events—happenings without any intrinsic meaning. However, human beings are not just bodies in motions; they perform actions, and actions can only be understood by an act of interpretation in which one "thinks oneself into the action."[68] One must look at the action not from the outsider's point of view, but from the insider's. Thus, the hermeneutical method of interpretation and re-interpretation within the continuity of a tradition is the method not only for securing understanding of another culture but for also exhibiting respect for that culture.

A culture is a fabric of meaning that has arisen as a result of a historical process of interpretation and re-interpretation. When two cultures meet, alternative systems of meaning are juxtaposed. Where one sees meaning the other sees meaninglessness; where one sees the sacred the other sees the profane. As was argued above, it is out of the interplay of these two cultures that externally-assigned meanings and identities are given to members of the other culture. These identities become the means for interpreting and understanding the other. However, being externally assigned identities, they are constructed more on the basis of the needs and demands that are internal to that culture than upon any understanding of the other. Real cultural understanding requires that one, to borrow and slightly modify a phrase from Collingwood, "think oneself" into the system of meaning of the other. One must become the other in order to see how he/she understands things. The fundamental condition for this type of knowledge is respect for the other and the systems of meaning that the other utilizes. Only by maintaining the integrity of the meaning system and then placing oneself within that system can one even begin to understand the world the way that the other does.

If one culture did not exercise force upon another, then presumably aspects of one would be reworked to fit inside the system of meanings of the other and by diffusion certain aspects of the external, and possibly even the internal, culture of one could come to exist within the other. Indeed, cultures seem to differ in the extent to which they will adopt aspects from another culture. Some have quite permeable boundaries, while others have quite impermeable ones.[69] Prior to the contact with the Europeans, there was in the Americas considerable borrowing and re-working of aspects of one culture by another so as to make them fit into its cultural configuration. However, when one groups uses force against another in order to eliminate it or to force its assimilation, cultural exchange becomes replaced by cultural imperialism.

In the Latin civilizing process, this manifested itself initially in mass and forced conversions. Later, as the limitations of these methods became apparent, it manifested itself in more subtle forms, such as in the attempt to find the hidden and original Christianity behind the Native world views. A good example of this would be Father Tempels' work, *Bantu Philosophy*. In this text, Tempels undertakes an examination of Bantu philosophy with the aim of uncovering its hidden Christian core so that the Bantu might more easily be civilized, i.e., led to Christianity. In this case the Bantu system of meaning was re-worked in terms of the Latin cultural complex and them re-imported to the Bantu as the true meaning of their system of thought. In this way the original system of meaning would be replaced by a new one that clothed itself in the appearance of the original one.[70] Insofar as coercion was used to promulgate this new system of thought so as to further assimilation, cultural imperialism would be at work.

In the Anglo/Saxon civilizing process, cultural imperialism took on a different form. It was less concerned with converting the Natives to a particular religion, (though Christianity was assumed to be superior) than with converting the indigenous people to competitive individualism. Thus, it took the form of converting the land and then the culture of the Natives into commodities. To have meaning within the Anglo/Saxon cultural configuration, something must become a object of contention among competing individuals in a rule-governed competition and prove itself on the battlefield of the marketplace of ideas or of things in relation to other similar objects.

Neither one of these civilizing processes appropriate the cultural meanings of the indigenous cultures. Indeed, if meaning is a matter of context and systematic relations with a system of signs, then it is doubtful that one culture could appropriate the meanings of another. Nevertheless, what can be appropriated are the vehicles that carry these meanings, i.e., certain aspects of external culture. In cultural imperialism, one culture undertakes to destroy these indigenous meanings by appropriating the external vehicle that carries these meanings, imbuing them with a new meaning derived from their own cultural configuration, and then setting them up as paradigms for the understanding of the indigenous culture in order to facilitate the assimilation of individuals from the subordinate culture into the dominant one. The dominant culture thereby attempts to define the social identity of the subordinate culture. There are three issues here. The first arises from the manner of appropriation of the vehicle, the second arises from the way in which this vehicle is reworked, and the third from the attempt to define the cultural identity of another group. With regards to the first question, the issue is, when can one group or individual come to legitimately possess a cultural artifact from another culture, and, alternatively, when is such a possession illegitimate and hence a form of cultural theft? With regards to the second question, the issue in the Anglo/Saxon context is, when is the commodification of a cultural artifact from another culture legitimate and when not? More precisely, if the sacred is taken as that which is intrinsically valued by one culture, then is the commodification of the sacred a form of cultural profanation and hence morally illegitimate? With regards to the last question, the issue is, doesn't the attempt by an outside group to determine the identity of those within another group violate the latter group's legitimate claim to self-determination and self-definition?[71] Is it legitimate to appropriate something from another culture, re-work it, and then claim to be selling something that genuinely reflects the original culture? Isn't this a type of fraud? This is an especially poignant point when the image promulgated by the dominant culture serves to hide the actual struggles faced by members of the subordinate group. These are the issues raised by Whitt's discussion of the knowledge system of the dominant culture and its devaluation of indigenous perspectives.

IV. Cultural Identity and Self-determination: The Problem of the Twenty-First Century

Cultural identity is going to be primary to the human condition. If the arguments of the previous section are accepted, then it must be agreed that the various frameworks that claimed to be developing the universal perspective of humanity were actually developing a culturally-bound and ethnically-centered one. Thus, as the new century approaches, particularism and pluralism are replacing this pseudo-universalism as various ethnic groups that have been repressed are undergoing cultural revivals. The important problems of the coming foreseeable future will be to build a framework in terms of which these different cultural groups can each pursue their own development free from the interference of others.

What is the basis for this moral claim of a people to develop its own cultural identity as well as the institutions required to give support to this identity? A nation is organized so as to preserve a certain way of life or culture. It will wish to preserve and develop its technology and its social, economic, and political institutions. It will wish to preserve and develop its religion, art, philosophy, and science as well as its cultural, educational, and religious sites. However, no nation can expect other nations to grant these protections to it unless it is willing to grant similar protections to them through formal agreements. Nations wish the perpetuation and furtherance of their own way of life. Since they claim self-perpetuation and self-determination for themselves, and since fairness and consistency requires that similar cases be treated similarly, it follows that they must grant similar self-perpetuation and self-determination to other nations insofar as they respect other nations and their right to self-determination. Thus, nations have a moral obligation to attempt to create through formal agreements a community of nations, that is, an international system within which each and every nation has a place and may flourish. This is done by formalizing the relations among nations by subjecting them to rules and regulations so that a common core of expectations and procedures can be developed upon which mutual trust, understanding, communication, and assistance can hopefully be built.[72]

Thus, the right of each people and nation to self-determination must be acknowledged. Each people has a right to determine their own fate without external interference and to pursue their own economic, political, social, and cultural development. Thus, a framework must be developed in which the integrity of nations and peoples are recognized and respected. Some people will be able to realize their aspirations only through the formation of their own nation-state. Self-determination for them requires sovereignty. Other people will be able to realize their aspirations within a federalist framework in which ethnic and nation-state aspirations are de-linked. Others, in which more than one cultural group occupies the same territory, provide more difficult problems.[73] Either way, the tendency toward creating strong centralized states must be reversed and the right to succeed must be recognized.

The United Nations has taken some steps in this direction. The United Nations charter recognize that all peoples have a right to self-determination. However, it has been reluctant to state that indigenous individuals are people and thus qualify for self-determination. However, the United Nations has also been working on a draft of a Working Paper on the Rights of Indigenous People. According to this, indigenous peoples have certain collective rights, which include the right to exist and to be free from genocide, ethnocide, discrimination, or forced assimilation. They have rights to their territories, to self-determination, and to international legal recognition.[74] The problem remains, though, of implementing this document and of decentralizing the many states that are suppressing the various peoples and nations of the world that are seeking cultural renewal. In many cases it is unlikely that states will on their own decentralize. Thus, pressure will have to be brought upon them from some form of international framework and bodies whose main function is to protect and cultivate nations, especially of nations within nations.

M. Annette Jaimes in "Native American Identity and Survival: Indigenism and Environmental Ethics" presents and analyzes several approaches to the creation of a Native American identity grounded in the concept of Indigenism and relates them to the environmental problems currently facing humanity. Bioregionalism is an important part of an identity based on Indigenism. From the point of view of bioregionalism, the earth consists of many unified wholes, which have arisen through historical processes. Thus, Indigenism requires a pluralistic and dynamic approach to the world and hence is directly opposed to universalistic and static approaches. Each whole consists of intra-dependent and reciprocally related parts, and each whole is specifically different from every other whole. A second important part of Indigenism is the Native Land Ethic. According to this, human beings have kinship relations with other organisms and natural features within their environment. One can develop one's capacities only up to the point at which they infringe on the ability of one's other relations in the environment from developing their capacities. A third important aspect of Indigenism arises from the special responsibilities that indigenous peoples of the former colonies, as guardians of the natural world, have for preserving and protecting the environment. As members of the Fourth World, which has been suppressed but which is reconstituting itself, the indigenous people will lead humanity through a process of renewal in which the environment and humanity's proper relation to it will be restored. Self-determination and self-sufficiency are needed by the Native Americans in order for them to be able to work out for themselves a form of life based on Indigenism and thus for them to work out their own creative solutions to the social, cultural, economic, and political issues that confront them.

In the twenty-first century, centralized states will come under increasing pressure from two different directions. They will come under pressure from below as a result of the various movements of cultural revival on the part of peoples and nations whose cultures have suffered as a result of the various civilizing processes that have swept the world over the last five hundred years, claiming to speak for mankind. On the other hand, they will come under pressure from above as a result of the further development of international law and international organizations, such as the United Nations. The challenge for the next century will be to develop processes and institutions by which this decline of the nation-states that have been built up through the various civilizing process can occur in a peaceful manner. Given, though, the state's ability to amass large military weapons and might, the prognosis for peace seems doubtful.

**Michael K. Green is associate professor of philosophy at the State University of New York at Oneonta.*

Notes

1. Michael Hechter, 1975, *Internal Colonialism The Celtic Fringe in British National Development, 1536-1966*, Berkeley: University of California Press, and Anthony D. D. Smith, 1979, *Nationalism in the Twentieth Century*, New York: New York University, p. 153.

2. William Safran, 1992, "Language, Ideology, and the State in French Nation-Building: The Recent Debate," *History of European Ideas*, vol. 15, no. 4-6, pp. 795-800, and Smith, 1979, *Ibid.*, at p. 153.

3. Linda Frey and Marsha Frey, "'I Have Become A Stranger To My Brethren:' The Role of Religious Dissent in Early Modern European Revolts," *History of European Ideas*, vol. 15, no. 1-3, pp. 437-441, and Smith, 1979, *Ibid.*, at p. 153.

4. Anthony D. Smith, 1987, *The Ethnic Origins of Nations*, New York: Basil Blackwell Inc., p. 28, and Smith, 1979, *Ibid.*, at p. 153.

5. Peter Loewenberg, 1992, "The Psychodynamics of Nationalism," *History of European Ideas*, vol. 15, no. 1-3, pp. 93-103, Smith, 1979, *Ibid.*, at p. 153.

6. Ronald S. Cunsolo, 1993, "Italian Nationalism in Historical Perspective," *History of European Ideas*, vol. 16, nos. 4-6, pp. 759-766.

7. Nicholas Xenos, 1992, "The State, Rights, and the Homogeneous Nation," *History of European Ideas*, vol. 15, nos. 1-3, pp. 77-82.

8. Gudmundur Alfredsson, 1982, "Greenland and the Law of Political Decolonization," *German Yearbook on International Law*, no. 25, pp. 290-307.

9. Joseph Schechla, 1993, "The State as Juggernaut: The Politics of India's Tribal Nations," Marc A. Sills and Glenn T. Morris, 1993, *Indigenous Peoples' Politics: An Introduction*, University of Colorado at Denver: Fourth World Center for the Study of Indigenous Law and Politics, pp. 46-74.

10. Amin M. Kazak, 1993, "The Kurds and Kurdistan: The Struggle for Statehood," Sills and Morris, 1993, *Ibid.*, at pp. 147-162.

11. Joshua Rubongoya, 1993, "The Bakonjo-Baamba and Uganda: Colonial and Postcolonial Integration and Ethnocide," Sills and Morris, 1993, *Ibid.*, at pp. 75-86.

12. Michel de Certeau, 1986, *Heterologies Discourse on the Other*, translated by Brian Massumi, Minneapolis: University of Minnesota Press.

13. Clausia González-Parra, 1993, "Aukin Wallmapu Ngulam: The Mapuche Nation and Its Struggle to Survive," Sills and Morris, 1993, *supra* note 9 at pp. 87-102.

14. Ana Valéria Nascimento Araújo Leitão, "Economic Development and Indian Peoples: Three Cases of Colonizing Indian Lands in the Amazonian Rainforest," Sills and Morris, 1993, *supra* note 9 at pp. 163-176.

15. Ward Churchill, 1993, *Struggle for the Land*, Monroe, Maine: Common Courage Press.

16. J. J. Rousseau, 1988, *On Social Contract*, translated by Julia Conway Bondanella, *Rousseau's Political Writings*, Alan Ritter and Julia Conaway Bondanella, eds., New York: W. W. Norton & Company, p. 98.

17. Rousseau, 1988, *Ibid.*, at p. 140.

18. Rousseau, 1988, *Ibid.*, at p. 109.

19. Rousseau, 1988, *Ibid.*, at p. 111.

20. Smith, 1987, *supra* note 4; Marc A. Sills, 1993, "Political Interac tion Between States and Indigenous Nations: A Point of Departure," Sills and Morris, 1993, *supra* note 9 at pp. 5-22; and Glenn T. Morris, "International Structures and Indigenous Peoples," Sills and Morris, 1993, *Ibid.*, at pp. 23-46.

21. Alvin W. Gouldner and Richard A. Peterson, 1962, *Notes on Technology and the Moral Order*, Indianapolis: Bobbs-Merrill Company, Inc., pp. 44-47; Peter Loewenberg, 1992, "The Psychodynamics of Nationalism," *History of European Ideas*, vol. 15, nos. 1-3, pp. 93-103; and Xenos, 1992, *supra* note 7.

22. Smith, 1987, *supra* note 4.

23. Marc A. Sills, 1993, "Political Interaction Between States and Indigenous Nations: A Point of Departure," Sills and Morris, 1993, *supra* note 9 at pp. 5-22.

24. For discussions of the concept of culture, see, Joseph Margolis, 1981, "Nature, Culture, and Person," *Theory and Decision*, vol. 13, December, pp. 311-330; P. J. Crittenden, 1986-87, "Kant As Educationist," *Philosophical Studies (Ireland)*, vol. 31, pp. 11-32; Gyorgy Markus, 1986, "The Hegelian Conception of Culture," *Praxis International*, vol. 6, July, pp. 113-123; Elena Gheorghe, 1981, "Culture from the Angle of Action and Creativity," *Philosophie et Logique*, vol. 25, pp. 95-103; Gregory Schufreider, 1986, "Heidegger's Contribution to a Phenomenology of Culture," *Journal of the British Society for Phenomenology*, vol. 17, no. 2, May, pp. 166-185; Nathan Rotenstreich, 1989, "Morality and Culture: A Note on Kant," *History of Philosophy Quarterly*, vol. 6, no. 3, pp. 303-316; Rita Gupta, 1982, "A Note on the Definition of Culture," *Indian Philosophical Quarterly*, vol. 10, October, pp. 65-84; Antonina Kloskowska, 1983, "The Autotelic Character of Symbolic Culture," *Dialectics and Humanism*, no. 1, pp. 153-163; and David Edward Shaner, 1987, "The Cultural Evolution of Mind," *The Personalist Forum*, vol. 3, Spring, pp. 33-69.

25. A. L. Kroeber, 1963, *A Anthropologist Looks At History*, Berkeley: University of California Press, p. 59 and A. L. Kroeber, 1963, *Configurations of Cultural Growth*, Berkeley: University of California Press.

26. Michael K. Green, 1993, "Images of Native Americans in Advertising: Some Moral Issues," *Journal of Business Ethics*, 12, pp. 155-162.

27. Claude Levi-Strauss, 1969, *The Raw and the Cooked*, translated by John and Doreen Weightman, New York: Harper & Row, Publishers.

28. This is implicit in Locke's treatment of ownership in the *Second Treatise* in which since the Native Americans do not mix their labor with the land they do not possess it. The same belief can be seen in Kant, who attributes the change from barbarity to civilization to agriculture. The belief that Native Americans were

"savages" and "barbarians" because they did not cultivate the land was widespread despite the fact that a great number of Native American cultures were based on agriculture. For discussions of the concept of the savage in respect to Native Americans, see, Roy Harvey Pearce, 1965, *The Savages of America: A Study in the Indian and the Idea of Civilization*, Baltimore: John Hopkins Press; Francis Jenning, 1976, *The Invasion of America Indians, Colonialism, and the Cant of Conquest*, Chapel Hill: The University of North Carolina Press; James Axtell, 1981, *The European and the Indian Essays in the Ethnohistory of Colonial North America*, Oxford: Oxford University Press; and Olive Patricia Dickason, 1984, *The Myth of the Savage and the Beginnings of French Colonialism in the Americas*, Edmonton, Alberta: The University of Alberta Press.

29. Jeffery R. Hanson and Linda P. Rouse, 1987, "Dimensions of Native American Stereotyping," *American Indian Culture and Research Journal*, vol. 11, no. 4, p. 40 and James R. Smith, 1981, "Native American Images and the Broadcast Media," *American Indian Culture and Research Journal*, vol. 5, no. 1, 1981, p. 83.

30. Hanson and Rouse, *Ibid.*, at p. 34.

31. Christian F. Feest, 1990, "Europe's Indians," *Society*, May/June, p. 46.

32. David D. Smits, 1987, "'We Are Not to Grow Wild': Seventeenth-Century New England's Repudiation of Anglo-Indian Intermarriage," *American Indian Culture and Research Journal*, vol. 11, no. 4, pp. 1-32.

33. Feest, 1990, *supra* note 31 at p. 46.

34. Hanson and Rouse, 1981, *supra* note 29 at p. 34.

35. *Ibid.*, at p. 36.

36. Feest, 1990, *supra* note 31 at p. 46. Also, see Thomas D. Matijasic, 1987, "Reflected Values: Sixteenth-Century Europeans View The Indians of North America," *American Indian Culture and Research Journal*, vol. 11, no. 2, pp. 31-50.

37. A. Keiser, 1970, *The Indian In American Literature*, New York: Octagon Books; R. E. Friar and N. A. Friar, 1972, *The Only Good Indian . . . The Hollywood Gospel*, New York: Drama Book Specialists; and G. M. Bataille and C. L. P. Silet, 1980, *Pretend Indians Images of Native Americans in the Movies*, Ames, Iowa: The Iowa State University Press.

38. Y. Lurie, 1991, "Wittgenstein on Culture and Civilization," *Inquiry*, 32, pp. 375-397.

39. William Safran, 1992, "Language, Ideology, and the State in French Nation-Building: The Recent Debate," *History of European Ideas*, vol. 15, no. 4-6, pp. 795. Also, see, Caroline C. Ford, "Which Nation? Language, Identity, and Republican Politics in Post-Revolutionary France," *History of European Ideas*, vol. 17, no. 1, pp. 31-46, and Linda Frey and Marsha Frey, "'I Have Become A Stranger To My Brethren:' The Role of Religious Dissent in Early Modern European Revolts," *History of European Ideas*, vol. 15, no. 1-3, pp. 437-441.

40. Jost Halfmann, 1992, "From Defeat to Demise: German Nationalism at the End of the Twentieth Century," *History of European Ideas*, vol. 15, no. 4-6, pp. 817-825.

41. Emiliana P. Noether, 1993, "The Intellectual Dimension of Italian Nationalism: An Overview," *History of European Ideas*, vol. 16, no. 4-6, p. 780.

42. On this see, Alter M. Bedard, O.F.M., S.T.L., 1951, *The Symbolism of the Baptismal Font In Early Christian Thought*, Washington, D.C.: The Catholic University of America Press, and J. D. C. Fisher, 1965, *Christian Initiation: Baptism in the Medieval West: A Study in the Disintegration of the Primitive Rite of Initiation*, London: S.P.C.K.

43. On this see, Joseph C. Plumpe, 1943, *Mater Ecclesia: An Inquiry into the Concept of the Church As Mother in Early Christianity*, Washington, D.C.: The Catholic University of America Press.

44. Joseph H. Lynch, 1987, "*Spiritale Vinculum*: The Vocabulary of Spiritual Kinship in Early Medieval Europe," *Religion, Culture, and Society in the Early Middle Ages*, Thomas F.X. Noble and John J. Contreni, eds., Kalamazoo, Michigan: Medieval Institute Publications, pp.165-181.

45. Etienne Gilson, 1983, translated by L. K. Shook, C.S.B., *The Christian Philosophy of St. Thomas Aquinas*, New York: Octagon Books.

46. St. Thomas Aquinas, *De Ente et Essentia*, c. 4.

47. Lewis Hanke, 1970, *Aristotle and the American Indians*, Bloomington, Indiana: Indiana University Press.

48. Thomas L. Pangle, 1988, *The Spirit of Modern Republicanism*, Chicago: The University of Chicago Press, p. 166.

49. John Locke, *Second Treatise on Government*, II, 32.

50. *Ibid.*, at II, 32.

51. Pangle, 1988, *supra* note 48 at p. 163.

52. *Ibid.*, at p. 142.

53. Richard Ashcraft, 1980, "The Two Treatises and the Exclusion Crisis: The Problem of Lockean Political Theory as Bourgeois Ideology," *John Locke*, Los Angeles: William Andrews Clark Memorial Library, p. 81.

54. Locke, *supra* note 49 at II, 43.

55. Glenn T. Morris, 1993, *supra* note 20.

56. Churchill, 1993, *supra* note 15 at pp. 46-47.

57. Victor W. Turner, 1969, *The Ritual Process Structure and Anti-Structure*, Chicago: Aldine Publishing Company, p. 92.

58. J. G. Merquior, 1980, *Rousseau and Weber*, London: Routledge & Kegan Paul, pp. 125ff.

59. Karl Marx, 1972, *Critique of the Gotha Program*, *The Marx-Engels Reader*, 2nd ed., Robert C. Tucker, ed., New York: W. W. Norton and Company, pp. 530-531.

60. Diane Paul, 1981, "'In The Interest of Civilization': Marxist Views of Race and Culture in the Nineteenth Century," *Journal of the History of Ideas*, 42, pp. 115-138.

61. H. Lorković, 1993, "Culture Conflicts and Types of Nationalism," *History of European Ideas*, vol. 16, no. 1-3, p. 241-245.

62. Daniel McIntosh, 1993, "The Crimean Tatars: Politics of National Identity and Return," Sills and Morris, 1993, *supra* note 9 at pp. 103-113.)

63. Smith, 1979, *supra* note 1 at pp. 115-149.

64. Jacek Lubecki and David Reichardt, 1993, "The Failure of Yugoslavia as a Multinational State: The Case of Croatia," Sills and Morris, 1993, *supra* note 9, pp. 115-134.

65. Asfaw Kumssa, 1993, "The National Question and the Right to Self-Determination in Ethiopia: The Case of the Oromo," Sills and Morris, 1993, *supra* note 9 at pp. 135-146.

66. Smith, 1979, *supra* note 1 at pp. 115-149.

67. C. K. Warriner, 1970, *The Emergence of Society*, Homewood, Illinois: The Dorsey Press, p. 20.

68. R. G. Collingwood, *The Idea of History*, Oxford: Oxford University Press, p. 215.

69. H. G, Barnett, 1953, *Innovation: The Basis of Cultural Change*, New York: McGraw-Hill Book Company, Inc., pp. 181-225.

70. For a discussion of the Catholic Church's latest attempt at understanding culture, see, Miroslaw Nowaczyk, 1983, "John Paul II's Concept of Culture," *Dialectics and Humanism*, no. 1, pp. 169-183.

71. For a discussion of some of these issues, see, Lynne Goldstein and Keith Kintigh, 1990, "Ethics and the Reburial Controversy," *American Antiquity*, vol. 55, no. 3, pp. 585-591.

72. Michael K. Green, 1992, "War, Innocence, and Theories of Sovereignty," *Social Theory and Practice*, vol. 18. no. 1, Spring, pp. 39-59.

73. John Howard Clinebell and Jim Thomson, 1978, "Sovereignty and Self-Determination: The Rights of Native Americans Under International Law," *Buffalo Law Review*, vol. 27, pp. 669-714.

74. Douglas Sanders, 1989, "The UN Working Group on Indigenous Populations," *Human Rights Quarterly*, 11, pp. 406-433; and Sills, 1993, *supra* note 23; and Morris, 1993, *supra* note 20.

NOBLE SAVAGES, SAVAGE NOBLES: REVOLUTIONARY IMPLICATIONS OF EUROPEAN IMAGES OF AMERINDIANS

*Thomas C. Fiddick

I. New Worlds and New Ways of Thinking

The debate over whether the impact of European exploration and exploitation of the New World was primarily positive or deleterious to the indigenous peoples has gone on for centuries. The myth of Eurocentered historiography, which eulogized the mission of Columbus and the subsequent missionaries in their civilizing and Christianizing of the savage infidels, was challenged by the so-called Black Legend school. The latter view, begun by de Las Casas and perhaps capped off by recent writers, such as Kirkpatrick Sale *(The Conquest of Paradise)* and David Stannard *(An American Genocide)*, has rightfully exposed the destructive results of Old World colonialism over the past five hundred years. Today, what needs to be explored is the ideological impact that the New World, and the indigenous people, had on Old World thinking. It is the contention of this writer that this impact, in the form of images that many Europeans received about the American natives, or Amerindians, seriously challenged and even undermined European institutions that we associate with feudalism; in exchange for seeing their way of life subverted by Old World conquistadores, the New World subverted old patterns of thought and helped give rise to revolutionary ideologies that culminated in a new Trinity replacing the Medieval myth of Father, Son, and Holy Ghost. I refer to Liberty, Equality, and Fraternity, or the self-evident truths that underlay that trilogy, and still underlie our most cherished and unexamined beliefs to this day, namely, Rousseau's statement that "man is born free" and Jefferson's declaration that "all men are created equal."[1]

II. European Images of Amerindians: Noble Savages

In his book, *The Columbian Exchange*, Alfred W. Crosby claims to be explaining the "biological and cultural consequences of 1492." However, he writes almost exclusively about the biological interaction between the Old and New Worlds, enlightening us about the different flora, fauna, and diseases that were "exchanged" after the first voyage of Columbus. Very little is mentioned about the images that Europeans brought back of the natives. What is mentioned is one-sided and misleading:

> The ancient and medieval pronouncements on . . . human behavior seemed to leave Europeans little choice but to condemn the Indians as allies of the Devil. For instance, Christians agreed that heterosexual monogamy was the way to handle the sex relationship. The Indians . . . practiced promiscuity, polygamy, incest and sodomy. The Europeans had either to conceive of . . . cultural tolerance . . . or to assume that Indians were in league with Hell. Most made the latter choice. The exception, of course, was Montaigne, who found nothing barbarous about what he heard of America, except insofar as "everyone gives the title barbarism to everything that is not according to his usage."[2]

There are several problems with the assertions made in this passage, aside from the fact that, except for the quote of Montaigne's, there is no substantiation for Crosby's claims. It is, of course, quite true that a popular portrayal by some Europeans of Native Americans as virtual demons was prevalent. However it had less to do with their actual, or alleged, sexual practices than their real or imagined savagery, wildness, or violence in battle. As Ray Billington has shown in his book, *Land of Savagery, Land of Promise*, such portrayals were prescriptions for genocidal campaigns against the "savages" and were often projections onto the Indians of the viciousness that Europeans exhibited in practice but denied in their psyches. As for Montaigne, he was certainly not alone in calling for cultural tolerance; moreover, as will be seen, he did not just call for tolerance toward New World peoples, but denounced European customs and policies, in both the New and Old Worlds. In doing so, he employed an image of the Amerindians diametrically opposed to the image of them as agents of Satan. To a great extent he might be said to have originated, or at least to have popularized, the image that has come to be called the Noble Savage. He did this in the sixteenth century, and he did so based on descriptions that European explorers made of the Indians.[3]

It is commonly believed that Jean-Jacques Rousseau coined the term, or created the concept of, the Noble Savage. That impression has been reinforced by the decision of Maurice Cranston to title the most recent volume of his multi-volume biography of Rousseau *The Noble Savage*.[4] In fact, though, the phrase was first used during the seventeenth century, long before Jean-Jacques was born. John Dryden wrote these lines in 1672 in his "The Conquest of Granada by the Spaniards:"

> I am as free as Nature first made man,
> Ere the base laws of servitude began,
> When wild in woods the Noble Savage ran.[5]

This is a lapsarian view of history, somewhat similar to the myth of the Fall, in which the idyllic paradise of the Garden of Eden is replaced by the expulsion, during which Adam and Eve were condemned to work by the sweat of their brows, i.e., to a life of servitude. It is the underlying assumption of the opening line of *The Social Contract*: "Man is born free, but is everywhere in chains." This assumption, that man's original, God-given rights to "life, liberty, and the pursuit of happiness" have been taken away in the course of history, buttressed our own Declaration of Independence, and also the promise that the French Republic made in 1792, when forced into war with the monarchies of Europe; I refer to the promise it made to offer "aid and fraternity to all peoples wishing to *recover* their *liberty*."[6]

The idea that man "in the state of nature" was freer than so-called "civilized" man—and thus also presumably happier—was not all that different from the views of men such as Calvin and Hobbes. (I refer to the theologian and political philosopher, not the cartoon characters.) However, they had assumed that such perfect freedom was bad; for Hobbes it led to a "war of each against all," since man was basically a "wolf to other men." (*Homo lupus hominem*) For Calvin and other churchmen, freedom of the will was what led to disobedience to God, the original sin that henceforth cursed all of Eve's children and led to innate depravity. However the new, secular version of the Fall posited a primitive society in which mankind enjoyed not only freedom but a state of harmonious equality and a relatively sinless existence. These qualities, along with a "Christian" attitude of compassion and a desire to share, were all observed, or imagined, by explorers who encountered Indians, beginning with Christobel Colon himself.

Although it is ridiculous to say that he "discovered" America, which had been found by Asiatic tribes crossing the land bridge connnecting modern day Siberia and Alaska thousands of years before 1492, he did "discover" something new to Europeans, namely, a lifestyle quite different from that of feudal, hierarchical Old World societies, which although Christian in name were scarcely Christian in practice. The peoples whom he mis-named Indians were described thus:

> whatever one had they all took shares of . . . They are so ingenuous and free with all they have that . . . of anything that they possess, if it be asked of them, they never say no; on the contrary, they invite you to share it and show as much love as if their hearts went with it.

They seemed to live in a state of what Marx and Engels would later term "primitive communism," for as Columbus noted, it was not possible to detect "whether they held private property."[7]

After thus describing what were essentially Christian values exhibited by these "pagans," Columbus proceeded to give this very un-Christian piece of advice. Since they "do not bear arms, and do not know them," he concluded: "They would make fine servants . . . With fifty men we could subjugate them all and make them do whatever we want." This, indeed, is what he and his successors did, or tried to do, over the next four or five centuries, in the name of, or the pursuit of, what Louis Wright has called "God, Gold, and Glory."[8]

Despite the resistance that was often put up against the European invasion of the New World, European explorers noticed those qualities of charity and compassion, which made the savages more "noble" than the ignoble Christians who tried to subdue them. In his book, *The Last Americans: The Indian in American Culture*, William Brandon cited the impressions of numerous explorers that reinforced the noble savage notion. Jacques Cartier in 1535 was landing on an island in the St. Lawrence and came upon hunters "who . . . freely . . . came to our boats without any fear, as if we had been brought up together," and actually helped carry them ashore. In 1541 Castenada described the "ferocious" Apaches as "a gentle people, not cruel, faithful in their friendship." In 1584 Sir Walter Raleigh's envoy, Captain Barlow, called them "most gentle, loving, faithful, void of all guile and treason," and he speculated that they seemed to live "after the manner of the golden age."[9]

This portrait of a "kinder, gentler America" may, of course, have been partly a PR tactic to induce more Europeans to venture across the Atlantic and to participate in colonial ventures. Hoxie N. Fairchild has suggested as much in his monumental work, *The Noble Savage: A Study in Romantic Naturalism,* wherein he notes that Raleigh was trying to "boom Virginia" as "a field for colonization" and that this "may account for the enthusiasm" of some descriptions of natives.[10] But such mundane motives would not seem to apply to missionaries. They were interested in saving souls, not making money; but some of their descriptions indicated that native Americans were already in a state of grace. One such missionary, writing about the Caribbean peoples in the 1650s, observed:

> They are all equal, without recognizing any sort of superiority or any sort of servitude . . . Neither is richer or poorer than his companion, and all unanimously limit their desires to that which is useful . . . and are contemptuous of all . . . superfluous things as not being worth to be possessed.[11]

A French missionary in 1721 marvelled at how the aborigines had maintained "the Simplicity and Freedom of the first Age of the World." In the 1750s Major Robert Rogers, writing about the Illinois and Missouri Indians, declared:

> These people of any upon the earth seem blessed . . . here is health and joy, peace and plenty while care and anxiety, ambition and love of gold . . . seem banished from this happy region.

A century later, as the Gold Rush and Manifest Destiny led to a greedy race for riches out West, anthropologist Henry Lewis Morgan was writing that Indian societies had "no gendarmes or police, no nobles, kings, regents, prefects or judges, no prisons, no lawsuits . . . All are equal and free." As for their political and economic systems, "Indian societies were socialist in character and governed, as a rule, by councils." Brandon and others have suggested that "the prevalent Indian institution of government by council . . . may have been one of the various factors contributing to the form of modern American republics," perhaps inspiring our "town councils." Some other authors have argued that our Constitution may also have been patterned after that of some Indian tribes, such as the Iroquois Confederation. For example, the fact that we were the first country to decide that questions of war or peace should be determined by an elected body, Congress, may have been influenced by our noticing that Indians had war "councils" making such momentous decisions, not "chiefs"—which were largely invented by European imaginations. Our constitutional prohibition against titles of nobility was likewise a conscious or unconscious emulation of our noble savage societies, which dispensed with the feudalistic hierarchies that often made nobles so savage toward their "underlings." The freedom and equality seemingly enjoyed by Native Americans were our ideals; but they were also increasingly becoming ideals of some Europeans.[12]

III. The Savageness of Civilization: Savage Nobles

Observations by New World explorers were instrumental not only in promulgating revolutionary notions about liberty, equality, and fraternity; but, by contributing to a contrast or comparison between lifestyles, they led to feelings that European societies were corrupt. As Fairchild argued, explorers who compared the New World to an idyllic, earlier period of history, whether the Biblical Garden of Eden or the classical belief in a primordial Golden Age, had a revolutionary impact on Old World beliefs:

> such a comparison with the Golden Age is particularly interesting. When men began to think of the American Indian in such terms, they were well on their way toward the formation of the Noble Savage idea.

That idea resulted "from the fusion of three elements: the observation of explorers; various classical and medieval conventions"—including works by men such as Ovid and Tacitus—and "the deductions of philosophers." The Noble Savage was, as Fairchild defines him, "any free and wild being who draws directly from nature virtues which raise doubts as to the value of civilization." Thus the "Noble Savage idea is to the modern world" what the "conception of a Golden Age" was to the ancient world, namely, a "protest against the evil incidental to human progress," which "looks yearningly back from the corruptions of civilization to an imaginary primeval innocence."[13]

It may be that this protest against the corruption of so-called civilization also contributed to the Protestant Reformation, which followed hard on the heels of the first explorations of the New World. Fairchild noted that throughout "the sixteenth century the feeling that civilization is corrupt is plainly evident." That revolutionary century that witnessed a rift in the [illegible]istian world, with its hierarchical and corrupt institutions, was [illegible]d by the discovery of different and decidedly admirable native

Americans. As Geoffrey Atkinson noted: "Many travellers and missionaries, even in the sixteenth century, mentioned the lack of private property among the primitive peoples" they observed, and "called attention to the generally happy condition of a primitive society founded upon equality and liberty." Such egalitarianism and happiness were in stark contrast to feudal and ecclesiastical institutions, which in turn caused much human unhappiness.[14]

The Noble Savage notion challenged traditional hierarchies and the assumptions of traditional Christian theology in another, more profound, way. A belief that man's basic nature, his impulses, were base and sinful was fundamental to Christian doctrine in both the Catholic and Protestant theologies, leading to the need for sacraments, priestly intercession, subordination to authorities, and the belief that happiness could only be achieved in the hereafter, since this world was a vale of tears and tribulations. Irving Babbitt, in what he dubbed *Rousseau and the Idyllic Imagination*, wrote that "one should note as far back as the sixteenth century an incipient glorification of instinct . . . that was later to culminate in the cult of the noble savage." This so-called "cult" assumed that man was by nature imbued with essentially Christian virtues, namely compassion—an "instinctive dislike of seeing . . . fellow creatures suffer." Thus, natural man, moved by pity, had impulses of "generosity . . . benevolence, and friendship itself," in Rousseau's words. Further, this:

> emphasis on pity leads to the setting up of a sort of inverted hierarchy . . . in the new evangel man is to be rated by his nearness to nature . . . As one ascends in the social scale, love diminishes, and as one approaches the top, it gives way to the opposite. As for the rich, Rousseau compares them to "ravening wolves," who once having tasted human flesh, refuse every other food, and henceforth desire to devour only men.[15]

What bothered Babbitt about Rousseau and his views was that they "flattered those at the bottom of the social hierarchy." The Noble Savage idea tended to "make the poor man proud, and at the same time to make him feel that he was the victim of a conspiracy." Thus Rousseau's was "the voice of the angry and envious plebian, who in the name of love is actually fomenting hatred and class warfare."

However, Rousseau had sixteenth century precursors in Sir Thomas More and Michel de Montaigne. *Utopia* contrasted the idyllic, New World community described by explorer Raphael Hythloday with contemporary,

Old World societies:

> where each man by fixed titles appropriates as much as he can, and a few share out all the wealth and leave poverty for the rest. It usually happens that the one class of men deserves the lot of the other. For the rich are greedy, wicked and useless, while the poor are modest and simple men, and by their labor contribute to the public rather than their own.

More also noted: "when I consider all" the governments "in the world today . . . nothing comes to mind except a conspiracy of the rich, who seek their own advantage under the name . . . of the republic."[16]

Montaigne's essays, especially "On Cannibalism" and "On Coaches" (sometimes translated "On Vehicles"), also contrasted two opposite societies, if not classes of the population, in revolutionary ways. In the latter essay, he had apparently read the denunciations of Iberian imperialism written by de Las Casas and other Dominicans, for he wrote concerning the newly discovered Western hemisphere:

> I very much fear that we have greatly hastened the decline and ruin of this hemisphere by our contact, and that we shall have made it pay very dearly . . . It is an infant world . . . we have taken advantage of their ignorance and inexperience to bend them more easily to treachery, lust, covetousness, and to every kind of inhumanity and cruelty . . . after the example of our own manners.[17]

Montaigne's sympathy for New World natives naturally translated into what could be called an anti-imperialist diatribe. In "On Cannibalism," written after reading *History of the Indies*, by the Spanish priest Francisco Lopez de Gomara, he praised the:

> courage with which so many thousands of men, women and children so often advanced and flung themselves against certain dangers, in defense of their gods and their liberty; and their noble persistence in withstanding every ordeal and hardship, even death, rather than submit to the domination of the men who had so shamefully deceived them.

In other words, the "noble savages" could fight, even though they preferred living in peace.

This aspect of the image of the noble savage has been overlooked, or distorted, by those interested in showing that Indians were warlike, not peaceful paragons of pacifism, before Columbus. However, this strawman image misses the point and ignores the radical ramifications of the myth.[18] Many scholars have noted that one of the passages from Montaigne's essay reappeared, almost verbatim, in Shakespeare's *The Tempest*, whose character Caliban, being a near-acronym for cannibal, indicates how Shakespeare had read Montaigne. The latter had described the New World natives and their societies as having:

> no knowledge of letters. . . no title of magistrate or of political superior, no habit of service, riches or poverty, no contracts, no inheritance, no divisions of property, only leisurely occupations.

Shakespeare's figure Gonzalo, describing what Aldous Huxley made famous, the "Brave New World," called it "innocent and pure"—a commonwealth in which there was "no name of magistrate," in which "Letters should not be known; riches, poverty, and use of service none," and in which "All things in common nature should produce" in such abundance as to "excel the golden age." Similarly, Montaigne, exercising his "idyllic imagination," wrote in that now well-known essay: "These nations are still very close to their natural simplicity . . . still governed by natural laws and very little corrupted by our own," in such "a state of purity" that they surpass "not only the pictures with which the poets have illustrated the golden age," with "mankind in the state of happiness, but the ideas and aspirations of the philosophers as well."[19]

One aspect of the Noble Savage and Golden Age myths that is sometimes noted is the incipient anti-intellectualism inherent in the emphasis on instinct rather than logic, simplicity rather than complexity. Fairchild, for instance, cites this passage from *The Praise of Folly* by that other sixteenth century humanist, Erasmus:

> The simple people of the golden age were funished with no . . . school-knowledge. Nature alone sufficed to guide them; instinct to prompt them how to live . . . so that by far the happiest people in the world are those who . . . . dispense with artificial training altogether, and . . . follow solely nature.

The idea expressed here "bears a rather strong resemblance to . . . Rousseau's first discourse," anticipating the Romantic revolt against the

Age of Reason. This, too, had revolutionary implications for the class structure of the Old World, for it implied that more virtue and happiness exist among the "lower orders" than among the presumably more learned, lettered upper classes. Or, as Erasmus put it, "no class of men is happier than that of those whom the world calls simpletons," for they allegedly "feel no shame . . . no ambition, no envy," whereas "besotted men of wisdom" are "racked by anxiety," such as "the dread of death" and other "impending evils." In short, "ignorance is bliss," while book-learning breeds misery.[20]

Erasmus, of course, the great humanist and classical scholar, was not advocating this viewpoint but merely presenting it as one of several "follies" to which humans are heir. What Fairchild wrote of Montaigne is probably not true of Erasmus: "He himself was quite civilized . . . and learned enough to feel the futility of civilization and learning." However, Montaigne was not so interested in the "futility" of "civilization and learning" as he was in the "utility" of the New World, which he used as a kind of fencing foil with which to prick the balloon of Old World pride and self-righteousness. What he did was to expose the hypocrisy of his contemporaries, saying even cannibals were noble compared to the "treachery, disloyalty, tyranny, and cruelty, which are our common faults."

In dealing with the reports of cannibalism among natives of Brazil, the Frenchman wrote:

> We are justified . . . in calling these people barbarians by reference to the laws of reason, but not in comparison with ourselves, who surpass them in every kind of barbarity . . . I do not believe that there is anything barbarous or savage about them.[21]

After vividly describing how they would take a prisoner, "despatch them with their swords . . . roast him, eat him . . . and send portions to their absent friends," he then compared that to an *auto da fe*:

> I consider it more barbarous . . . to tear by rack and torture a body still full of feeling, to roast it by degrees—a practice we have seen in recent memory . . . under the cloak of piety and religion—than to roast and eat a man after he is dead.

This essay may well have influenced that other French cynic and critic, Voltaire, whose *Candide* catalogued every conceivable example of human cruelty done under the "cloak of piety and religion," including burnings at the stake by the Inquisition. Moreover, the practice of cannibalism, in Voltaire's treatment of it in the famous novelette, is more or less excused, or explained, as a natural response to the treatment meted out by Jesuits in Paraguay. By contrast, the inaccessible kingdom of El Dorado had been "safe from the rapacity of European nations." There the people were living like the noble savages as described by so many explorers, and by Montaigne, More, Shakespeare, and others; there were neither courts, nor lawsuits, nor prisons, as though they had taken that piece of Shakespearean advice: "first we kill all the lawyers."[22]

This vision of a utopian El Dorado in which all are treated in humane fashion resembled descriptions made by that early historian of the New World, Peter Martyr, who "rhapsodized on the absence of deceit and pestiferous money" among natives, and also the lack of "laws and quarreling judges," concluding that the "Indians seemed to live in that golden world of which the ancients had spoken"—which in the case of El Dorado literally included so much gold that it was not considered valuable or worth grabbing.

This view of a pristine world, free from human greed and vice, was not simply a harmless myth, or, what Gilbert Chinard termed, an "American exoticism." It led to a Sorelian myth, that is, a vision of the future which could also become a call to revolutionary action and be directed against forms of property as well as against classes. The famous Encyclopedist, Denis Diderot, expressed it this way:

> I am convinced that there cannot be true happiness for the human species except in a social state in which there is neither king nor magistrate nor priest nor laws nor thine nor mine nor property moveable or real, nor vices.[23]

This vision of what an ideal society should *dispense with* inspired in later years a kind of anarcho-communist movement in Europe. As James Joll noted in his history of Anarchism, "the notion of the Noble Savage" became:

> dear to all anarchists' hearts . . . The idea of a happy primitive world, a state of nature in which, so far from being engaged in a struggle of all against all, men lived in a state of mutual cooperation, was to have an appeal to anarchists of all kinds.

Joll attributes the noble savage idea exclusively to Jean-Jacques Rousseau. However, as we have seen, the idea long predated that political philosopher, who after all had a rather pessimistic view of what humans could accomplish. In explaining how it was that freeborn men could end up in chains, he described the "origins of society" as a "system of laws that imposed new chains on the weak," a contract which:

> gave new power to the rich; which destroyed natural liberty forever and permanently established . . . inequality . . . subjecting mankind to labor, slavery and misery for all time, to the advantage of a few ambitious men.[24]

This was a radically new view of that "Great Chain of Being" idea which justified hierarchy for so many centuries as representing the will of God.

This view of how man has "progressed," or rather regressed, from a state of freedom and equality to a society based on a tiny minority at the top enslaving the vast majority had obvious revolutionary implications. It fostered a sense of class consciousness and class hatred. Such a sense of injustice was even expressed by the Native Americans themselves. As Montaigne noted, when some of those New World "natives" were brought back to Europe, they "found it strange that the poverty stricken" peoples "should suffer injustice, and . . . not take the others by the throat and set fire to their houses." This, of course, is exactly what happened in 1789, as serfs burned down the nobles' manor houses, and later, in the Reign of Terror, the nobles were not only "taken by the throat" but had their throats operated on by the revolution's razor.[25]

IV. Revolution: The Return to the Natural Nobility of Humanity

What the idea of the Noble Savage led to was a rather savage treatment of the nobility in Europe, which got a taste of its own savage treatment of the poor. On a more elevated level, in terms of the history of ideas, the Noble Savage notion supplanted the old medieval belief in a Great Chain of Being. That idea had buttressed the political and religious hierarchies for centuries, by instilling in the populace a feeling that all blessings flowed from above, from God, Pope, King and from Lord, Prince, and Priest. Now, thanks in large part to a sympathetic portrayal of American natives, those at the bottom of the social pyramid were seen as more virtuous than those higher up. "Nobility" was not a quality reserved for a tiny handful of men, due to accidental birth or by virtue of inherited title and land; nobility was bequeathed to all mankind by Nature, and "natural man" was freer, more equal, and more admirable than the supposedly civilized men of status in Christian Europe. Man in the "state of nature" did not live a "nasty, poor, brutish and short" existence, as Hobbes described it; on the contrary, such a man was more likely to be compassionate toward his fellow man than so-called Christians, and life for him was seemingly a "terrestrial paradise," as Columbus himself first described the New World.

The way in which Europeans plundered that "paradise," and enslaved millions of Africans as well as native Indians to help in that plunder, also contributed to the revolutionary ramifications of the Noble Savage idea. If Columbus and his descendants had not descended like disease-spreading locusts on the Americas, ravaging the people and the environment in pursuit of gold, images might have been quite different. However, when atrocities committed by Old World conquerors were compared with the relatively innocent, idyllic societies that suffered from European colonization, "invidious distinctions" were bound to be made and a radical critique of the class-ridden societies of the conquerors resulted.

What happened to the Noble Savage idea was somewhat similar to the way the Great Chain of Being concept became transformed into a theory of evolution. Arthur O. Lovejoy, the father of Intellectual History, began the tenth chapter of his magnum opus, *The Great Chain of Being*, with words which might also be applied to the history of the Noble Savage notion.[26]

> It is one of the instructive ironies of the history of ideas that a principle introduced by one generation in the service of a . . . philosophic mood congenial to it often proves to contain the germ of a contrary tendency—to be, by virtue of its hidden implication, the destroyer of that *Zeitgeist* to which it was meant to minister.

Lovejoy went on in this chapter, titled "Romanticism and the Principle of Plenitude," to show how the static, hierarchical idea of a Chain of Being was "temporalized," placed in a time continuum. When that occurred, a transformation took place leading from "emanationism and creationism to . . . what may best be called radical evolutionism." A dynamic, romantic idea that all beings are striving, or evolving, from lower to higher forms, or toward Perfection, was derived from, but destructive toward, the older hierarchical idea.

In the same way the Noble Savage concept destroyed a feudalistic *Zeitgeist*. What began as a simple observation that people in the New World were exotically different, leading a simpler lifestyle that could be "used" or exploited by more sophisticated, powerful peoples from the Old World, became transformed by being "temporalized." In other words, when Amerindian societies began to be seen as representing a mythical, primitive *period of history*—a Golden Age or primordial paradise which preceded later, more "civilized" society—the idea developed that man was born to be free and equal, endowed with certain inalienable rights. Since those rights had been taken away by tyrannical kings or classes, the logical conclusion was that revolution was needed—not evolution. Like revolutions of the planets, which return from where they began, political revolutions were a process in which people and their societies would return to that state of things in which, like primitive man, all would have their rights restored, their rights to life, liberty and pursuit of happiness.[27]

**Professor Thomas C. Fiddick is Professor of History at the University of Evansville, Evansville, Indiana.*

Notes

1. A brief but insightful discussion of the Black Legend school, which includes a good annotated bibliography, is to be found in Daniel C. Scavone's, 1992, *The Importance of Christopher Columbus*, San Diego: Lucent Books, pp. 67-70 and 90-92. Unfortunately, it does not mention David Stannard's recent study of European genocidal policies toward American peoples. See his, 1992, *American Holocaust: Columbus and the Conquest of the New World*, Oxford U. Press, or his article in the October 19, 1992 issue of *The Nation*, in which he reiterates his assertion that between sixty and eighty million Amerindians perished by the end of the 16th century, "the most thoroughgoing genocide in . . . history" (p. 430).

2. Alfred W. Crosby, 1972, *The Columbian Exchange*, Westport, CT: Greenwood Press, p. 10.

3. Ray Billington, America's foremost historian of the U.S. West, in, 1981, *Land of Savagery, Land of Promise: The European Image of the American Frontier in the Nineteenth Century*, New York and London: W.W. Norton & Co., has shown how European writers "demonized" the indigenous peoples in the process of exterminating them, especially in the nineteenth century "Indian Wars," although some writers idealized their "noble" way of life. See especially Chapters 1, 2, and 5. Contrary to Crosby, it was not the discovery by voyeuristic voyagers of the Natives' alleged sexual perversity and practices that led Europeans to demonize the Indians; the central cause according to Billington lay in a series of sensational and fictional "captivity narratives." Sympathetic portrayals were reinforced by "the findings of American scientists" who observed and studied their cultures (p. 16). Another work dealing with this subject is Gaile McGregor, 1988, *The Noble Savage in the New World Garden*, Toronto: Toronto U. Press. Neither work analyses the revolutionary implications of Noble Savage ideologies, or their impact on European institutions.

4. Cranston's meticulously researched volume, 1991, *Noble Savage*, Chicago: U. of Chicago Press, does not explicitly explain how views of Native Americans influenced Rousseau's outlook; nor does it indicate how Montaigne's writings on the subject may have been an influence. However, one may infer such influences implicitly in his analysis of *Emile* and the *Discourse on Inequality*.

5. Cited in Hoxie N. Fairchild, 1961, *The Noble Savage: A Study in Romantic Naturalism*, New York: Russell & Russell, p. 29.

6. Cited in R.R. Palmer, 1964, *The Age of Democratic Revolution, II: The Struggle*, Princeton: Princeton U. Press, p. 3.

7. Cited in Fairchild, 1961, *op. cit.*, pp. 8-10; Billington, 1981, pp. 1-3; Scavone, 1992, pp. 35-38. See also Zvi Dor-Ner, 1991, *Columbus and the Age of Discovery*, New York: William Morrow and Co., pp. 151-3.

8. Another, more recent book employing those three "G" words in its title is John Dyson's, 1991, *Columbus: For Gold, God and Glory*, New York: Simon and Schuster.

9. These and subsequent quotations from explorers are cited in William Brandon, 1974, *The Last Americans: The Indian in American Culture,* New York: McGraw-Hill, Chapter 1.

10. Fairchild, 1961, pp. 12-13. Other sympathetic portraits of what were sometimes called the "naturals" by adventurers, like Drake, stressed how they were "civil and gentle folk"—even the peoples of Brazil, later reputed to be cannibals. If there were ulterior motives behind such descriptions, as part of an early advertising blitz for purposes of future colonization, one might conclude that Europe's "advancemen" almost invariably pointed to the natives' nudity in hopes of inciting lust among potential recruits seeking sexual as well as financial satisfactions. The Pocahontas story was a central aspect of such "bait" that lured European men in search of Indian maidens. One need not be a Freudian to note the libidinous urges underlying a passion for "civilizing missions."

11. The contrast between such idyllic descriptions and later reputa tions that Carib Indians acquired for vicious savagery suggests a change resulting from contact with Europeans. A fierce reputation may have been designed by natives hoping to frighten away rapacious intruders from overseas.

12. Brandon, 1974, *loc. cit.*; Billington, 1981, also noted that Europeans were favorably impressed by the fact that "Indians enjoyed a degree of freedom and equality unknown to less favored people." Furthermore: "Their whole constitution breathes nothing but liberty," since they insisted on "such Absolute Notions of Liberty that they allow no kind of Superiority of one over another." Their leaders had to "persuade, rather than command, their followers to obey" (pp. 16-17). Perhaps it is symbolic that the Boston Tea Party was staged by Sons of Liberty in Indian garb.

13. Fairchild, 1961, pp. 1-3.

14. *Ibid.*, at p. 17; Brandon, 1974, p. 5.

15. Irving Babbitt, 1924, *Democracy and Leadership*, New York and Boston, Houghton Mifflin Co., Chapter II, "Rousseau and the Idyllic Imagination," pp. 74-77. Fairchild rightly notes how

Babbitt exaggerated Rousseau's alleged "cult of the sub-rational" and the Noble Savage (p. 131).

16. Thomas More, *Utopia*, tr. Peter K. Marshall, 1963, New York: Washington Square Press, pp. 123-4. It has been argued that More was not attacking medieval institutions but actually defending monastic bodies. However, *Utopia*, was aimed at the feudal nobility as well as the new class of commercial capitalists. "Is this not an unjust . . . republic which lavishes such riches upon the nobles . . . and the goldsmiths and the others . . . who are idlers" (p. 123). Whether More modelled his ideal community on an imaginary place or on a New World society, such as Peru, as has been argued, is a moot issue.

17. Michel de Montaigne, *Essays*, tr. J.M. Cohen, 1958, Balitimore: Penguin Books, p. 279.

18. Concerning the question of how "warlike" the noble savages were see Francis Jennings, 1975, *The Invasion of America: Indians, Colonialism and the Cant of Conquest*, Chapel Hill, NC: University of North Carolina Press. Jennings exposed the "myth" of "savage war," which was allegedly unbridled and "uncivilized."

19. Montaigne, in Cohen, 1958, pp. 105-19; the comparison between *The Tempest* and "On Cannibalism" is explored by Fairchild, 1961, and Brandon, 1974.

20. Fairchild, 1961, pp. 18-19.

21. Montaigne, in Cohen, 1958, p. 114.

22. Voltaire, 1959, *Candide* [1759], trans. by Lowell Blair, New York: Bantam Books, Inc., Chapter 17.

23. Brandon, 1974, *op. cit.*, p. 5.

24. James Joll, 1964, *The Anarchists*, New York: Grosset & Dunlap, p. 30. Babbitt, 1924, asserted that this passage from Rousseau was "a direct source of inspiration to the bomb-throwing anarchist." (p. 76).

25. Montaigne, in Cohen, 1958, p. 113. This is not to suggest that Amerindians were responsible for class hatreds in the Old World. That had of course existed for centuries. For instance, Joll cites a twelfth century movement in Flanders whose leaders expressed a desire to "strangle the nobles and clergy, every one of them." Indians simply shared a common sense of outrage over injustice that all oppressed peoples feel.

26. A. O. Lovejoy, 1936, *The Great Chain of Being*, New York: Harper & Brothers, p. 288.

27. The admiration that many Euro-Americans had for Native Americans, their societies, and their way of life sometimes expressed itself not in revolutionary language but in actually becoming an "Indian." Hector St. John de Crevecoeur noted in *Letters From an American Farmer* that, although "we have no examples of even one of those Aborigines having from choice become Europeans," there were "thousands of Europeans" who "are Indians." See James Axtell, 1975, "The White Indians of Colonial America," *William and Mary Quarterly*, 3rd series, Volume 32, pp. 55-88 for more evidence of this amazing reversal which occurred, wherein the "civilized" Westerners rejected their own cultures in favor of a more noble, if "savage," culture.

"THE VOICE OF THE LAW": JOHN MARSHALL AND INDIAN LAND RIGHTS

*Stephen D. Osborne

I. The Rule of Law and Indian Removal

Vine Deloria, Jr. has recently complained that scholarly analyses of federal Indian law have tended to remain ahistorical and formalistic, focusing on correct explication of "the law" to the exclusion of the evolving social contexts from which that law derives and within which it has been applied. Like Biblical literalists or literary New Critics, "the propensity of legal scholars [is] to avoid the historical context in which events occurred and to concentrate instead on the documents themselves."[1] The result is a hermetic discourse of specialists aspiring to a kind of Newtonian textual science divorced from concrete social practice.

> Most of the new literature reads like a mechanic's manual, describing a machine with only three moving parts and using some multisyllabic words that are assumed to communicate some meaning beyond their ordinary meaning in common usage. No effort is made to examine the larger philosophical context of law and ask whether or not federal Indian law actually fits into this context. The tortured reasoning of various Supreme Court opinions receives no criticism and the idea that historical incidents may well have determined the context and content of the law, regardless of what either the Congress or Supreme Court might have intended, are quite foreign thoughts in modern federal Indian law. When law is made in this fashion, it becomes the exclusive province of the practitioner, and he acts pretty much the way a priesthood demands that he act. Law develops a language all its own and is no longer perceived to have any relationship with the lives of ordinary people. [2]

In part Deloria is calling for a multidisciplinary approach to the study of federal Indian law, suggesting that it must engage economic, political, sociological, and ethical issues rather than retreat into legalism.[3] I hope to do this by historicizing and criticizing the "tortured reasoning" of two Supreme Court opinions from the early republic, both penned by Chief Justice John Marshall in the early nineteenth century, that helped determine the rights (and their lack) of Indians to this day.

However, Deloria also points to a more complex issue involving the connection between the attempted detachment of legal discourse from history and society, and the role of law in legitimizing the imperial aspirations of the young United States. By denying or mystifying its social origins, legal discourse tries to ground itself in Reason, and thus ultimately in Nature itself. Marshall speaks with the quintessential voice of Manifest Destiny; like "civilization" in its conquest of "savagery," Marshall's reasoning presents itself, in Judge Benjamin Cardozo's words, as "the inevitable progress of an inexorable force."[4] A philosophical commitment to objectivity and neutrality becomes an insidious ideology when it is taken from the mechanics' manual and applied to the lives of "ordinary people" like Indians. The metaphysics of American law played its part in what Herman Melville[5] in 1857 famously called "the metaphysics of Indian-hating." I would like to pursue this argument first by using Alexis de Tocqueville's reflections on Indian policy in the young republic to frame the central problem of the rule of law, then by drawing out the theoretical issues raised by this problem, and finally by testing that theory through a detailed analysis of the texts and contexts of John Marshall's most important Indian cases.

It is useful, I think, to begin at the end of the story, with the physical results of the Removal policy legitimized by the legal system, before ascending to its "metaphysics." One of the more famous first-person accounts of a removal march was given by a French traveler who, in reflecting on the scene and the policy it represented, used the occasion to pose one of the most haunting questions in the history of liberal democracy. In 1831, a saddened and bewildered Tocqueville witnessed the removal march of a band of Choctaw Indians passing through Memphis en route to the new home in Indian Territory granted them by the Indian Removal Act of 1830. It was the dead of winter; the Choctaws were freezing, sick, destitute, many appearing "on the verge of death." Tocqueville recalls the scene in *Democracy in America* (1835): "never will that solemn spectacle fade from my remembrance," he declares. The stoic, or fatalistic, band trudged onto the bark that would take them across the

Mississippi. "No cry, no sob, was heard among the assembled crowd; all were silent. Their calamities were of ancient date, and they knew them to be irremediable."[6]

The scene is not an isolated one, Tocqueville assures his readers. "The expulsion of the Indians often takes place at the present day in a regular and, as it were, a legal manner."[7] In fact, the removal march comes to exemplify American policy toward its indigenous population: methodical, "regular," legal, rational—and deadly. In a famous passage, Tocqueville concludes his analysis of the history and destiny of American Indians in chilling tones:

> The Spaniards were unable to exterminate the Indian race by those unparalleled atrocities which brand them with indelible shame, nor did they succeed even in wholly depriving it of its rights; but the Americans have accomplished this twofold purpose with singular felicity, tranquilly, legally, philanthropically, without shedding blood, and without violating a single great principle of morality in the eyes of the world. It is impossible to destroy men with more respect for the laws of humanity.[8]

These words continue to haunt students of American culture and history; they are among the most oft-quoted in all of Tocqueville's eminently quotable tome.[9] I am glad to follow in this worthy tradition, but I wish to linger a bit longer on the passage than is customary, because I think it has often been misread, obscuring its true power and its troubling implications for liberal democracy. Where most scholars hear sarcasm, "bitterness"[10], or "mock admiration,"[11] I hear genuine ambivalence. Tocqueville's story is less satirical than tragic. Of course it is critical of American policy, but that policy comes to seem inevitable; even the Choctaws understood their woes to be "irremediable," a word Tocqueville uses three times in the section on Indian policy.[12] Tocqueville is not denouncing genocide cloaked in sham legality; his tale is still more chilling. The "extermination" of the Indians *is* legal and, in a particular sense, rational. The story of irrational hatred, fear, and prejudice on the part of whites is an important one, but distorting to the extent that it ignores the *systematic* racism of the legal "metaphysics of Indian-hating." In a sense, Tocqueville's analysis is the intellectual ancestor of Hannah Arendt's thesis on "the banality of evil:"[13] while the Spanish were guilty of shameful atrocities, it was left to a network of impersonal Anglo-American bureaucracies to perfect the political art of genocide. America was, to coopt the phrase of James Harrington in *Oceana* (1656), an "empire of laws and not of men."[14] The haunting question Tocqueville bequeaths us is how to reconcile the rule of law, with all of its unquestionable benefits, with the trails of tears walked by the displaced tribes of the Southeast.

One of "the laws of humanity" with which the Americans were acting in accord was Manifest Destiny, the supposedly inevitable expansion of the white race across the North American continent. The history of this idea and its disastrous effects on native populations is well known thanks to the pioneering work of Roy Harvey Pearce, and more recent writers,[15] and my focus is on "the formalities of law" which so impressed Tocqueville[16] rather than the less formal ideology of savagism *per se*. As we will see, though, the two cannot be separated so cleanly, so I will set forth a brief summary of this cultural narrative, this self-defining and -justifying tale of identity and difference that figured so prominently not only in popular culture but in political and legal discourse as well.

Structuring the ideology of "progress" at the heart of Manifest Destiny was the opposition of "savagery" and "civilization" analyzed so well by Pearce. Pseudo-anthropological study, combined with emerging evolutionary theory, had convinced Europe and white America by the end of the eighteenth century that the human races could be organized in a hierarchy according to how far they had progressed along the road to civilization—the latter term always being defined, of course, exclusively in terms of Euroamerican culture. In America, the progress of civilization could be seen along spatial and temporal axes at once, as Thomas Jefferson indicated in 1824:

> Let a philosophic observer commence a journey from the savages of the Rocky Mountains, eastwardly towards our seacoast. These he would observe in the earliest stage of association living under no law but that of nature, subsisting and covering themselves with the flesh and skins of wild beasts. He would next find those on our frontiers in the pastoral state, raising domestic animals to supply the defects of hunting. Then succeed our own semi-barbarous citizens, the pioneers of the advance of civilization, and so in his progress he would meet the gradual shades of improving man until he would reach his, as yet, most improved state in our seaport towns. This, in fact, is equivalent to a survey, in time, of the progress of man from the infancy of creation to the present day.[17]

At the same time, James Fenimore Cooper was beginning to dramatize this cultural topography in his Leatherstocking Tales. The idea itself was hardly new, however; Crevecoeur had sketched the same "progress" some forty years before in his *Letters from an American Farmer.*[18] The important point here is that this story, no less mythical in Jefferson than in Cooper, not only explains the demise of the red man and the ascendance of the white, but justifies them. In this ideological function the story can be seen not as the "natural" emplotment of empirical observations but as a descendent of John Locke's influential chapter on "Property" in the *Second Treatise of Government*—almost certainly part of the baggage Jefferson's "philosophic observer" would carry on his rambles. Locke used American Indians as his example of primitive societies who forfeit their rights to land by using it wastefully, by failing to invest the labor that would improve it through cultivation and thus allow it to support more people in greater comfort. As Locke states:

> And hence subduing or cultivating the Earth, and having Dominion, we see are joyned together, The one gave Title to the other. So that God, by commanding to subdue, gave Authority so far to *appropriate.*[19]

The natural law of property thus dictated that Indians, mistakenly believed to be unwilling or unable to cultivate, give way before European agrarian expansion.

Later versions of Manifest Destiny did not require Locke's more or less explicit moral censure of the Indians as contrasted to the industrious, rational English; instead, they could accommodate the benevolent concern of Jefferson and Tocqueville, or the noble savagism of Cooper. Still, however one might be inclined to regard it, the Indian's fate was inscribed in the natural laws of property and progress. However, to what extent did human law—specifically, American law in the Removal era—conform itself to these supposedly natural ones? It is hard to overstate the influence of Manifest Destiny on the thinking of the period, and yet, with respect to Marshall at least, I think it has sometimes been done. It is easy enough to extract a racialist metaphysics from his opinions—though not so easy that I will disdain the demonstration here—while ignoring the competing discursive strands that call into question the admittedly dominant cultural narrative of Manifest Destiny. Marshall does, however, exemplify and even epitomize a classical legal philosophy that claims for law a privileged place, and voice, in civilized society.

II. The Metaphysics of Law

Perhaps the fundamental legitimizing claim of liberal democracy is to be "a government of laws and not of men." Rather than being subject to the arbitrary caprice of their rulers, citizens are subject only to the law—as are the rulers themselves. Government retains for itself a monopoly on the legitimate use of coercive force, but only within democratically-determined legal parameters. The cardinal virtues of the law are neutrality and objectivity; "justice is blind" to individual wealth, beauty, and power (or lack thereof). The gulf between this ideal and the actual workings of any real legal system is all too painfully apparent to anyone of good faith, but the ideal itself remains a dominant ideological form, embraced by the conventional politics of left and right alike. Whether this is for good or ill, my concern now is to point out that the ideal of the rule of law entails more than a simple, transparent, culturally-neutral social contract.[20] Instead, it expresses the fundamental aspirations of Euroamerican civilization. The doctrine of the rule of law, as Fred Dallmayr writes,

> is not simply an accidental political bias but is linked with central premises and hierarchical postulates endemic to Western civilization: particularly the rule of reason over arbitrary will, of universal principle over particular circumstance, and ultimately of idea over matter.[21]

As we will see, each of these binary oppositions, with their privileged and their repressed terms, associated of course with whites and Indians respectively, figured prominently in the legal disposition of American Indians during the Removal period.

The doctrine of the rule of law is most obviously metaphysical in its elevation (in Dallmayr's terms) of idea over matter. In other words, law is taken to be a transcendent principle rather than the contingent product of concrete social and historical processes. Its authority derives precisely from its presumed independence from such local activity: it is universal, "natural," not "of men" in the sense of being (merely) a cultural product. Instead (or in addition) it is a product of reason (as opposed to "arbitrary will"), and the inevitable, if sporadic, evolution toward a universal conception of human rights in the just society. Thus law can be distinguished from politics, the realm of contending interests and powers, by its disinterestedness. Constitutionally separate from the other branches of government, the law is neutral referee to the social struggle, an arbiter rather than a participant.

A corollary claim involved in the elevation of idea over matter is that law transcends language, the material medium of its expression. More properly, the claim is that law distills its language of social/historical impurities, becoming an analytical or propositional discourse grounded not in a concrete culture but in logic or Reason itself. Just as it must rise above ideology, law must also rise above the messiness (and richness) of everyday language, its essentially metaphoric and allusive quality, its implication in cultural mythologies (in Roland Barthes' expanded sense of the term).[22] "A language of its own," in Deloria's terms, it aspires to self-identity, again through the privileging of idea over matter, of content over vehicle or, in another standard formulation, of logic over rhetoric.[23] More sophisticated versions of this argument acknowledge that such an aspiration has not been and may never be fully realized, but insist that although legal interpretation may never entirely "work itself pure," it does exhibits a discernible progress toward determinate, objective rulings as the weight of precedent accumulates and constrains the authors of judicial opinions. Over time, the law acquires an ever-greater integrity and coherence.[24]

American Indians might be tempted to reply using the words of Clifford Geertz in his essay "Thick Description" when he criticized structural anthropology for its preoccupation with abstracting formal systems from the concrete "flow of behavior," the social "drama" played out within and against these forms. The structuralists produced patterned, "impeccable," quasi-scientific descriptions whose truth-claims depended in large part on the formal coherence of their systems. "But there is nothing so coherent," Geertz wryly observed, "as a paranoid's delusion or a swindler's story."[25] But, if the effect of the story told by American law was to swindle the Indians, it was also to delude itself as to its own nature, to reassure itself of its own logical coherence by mystifying its origins in, to use Cardozo's pregnant phrase, "the empire of inarticulate emotion."[26]

Needless to say, arguments about the distinctiveness, integrity, and coherence of legal discourse could be elaborated in much more detail.[27] My purpose here, though, is not to rehearse a longstanding and ongoing theoretical debate, but to provide a brief background relevant to an analysis of John Marshall's rulings in cases involving Indian land rights. My theoretical claim, to be tested in the analysis, can be stated fairly simply: legal discourse, like any other, is both political and "literary" in that it unavoidably employs the metaphors and narrative conventions and traditions of the culture in which it is embedded. This position, in turn, encourages a certain critical method similar to that suggested by Deloria, and articulated well by Gerald Bruns:

> Understood . . . as social rather than propositional discourse, the law is without ground ("without why"); it is not a system working itself pure but a play of surfaces, a heterogeneous cultural practice that cannot be formally reduced but needs to be studied locally in terms of its position and effects within specific social and political situations.[28]

I hope to show, within the fairly circumscribed "social and political situation" of the Removal period, that the repression of politics and language in the legal discourse of the time was fundamental to the legitimation of the imperialist enterprise of an expanding America. However, as generally happens when one applies theory to history, the result is far from predictable. If Marshall does indeed speak with the voice of empire, as I claim, it is with the fully human voice of one grappling with guilt and contradiction as well as certainty. Like any social discourse, legal discourse draws on many "languages," some contradictory and hence potentially subversive of the ideal of a "pure" propositional discourse.

III. John Marshall and Legal Discourse

Marshall, the first Chief Justice of the U.S. Supreme Court, was among the very most thoughtful, learned, ethical, and eloquent men of his age. He also did more to destroy American Indian cultures than even his contemporary, the noted Indian-hater Andrew Jackson. Marshall had great personal respect and sympathy for the Indians, yet he authored a series of opinions that have impaired their legal rights to this day. A close examination of the rhetoric and historical context of these opinions reveals the quandries and contradictions of a man seeking to reconcile the historical process of imperialism with the trancendental mandate of justice. In the attempt, Marshall employs conventional cultural narratives, the master plots of imperial historiography, but unlike many of his contemporaries he does not (always) try to ground these narratives in the eternal laws of nature. On the contrary, he sometimes highlights the contingent, if not arbitrary, quality of these stories and the laws that must ultimately be extracted from them. If he finally remains trapped in the ideology of savagism (as elaborated by Pearce), it is because he is constrained not only by the institutional imperatives of his position, but by the very language available to him. In his struggle to define the rights of a subject people, he defines himself as subject.

In his essay on "Law and Literature," Cardozo, himself one of the greatest judicial stylists, remarked on Marshall's "magisterial" writing style—a type Cardozo ranks "first in dignity and power." The passage is worth quoting at some length, for it provides a classic description of the judge's role in executing the Law: not to create it, not even to interpret it really, but to become its disembodied voice:

> We hear the voice of the law speaking by its consecrated ministers with the calmness and assurance that are born of a sense of mastery and power. Thus Marshall seemed to judge, and a hush falls upon us even now as we listen to his words. Those organ tones of his were meant to fill cathedrals or the most exalted of tribunals. The judicial department, he tells us, "has no will in any case,. . .Judicial power is never exercised for the purpose of giving effect to the will of the judge; always for the purpose of giving effect to the will of the legislature; or in other words, to the will of the law." The thrill is irresistible. We feel the mystery and the awe of inspired revelation. His greatest judgments are framed upon this plane of exaltation and aloofness. The movement from premise to conclusion is put before the observer as something more impersonal than the working of an individual mind. It is the inevitable progress of an inexorable force.[29]

As a slave-holding Virginia gentleman, Marshall was certainly born to "a sense of mastery and power"—nothing "impersonal" there. However, the claim is that, rhetorically, Marshall's power derives from his transcendence of personal and historical position, of the "metaphysical" suppression of will and particular circumstance. Cardozo's pervasive religious imagery brings to mind Deloria's seemingly odd description of a priesthood of mechanics in the quote that begins this essay. Both the spiritual and the material technician operate within the parameters of a design supposedly fixed and eternal, "inexorable"—the laws are found, not made. Mediating the two realms is Reason, "the movement from premise to conclusion," figured as a universal principle with no premises of its own rooted in a particular social history.

However, Cardozo, as a kind of proto-realist in the history of legal theory, goes on to note that, powerful as it may be, this rhetorical effect is based on the "illusion" of judicial objectivity.[30] As he says elsewhere, despite all necessary efforts to attain impartiality, "we shall be far from freeing ourselves from the empire of inarticulate emotion, of beliefs so ingrained and inveterate as to be a portion of our very nature."[31] The following section of this essay seeks not simply to show that John Marshall was the subject of a particular ideological "empire," but to suggest the discursive foundations upon which the legitimacy of that empire was built and which Marshall helped build.

IV. John Mashall and *Johnson v. McIntosh*

In 1823, a settler and a land speculator in present-day Illinois found that they both "owned" the same piece of land, the former having received it via federal grant, the latter having purchased it from an Indian tribe. Who had the right to dispose of territory claimed by the United States, but also claimed, and occupied, by Indians? In the case of *Johnson v. Mcintosh*, Marshall ruled that only the federal government could lease or sell Indian lands. The Indians possessed merely "a right of occupancy," not "absolute title." The international (European) doctrines of discovery and conquest were affirmed: whichever nation gets there first and is able to assert military control over the area becomes its owner. (In this case, Britain had received the land from France through the treaty of 1763, while the United States had taken control following the Revolution.) Although Marshall calls these doctrines "pompous" and "extravagant," they are nonetheless authoritative and binding on the Court.

> Conquest gives a title which the Courts of the conqueror cannot deny, whatever the private and speculative opinions of individuals may be, respecting the original justice of the claim which has been successfully asserted.[32]

Here Marshall makes two distinctions fundamental to colonialist discourse—between "private" sentiment and public law, and between "original justice" and present legality. The former seems to assert the objective nature of legal reasoning—it is above and beyond personal "opinion" or "speculation." However, the latter distinction admits that there is really no ground for objective determination; "original justice" remains irrelevant and inaccessible. Marshall does not labor under the popular fiction that human rights are extralinguistic, metaphysical properties inhering in people—that "all men are endowed by their creator with certain inalienable rights." The Europeans' "original" claim to Indian land is pompous and extravagant because impracticable; the Indians possessed superior force at the time of discovery. However, as the tide of expansion and conquest—to use the favorite metaphor of nineteenth-century historians—swept across the land, the claim becomes reasonable and even lawful. "Rights" appear and disappear as products of history and juridical historiography.

Marshall makes it clear that law is a narrative art and not a science. In effect renouncing Locke's philosophy of property, Marshall does not wish to decide "on abstract principles" whether "agriculturalists, merchants, and manufacturers" have a greater right to land than mere "hunters," who do not improve or settle it. Still, having invoked this conventional (and mistaken) opposition between savagery and civilization (see Pearce) only to dismiss its force, he nonetheless feels compelled to discourse on "the character and habits" of the Indians: they were "fierce savages, whose occupation was war, and whose subsistence was drawn chiefly from the forest." To leave them in possession of the country, was to leave the country a "wilderness."[33] This gratuitous moralism and racialism—unnecessary once the doctrine of conquest has been affirmed, and designated previously as too "abstract" to be relevant—suggests a profound ambivalence on the part of Marshall toward the imperialist process. He states:

> However this restriction [on Indians transferring title to lands they occupy] may be opposed to natural rights, and to the usages of civilized nations, yet, if it be indispensable to that system under which the country has been settled, and be adapted to the actual condition of the two people, it may, perhaps, be supported by reason, and certainly cannot be rejected by Courts of justice.[34]

Admitting that legality has little to do with "natural rights" or even rationality, Marshall brackets both personal sympathy and logic, deferring to and reinscribing various cultural narratives or master plots: the inevitable "progress" or expansion of the white race in its civilization of the "wilderness;" the corresponding decline of the savage Vanishing American; and the evolutionary justice of the strong prospering at the expense of the weak. Locke's justification for the colonialist appropriation of native land, kicked out the front door, returns through the back.

I do not wish to suggest that Marshall should, or even could, have ruled otherwise. Constrained by the historical and political realities of his time, his ruling was indeed "indispensable to that system" within which he worked—or at least indispensable to that system's proceeding in relatively good conscience. To have ruled for the plaintiff Johnson, who bought the land from the Indians, would have been to undermine the title of the entire United States. However, beyond these pragmatic considerations, compelling as they are, there is really no legal justification for the decision, as Marshall himself admits, until he produces it himself in the ruling. "He created a theory to correspond to what had already occurred";[35] history, not "nature" or "reason," compels the verdict. In the Anglo/American common law tradition, there is no necessary ground for rulings in "abstract principles" of the kind Marshall eschewed in *McIntosh*. For better or worse, the law is unabashedly narrative or even literary in nature—as analogies are drawn with past cases, metaphorical reasoning becomes dominant—rather than "scientific," in the fashion of the Napoleonic Code or other Continental systems. Thus, as Marshall was well aware, his ruling not only clarified and codified existing law, placing a legal construction on past history, but influenced future rulings, and indeed the tenor of American expansion generally. In 1835 the historian James Hall reflected on the westward thrust:

> America was settled in an age when certain rights, called those of *discovery* and *conquest*, were universally acknowledged; and when the possession of a country was readily conceded to the strongest. When more accurate notions of moral right began, with the spread of knowledge, and the dissemination of religious truth, to prevail in public opinion, and regulate the public acts of our government, the pioneers were but slightly affected by the wholesome contagion of such opinions.[36]

One must wonder, however, when the symptoms of this moral epidemic began to show themselves—and when it was cured. In 1955 the doctrines of discovery and conquest (as affirmed by Marshall in *Mcintosh*) were cited in a ruling against Alaskan natives in *Tee-Hit-Ton Indians v. United States*; in 1980 the Sioux Nation was informed by the Supreme Court that "the taking of the United States of *unrecognized* or *aboriginal* Indian title is not compensable."[37] *McIntosh* was also cited by British courts in Africa and India, helping to legitimize England's sovereignty over its colonies.[38] Marshall's carefully worded opinion, which renounced claims to the authority of "natural right" and even "reason," became a canonical text of imperialism nonetheless. For this he can hardly be blamed, except insofar as he cast the history of European expansion in impressively "impersonal," "magisterial" tones, in Cardozo's terms, articulating "the empire of inarticulate emotion" in a way that denied both emotion and empire.

V. John Marshall and *Cherokee Nation*

Marshall's next important case regarding Indian rights presented him with a different "literary" problem, one of textual interpretation. In 1829, when the state of Georgia extended its laws over the Cherokee Nation, formerly an independent political entity having treaties only with the federal government, the tribe perceived this move quite rightly as an attempt to destroy its sovereignty and seize its lands. In 1831 the Cherokees' suit against Georgia, contesting its authority over them, was considered by the Supreme Court. The Court denied the suit on the grounds that it lacked jurisdiction. The Cherokees, of course, were not American citizens; neither were they a "foreign nation," which the Constitution empowers to bring suit in federal courts against American citizens or institutions. Instead, as Marshall declared in the majority opinion to the case, Indian tribes were to be considered "domestic dependent nations," "in a state of pupilage." Their relation to the United States "resembles that of a ward to his guardian."[39] This reading depends on a highly questionable interpretation of the Constitution, which in turn seems to depend upon Marshall's appropriation of the conventional cultural narratives of Manifest Destiny and the Vanishing American. As in *McIntosh*, Marshall creates a theory to fit the facts, but also construes the facts so as to fit the theory. He begins by suggesting sympathy for the Cherokee plight:

> If Courts were permitted to indulge their sympathies, a case better calculated to excite them can scarcely be imagined. A people once numerous, powerful, and truly independent, found by our ancestors in the quiet and uncontrolled possession of an ample domain, gradually sinking beneath our superior policy, our arts and our arms, have yielded their lands by successive treaties, each of which contains a solemn guarantee of the residue, until they retain no more of their formerly extensive territory than is deemed necessary to their comfortable subsistence. To preserve this remnant, the present application is made.[40]

Again Marshall's sympathy is useless and even illegal; he adheres to the ideal of judicial objectivity, the ascendence of reason over arbitrary will. This time, though, he has specific textual evidence upon which to base his reasoning.

The contract binding Marshall and the Cherokee nation is the Constitution. (Never mind the fact that no Cherokee delegates were included in the Constitutional Convention.) Article III, Section VIII provides that Congress may "regulate commerce with foreign nations, and among the several states, and with the Indian tribes." The intent of the clause, with regard to the Indians, was to avoid the chaos that would ensue should each state cut separate deals with the tribes, many of which existed in more than one state. Moreover, for national security purposes, the federal government needed to insure the exclusive right to negotiate treaties and alliances with the tribes, just as with foreign nations. Ironically, however, the acknowledgement of Indians as separate and powerful peoples in 1789 allows the Court to dismiss them in 1831.

> In this clause they are as clearly contradistinguished by a name appropriate to themselves, from foreign nations, as from the several states composing the union. They are designated by a distinct appellation; and as this appellation can be applied to neither of the others, neither can the appellation distinguishing either of the others be in fair construction applied to them.[41]

Marshall's argument does more than simply justify the Court's refusal to "indulge [its] sympathies." By displacing the authority for his decision onto the Founding Fathers, Marshall seems to avoid "construction," "fair" or otherwise, altogether: his decision is found, not made.

What seems a tenaciously literal reading of the Constitution, however, is in fact a questionable interpretation. The commerce clause can quite reasonably be read as establishing "tribes" and "nations" as parallel or analogous rather than contradictory designations, as Justice Thompson suggested in his dissenting opinion.[42] Thus the tribes would have the same rights to sue. Moreover, this ahistorical reading, which ignores the remarkable evolution of the Cherokee nation[43] and hypostatizes the categories established in one sentence of the Constitution coexists paradoxically with an appeal to the historical conditions of 1789.

> In considering this subject, the habits and usages of the Indians, in their intercourse with their white neighbours, ought not to be entirely disregarded. At the time the constitution was framed, the

> idea of appealing to an American Court of justice for an assertion of right or a redress of wrong, had perhaps never entered the mind of an Indian or of his tribe. Their appeal was to the tomahawk, or to the government.[44]

"History" is used antihistorically: Indian "habits and usages" are fast-frozen in time; their collective "mind" is not allowed to change. No distinction is made among tribes; the Cherokees are simply "Indians." Again we see the "metaphysical" elevation of a universal principle of "Indianness" over the particular circumstance of the petitioning tribe. Moreover, as in *McIntosh*, the historical and racialist discourse is gratuitous; having established the legal status of the tribes through textual analysis of the Constitution, there should be no need to consider their habits. If such consideration demonstrates Marshall's dedication to weighing all aspects of a case, it also seems to signal insecurity or uncertainty as to the verdict and the reasoning supporting it.

Marshall's abdication of his responsibility to interpret the Constitution in light of changing historical circumstances allows him to act without seeming to act—or rather, to act only in accordance with the mechanical principles (to use Deloria's image) set forth in the constitutional blueprint. He presents the legal system, the structure of power relations over which he presides, as a transparent text in which the history of Cherokee social evolution is merely an interesting aside. In his reading of white/Indian conflict, the structures of language and power intersect in particularly clear ways. The Cherokees are denied access to the legal system because of the syntactical differentiation between "foreign nations" and "Indian tribes" in the formal structure of a clause in a document.

This is not to say that the final appeal against the policy of Removal was entirely a casualty of formalist metaphysics, of the elevation of idea over matter. Marshall's decision, as Joseph C. Burke has shown, was the product of a complex process of mediation among legal, political, and moral considerations. Marshall's sympathy for the Cherokee cause was genuine, and he wanted dearly to assert the authority of the Court against the open defiance of Georgia, which did not even deign to present counsel in its behalf and publicly declared that it would ignore an unsatisfactory ruling.[45] The following year, 1832, Marshall was able to indulge his sympathies for the Cherokees. In *Worcester v. Georgia* his majority opinion recognized the Cherokees as a distinct "nation" and asserted "their title to self-government." The Court ruled that Georgia's imprisonment of Samuel Worcester, a white missionary living with the Cherokees, an unconstitutional extension of the state's laws into the political community of the tribe, which was subject only to federal authority. Marshall's courageous ruling threatened to destroy whatever authority the Court had built in its first half-century, for President Jackson had no intention of enforcing its decision. Privately Marshall feared for the survival of the constitutional system as a result of this clash of governmental branches, but the situation never came to a head. South Carolina's Nullification Ordinance of the same year united Jackson, the Court, and Georgia, making the Cherokees a political "embarrassment."[46] Worcester was pardoned, and the Cherokees were removed. The Court retained its authority, and, yet, with regard to its protection of Indians, showed itself impotent.

Establishing the authenticity of Marshall's sympathy for the Cherokees and sketching the political climate constraining his decisions in their cases is crucial for a number of reasons beyond fairness to the great Chief Justice himself. Most obviously, such an analysis indicates that politics and jurisprudence are inextricably entwined.[47] Marshall feared that granting the injunction against the Georgia legislature would "savor too much of the exercise of political power to be within the proper province of the judicial power,"[48] but the ruling obviously enhanced Jackson's political power and destroyed the Cherokees', as Marshall was well aware. One does not have to embrace a the critical legal studies position—"Law is simply politics by other means"[49]—to insist that Marshall's clean distinction between "provinces" is both mistaken and dangerous to the extent that it ratifies the formalist ideology of the rule of law which proclaims itself beyond ideology.

Second, the ruling shows that, for better or worse, a government of laws not men can "protect" us from our best impulses as well as our worst, as it did Marshall in *Cherokee Nation*. Marshall's "impersonal," "magisterial" impulse seems to have distanced him from the real suffering his ruling was bound to produce. Ironically, his scrupulous interpretation of the Constitution compelled him to adopt the paternalistic rhetoric of his archnemesis, President Jackson.[50] As Felix Cohen pointed out, Marshall's trope—Indians "resemble" wards—continued to impair Indian rights well into this century. Even today Native American tribes struggle to articulate and realize new models of interaction with their old "guardians."[51]

Finally, Marshall's clash with Jackson can be seen to represent the historical crossroads of rule by force and rule by law. In a more precise and accurate formulation, the Cherokee cases mark the conflict between an emergent model of authority based on legal and bureaucratic procedures and a residual heroic ethos. In principle, Jackson, the charismatic warrior hero but also the Chief Executive, must be bound by the same "impersonal" strictures, the same procedural limitations outlined in the Constitution, as Chief Justice Marshall. In fact, however, the rulings of Marshall are meaningless without the collaboration, the "personal" endorsement, of Jackson. Jackson's alleged reaction to the *Worcester* ruling—"John Marshall has made his decision; now let him enforce it"—is apocryphal. But it rings true, because it expresses the period's genuine tension between rule by force and by law. All of Marshall's pretty words and elegant arguments in *Worcester* were impotent; the Cherokee's appeal would still be to the tomahawk. A shared impotence links Marshall and the Indians; unable to hear their suit in *Cherokee Nation,* he wistfully recalls the days when the plaintiffs took arms against their opponents. Tocqueville's contrast between the Spanish and the Anglo/Americans comes to mind; "the formalities of law," not naked force, are the new basis of domination in the American empire. However, when the Indians attempt to engage this legal authority on its own terms, they are denied access to the process and advised to revert to arms. "Thus it is," to quote Melville somewhat out of context, "that they whom we denominate 'savages' are made to deserve the title."[52]

"The Indian" of early American law, then, was constructed from various narrative strands I have called master plots or cultural narratives. Unable to find any basis for appropriation of Indian lands in "abstract principles" or "original justice" and compelled to retreat from his personal "sympathies," Marshall fell back on savagist cliches about the "habits and usages" of Indians, and the ideologically saturated plotlines of Manifest Destiny and the Vanishing American. Furthermore, in his own literary production of the law, Marshall generated and codified a new vocabulary, a new metaphorics of paternalism legitimizing the emerging bureaucratic domination of native peoples. If this domination took place "in a regular and . . . legal manner," with "a singular attachment to the formalities of law," as Tocqueville observed, it should compel us, as historians and citizens, to probe continually the "empire of inarticulate emotion" beneath the surface coherence of those forms. No more than Marshall, of course, will we ever entirely free ourselves from that empire; like him, though, we can resist the reification of cultural narratives into the "abstract principles" underwriting the sham coherence of Geertz's "swindler's story." For, as Deloria says, "it is in the specifics, in the more accurate historical statement, that law begins to approach a measure of justice."[53]

**Stephen D. Osborne is Lecturer in the Writing Program at the University of California at Los Angeles.*

Notes

1. Vine Deloria Jr., 1989, "Laws Founded in Justice and Humanity: Reflections on the Content and Character of Federal Indian Law," *Arizona Law Review*, 31, 2, p. 210.

2. *Ibid.*, at 204

3. *Ibid.*, at 220. c.f. 206.

4. Benjamin Cardozo, 1986, "Law and Literature," *Law and Literature and Other Essays and Addresses*, Littleton, Colorado: Fred B. Rothman and Co., p. 11.

5. Herman Melville, 1964, *The Confidence-Man* [1857], New York: Holt, Rinehart, and Winston.

6. Alexis de Tocqueville, 1990, *Democracy in America* [1835], New York: Vintage Books, p. 340.

7. *Ibid.*, at p. 340.

8. *Ibid.*, at p. 355.

9. Brian Dippie, 1982, *The Vanishing American*, Middletown, Connecticut: Wesleyan University Press, 1982, p. 70; Ronald Takaki, 1979, *Iron Cages: Race and Culture in 19th-Century America*, Seattle: University of Washington Press, p. 81; and Robert A. Williams, Jr., 1989, "Documents of Barbarism: The Contemporary Legacy of European Racism and Colonialism in the Narrative Traditions of Federal Indian Law," *Arizona Law Review*, 31, 2, p. 240.

10. Dippie, 1982, *Ibid.*, at p. 70.

11. Williams, 1982, *supra* note 9 at p. 240.

12. Tocqueville, 1990, *supra* note 6 at pp. 342 and 354.

13. Hannah Arendt, 1963, *Eichmann in Jerusalem: A Report on the Banality of Evil*, New York: Viking Press, 1963.

14. Quoted in Fred Dallmayr, 1992, "Hermeneutics and the Rule of Law," *Legal Hermeneutics: History, Theory, and Practice*, Gregory Leyh, ed., Berkeley: University of California Press, p. 5.

15. Roy Harvey Pearce, 1965, *Savagism and Civilization: A Study of the Indian and the American Mind*, Baltimore: Johns Hopkins University Press. See Dippie, 1982, *supra* note 9, e.g., on the connection between Manifest Destiny and the companion narrative of the Vanishing American. Richard Drinnon in, 1980, *Facing West: The Metaphysics of Indian-Hating and Empire Building*, Minneapolis: University of Minnesota Press traces the savage/civilized colonial dynamic beyond the shores of the Pacific to the Phillipines and Viet Nam.

16. Tocqueville, 1990, *supra* note 6 at p. 355.

17. Quoted in Pearce, 1965, *supra* note 15 at p. 155.

18. Hector St. John de Crevecoeur, 1986, *Letters from an American Farmer* [1782], New York: Penguin, pp. 71-73.

19. John Locke, 1967, *Second Treatise of Government*, In *Two Treatises of Government*, Peter Laslett, ed., London: Cambridge University Press, p. 310; his emphasis. Anyone familiar with typical tribal views of the human place in nature can see how utterly foreign Locke's conception, rooted in *Genesis*, would be to them. N. Scott Momaday in, 1976, "Native American Attitudes Towards the Environment," *Seeing with a Native Eye*, Walter Capps, ed., New York: Harper and Row summarizes the American Indian attitude in what seems to be an implicit polemic against Locke which redefines one of his favorite terms, "appropriation:"

> [T]he native American ethic with respect to the physical world is a matter of reciprocal appropriation; appropriations in which man invests himself in the landscape, and at the same time incorporates the

> landscape into his own most fundamental experience . . . This appropriation is primarily a matter of the imagination. (p. 80)

The tacit contrast is to Western *material* appropriation, or expropriation, and "improvement" of the land. Momaday invokes appropriation in its archaic sense of "to make suitable;" he describes "appropriate" relations of harmony, of "alignment" (pp. 84-85), of mutual accommodation and adjustment, as opposed to Locke's "dominion." Extending Momaday's logic, if the relationship between humans and land can be described as "property," it would signify rightness, being proper, rather than ownership.

20. Even the notion of judicial objectivity, which seems so natural, is itself culturally determined and defined. Here is Chief Justice Tom Tso of the Navajo Supreme Court:

> In traditional Navajo culture the concept of a disinterested, unbiased decisionmaker was unknown. Concepts of fairness and social harmony are basic to us; however, we achieve fairness and harmony in a manner different from the Anglo world. For the Navajo people, dispute settlement required the participation of the community of elders and all those who either knew the parties or were familiar with the history of the problem. Everyone was permitted to speak. It was difficult for Navajos to participate in a system where fairness required the judge to have no prior knowledge of the case, and where who can speak and what they can say are closely regulated. (Tom Tso, 1989, "The Process of Decision Making in Tribal Courts," *Arizona Law Review,* 31, 2, p. 229.)

21. Dallmayr, 1992, *supra* note 14 at p. 4.

22. Roland Barthes, 1990, *Mythologies*, New York: Noonday Press.

23. Gerald Bruns, 1992, "Law and Language: A Hermeneutics of the Legal Text," *Legal Hermeneutics: History, Theory and Practice*, Gregory Leyh, ed., Berkeley: University of California Press, p. 34.

24. Ronald Dworkin, 1986, *Law's Empire*, Cambridge: Harvard University Press, pp. 400-407.

25. Clifford Geertz, 1973, *The Interpretation of Cultures*, New York: Basic Books, pp. 17-18.

26. Quoted in Richard Weisberg and Jean-Pierre Baricelli, 1982, "Literature and Law," *Interrelations of Literature*, Jean-Pierre Baricelli and Joseph Gibaldi, eds., New York: MLA, p. 162.

27. An important dialogue on this subject has been that between Ronald Dworkin and Stanley Fish. Dworkin draws an analogy between the progress of law and a chain novel. As the work proceeds, the writers become increasingly constrained by the logic of plot and characterization established by those who come before. As a result, interpretive latitude progressively diminishes as the story unfolds. Fish replies to the effect that since history/precedent—the early chapters—is itself always subject to the interpretive construction of later writers, Dworkin begs the issue of interpretation by imagining the judge alone with his texts rather than participating in an "interpretive community" with its own local/historical standards concerning how texts should be interpreted, what counts as textual evidence, what kind of argument is persuasive, etc. The relevant articles are reprinted in W. J. T. Mitchell, ed., 1983, *The Politics of Interpretation*, Chicago: University of Chicago Press.

28. Bruns, 1986, *supra* note 23 at p. 33.

29. Cardozo, 1986, *supra* note 4 at pp. 10-11.

30. *Ibid.*, at p. 11.

31. Quoted in Weisberg and Baricelli, 1982, *supra* note 26 at p. 162.

32. Francis Paul Prucha, ed., 1975, *Documents of United States Indian Policy*, Lincoln: University Press of Nebraska, p. 36.

33. *Ibid.*, at p. 26.

34. *Ibid.*, at p. 37.

35. Robert T. Coulter, and Steven M. Tullberg, 1984, "Indian Land Rights." *The Aggressions of Civilization*, Sandra L. Cadwalader and Vine Deloria, Jr., eds., Philadelphia: Temple University Press, p. 195.

36. James B. Hall, 1835, *Sketches of History, Life, and Manners in The West,* Vol. 2, Philadelphia, 2 vols, p. 75.

37. Coulter and Tullberg, 1984, *supra* note 35 at pp. 194 and 197.

38. *Ibid.*, at p. 189.

39. Prucha, 1975, *supra* note 32 at p. 59.

40. *Ibid.*, at p. 58.

41. *Ibid.*, at pp. 59-60.

42. Richard Peters, 1831, *The Case of the Cherokee Nation Against the State of Georgia,* Philadelphia: John Grigg, pp. 206-207.

43. This Cherokee evolution included the creation of a written alphabet, the establishment of a tribal newspaper and a democratic government, and the adoption of an agrarian lifestyle, including the use of black slaves. How much more "assimilated," for better or worse, to Southern America could they become? Still, all this was not enough to shake the conviction of even the best intentioned Removalists that Indian savages must roam free in the hunting grounds of the West, where their racial destiny could be fulfilled free from the corrupting influences of civilization.

44. Prucha, 1975, *supra* note 32 at p. 59.

45. In January of 1831 Georgia had executed George Tassel, "a Cherokee convicted by a Georgia court for murder committed in Indian territory," in defiance of a writ of error issued by Marshall himself. (Joseph C. Burke, 1969, "The Cherokee Case: A Study in Law, Politics, and Morality," *Stanford Law Review*, 21, pp. 530-531).

46. *Ibid.*, at p. 530 and Wilcomb E. Washburn, 1971, *Red Man's Land/White Man's Law*, New York: Scribner's, pp. 68-69.

47. For the modern cultural critic this proposition may appear self-evident. In legal theory, however, it remains somewhat controversial. The so-called "realists," who argue that personal and political considerations inevitably color a judge's reading of statutory or contract law, continue to debunk the "formalist" faith in the transparency of (well-written) statutes or contracts and the ability of the (good) judge to disinterestedly perceive their original intent. The formalists or "textualists" reply that if objectivity is an illusion, it is a necessary one if judges are ever to accomplish their business. Derrida on the bench would undoubtedly produce some interesting opinions, but in court "to write" is just as surely a transitive verb, and an activity that impacts upon people in the most immediate ways. For a lucid discussion of this controversy by a legal scholar heavily influenced by literary theory, see Gary Peller, 1985, "The Metaphysics of American Law," *California Law Review*, 73, pp. 1152-1290.

48. Quoted in John C. Cuneo, 1975, *John Marshall: Judicial Statesman*, New York: McGraw-Hill, p. 136.

49. David Kairys, "Legal Reasoning," in Kairys, ed. *The Politics of Law*, New York: Pantheon Books, 1982, p. 17.

50. See Michael Paul Rogin, 1975, *Fathers and Children: Andrew Jackson and the Subjugation of the American Indian*, New York: Knopf for an interesting, if methodologically controversial, psycho-historical reading of "the great white father's" relationship to his Indian "children" and his own Revolutionary "fathers."

51. See Felix Cohen, 1960, *The Legal Conscience*, New Haven: Yale University Press, pp. 328-334. A new model of white/Indian relations that seems to be gaining some currency as an alternative to Marshall's is the "mentor" relationship, particularly as applied to corporate consultant/investors in Native American-run businesses on reservations. While this new model appears promising in terms of financial benefits to certain tribes and suggests a somewhat less authoritarian hierarchy, its rhetorical shift from familial to corporate terms may simply express a modern version of Marshall's, and Jackson's, paternalism.

52. Herman Melville, 1958, *Typee* [1846], New York: Bantam Books, p. 26.

53. Deloria, 1989, *supra* note 1 at p. 219.

JUDICIAL "MASKS:" THEIR ROLE IN DEFINING AND REDEFINING THE TRIBAL/CONGRESSIONAL RELATIONSHIP 1870–1924

*David Wilkins

The condition of the Indians in relation to the United States is, perhaps unlike that of any other two people in existence. In the general, nations not owing a common allegiance are foreign to each other. The term foreign nation is, with strict propriety, applicable by either to the other. But the relation of the Indians to the United States is marked by peculiar and cardinal distinctions which exist no where else.[1]

I. The Problem: From Tribal Sovereignty to Government Ward

Chief Justice John Marshall penned this striking passage in the seminal case, *Cherokee Nation*, which defined in a politically peculiar way, the relationship between American Indian Tribes and the United States. The case and the passage are frequently cited even today by policy-makers, commentators, and scholars who wrestle with the question of how racially-based tribal nations, which for the most part are completely land-locked by both state and federal jurisdictions, are yet able to wield a myriad of governmental powers, some of which may legally conflict with the United States Constitution.[2] However, Marshall's quote compels one to ask a deeper and more important set of questions. What, more precisely, urged Marshall and succeeding generations of scholars, politicians, administrators, and jurists to conclude that "peculiar and cardinal distinctions" mark the tribal-federal relationship, and what are some of these peculiarities?

Marshall, of course, because of his enormous intellectual talent, his belief in federal supremacy, his compassion for tribes, and the important element of timing, is the principal federal figure responsible for the current state of tribal-federal relations. A number of writers have critically analyzed Marshall's comments in *Cherokee Nation* and his other important Indian law decisions.[3] Though differing, sometimes vehemently, in their interpretation of Marshall's doctrines, there is some concurrence that Marshall blended his federalist convictions, a sense of moral obligation to tribes, and a pragmatic need to find a way to reconcile tribal status with the constitutional framework.[4] While scholars will continue to debate the status of tribal sovereignty as it emerged from the Marshall Court era, one would be on firm ground to argue that tribes, in the words of dissenting Justice Thompson in the *Cherokee* case, were indeed "foreign" to the United States at the time. Thompson said:

> It is their political condition that constitutes their foreign character, and in that sense must the term foreign, be understood as used in the constitution. It can have no relation to local, geographical, or territorial position. It cannot mean a country beyond the sea. Mexico or Canada is certainly to be considered a foreign country, in reference to the United States. It is the political relation in which one government or country stands to another which constitutes it foreign to the other.[5]

Thompson's dissent, it should be noted, formed the basis of Marshall's follow up decision,[6] which affirmed the "distinct and independent" status of the Cherokees and the supremacy of federally-negotiated Indian treaties over state laws.

Indian sovereignty was recognized in other ways also. The principal source of congressional authority in the field of Indian affairs is the Commerce Clause of the Constitution. This is the only explicit source of power delegated to Congress. Theoretically, this clause should not extend to Congress any greater power over tribes than it exercises over states, though in historical practice such has not been the case.[7] In addition, there are two other important sources of authority; these are the power to make treaties and the power to make war and peace.[8]

The Commerce Clause provision as originally interpreted was narrowly construed by Congress. In an 1834 House Report, it was stated:

> The right of self-government in the Indian tribes does not exclude

> the right of the United States to make laws for the regulation of trade with the Indian tribes, so far as our citizens are concerned. This right is by the Constitution of the United States vested in Congress, and cannot be surrendered.[9]

The intent here was twofold. First, Congress, not the States, was to be the primary agent to negotiate with tribes. Second, Congress was involved in a laborious, almost futile, effort to restrict unscrupulous white traders from defrauding tribes. These were both essential goals to maintain a positive tribal/federal relationship.

That the United States respected tribal autonomy is evidenced by another comment voiced in the same House Committee on Indian Affairs Report regarding the legality of extending federal criminal laws into Indian country. The Committee reported the following:

> It will be seen that we cannot consistently with the provisions of some [of] our treaties, and of the territorial act, extend our criminal laws to offenses committed by or against Indians, of which the tribes have exclusive jurisdiction; and it is rather of courtesy than of right that we undertake to punish crimes committed in that territory by and against our own citizens . . . It is not perceived that we can with any justice or propriety extend our laws to offenses committed by Indians against Indians, at any place within their own limits.[10]

This exclusively federal authority was to be exercised by the legislative rather than the executive or judicial arms of the government.

The relationship between federal authority and tribes was, however, significantly transformed during the period 1870–1924. The half-century covered in this article witnessed, in Skowronek's words, "a rapid movement from social simplicity to social complexity."[11] It was an era in which the federal courts were granted expanded jurisdiction by Congress. In fact:

> the sweeping powers granted were an open invitation to the federal judiciary to assume the role of stern policeman for the new national economy . . . [and] with substantive due process, the Court asserted that the judiciary itself was the only reliable bastion of rational policy making in this volatile democracy.[12]

Nowhere is this more true than in the area of federal Indian law and policy. Before the turn of the nineteenth century, a conception of Indians as impoverished and helpless "wards" who were linked to their federal "guardians" together with a conception of property derived from an interpretation of the doctrine of discovery that can be traced back to *Johnson v. McIntosh*[13] virtually supplanted the Commerce Clause and Treaty-making Clauses. In fact, the so-called "plenary power of guardianship," as it was described by the Supreme Court in *United States v. Sandoval*,[14] led to a host of horrendous Supreme Court decisions and federal laws which lacked a constitutional mooring.[15]

The birth and reification of the doctrine of "guardianship" and the notion that federal ownership of the national domain somehow extended an omnipotent aura to congressional enactments and judicial decisions is, however, tempered with the reality that throughout this period a host of important Supreme Court decisions were handed down that reaffirmed the sovereign political status of tribes. While blacks were suffering major legal defeats in *The Civil Rights Cases*[16] and *Plessy v. Ferguson*,[17] while women were being denied civil rights in cases like *Bradwell v. Illinois*[18] and *Minor v. Happersett*,[19] and while certain Chinese individuals endured the embarrassment of deportation in *Fong Yue Ting v. United States*,[20] some tribal nations were carefully distinguished and sporadically had their own separate traditions and customs upheld by the Supreme Court.

The question driving this article is how did this change of status from tribal sovereignty to government wardship occur? How, if tribes indeed did have a "peculiar status" in relation to the federal government because of their "foreign" and extra-constitutional status even though they were linked to that government by treaties, did they acquire an "inferior" or dependent position to that of the United States government, which purports to have "superior" plenary power over them?[21] If tribes were indeed "foreign" and extra-constitutional, as the historical, constitutional, and judicial evidence indicates, and are still not subject to state or federal constitutional constraints, when and why did it come to pass that federal (and sometimes state courts), not tribal courts, became the center of dispute resolution? How, in fact, can the federal courts' decisions apply to tribes when federal law can ostensibly apply only to constitutional entities, which tribes are not?[22] If tribes were indeed distinct and independent political communities in the 1830s and beyond, when and why did it become federal law that the United States under the "Doctrine of Discovery," not tribes, became the absolute title holder to even aboriginal Indian lands, with tribes holding a less than absolute right of occupancy?[23] These are intriguing questions, and I propose to answer them by studying a brace of United States Supreme Court decisions[24] during the pivotal era 1870 to 1924[25] in which fundamental alterations occurred in the tribal/federal relationship. These changes were all unilaterally inaugurated by the federal government, led by Congress, acquiesced to by the Executive, and legitimated or manufactured by the Supreme Court. While each of the three branches were actively involved in this arrogation of power over tribes, the Supreme Court occupied, one could forcefully argue, the most pivotal role in this process, which focused first on the diminishment of tribal political status, then on the loss of tribal property, and then on a fundamental realignment of the tribal/congressional relationship, with Congress being vested with unlimited power over "dependent" tribes.

The Court's role is seminal because of the perceptions many Americans have of the Supreme Court as the purveyor of impartial justice. The United States is one of the most legalistic nations in the world. And the belief in "Law" or the "Rule of Law" is pervasive. While virtually all societies have law-making and law-enforcing institutions and legal systems, in the United States "law has become a reified entity."[26] By this, Medcalf means that Law:

> has become a thing unto itself. The process of reification—acquiring the appearance of an independent thing—involves forgetting origins and connections, loss of the past, and non-recognition of the many connections to forms of the present.[27]

Along with reification, where the abstract is treated as the real:

> the notion of Law in the United States has become deeply entrenched and revered, taking on a mystical, omniscient quality . . . result[ing] in the emergence of a semireligious social phenomenon that renders actual analysis extremely difficult.[28]

In other words, despite constitutional allocation of the management of the federal government's affairs with tribes to Congress (Commerce Clause), it has been the Supreme Court that in reality has elaborated and transformed in the most bizarre and dazzling ways the distinctive political/legal relationship between the federal government (and the constituent states) and tribal nations.

II. Theoretical Framework: Legal Consciousness and Legal Masks

The internecine struggles that have plagued the tribal/federal situation beg for clear, preferably simple, explanations. The complexity of the relationship, however, precludes simplistic answers. A broad, dual-theoretical framework should provide more plausible explanations for the Court's seemingly erratic decisions insofar as congressional power and tribal status are concerned. Critical legal theory[29] and the creative approach developed by John T. Noonan, Jr. provide the theoretical guideposts for this study.[30]

A. Critical Legal Theory: Legal Consciousness

Advocates of Critical Legal Theory (a.k.a. "Crits") posit that the Supreme Court operates with a distinctive "legal consciousness," which serves in the critical role as the perceptual screen, as well as the perceptual pool, that binds even apparently disparate decisions together.[31] This consciousness is not easily measured and so is unquantifiable. Duncan Kennedy suggests, however, that legal consciousness is an entity "with a measure of autonomy."[32] It refers:

> to the particular form of consciousness that characterizes the legal profession as a social group at a particular moment. The main peculiarity of this consciousness is that it contains a vast number of legal rules, arguments, and theories, a great deal of information about the institutional workings of the legal process, and the constellation of ideals and goals current in the profession at a given moment.[33]

It is, moreover, a combination of intellectual operations and terms that develop according to a unique pattern. CRITS stress, moreover, that legal consciousness wields an influence on results that are distinguishable from those of economic interest and political power. Kennedy went on to note the following:

> The notion behind the concept of legal consciousness is that people can have in common something more influential than a checklist of facts, techniques, and opinions. They can share premises about the salient aspects of the legal order that are so basic that actors rarely if ever bring them consciously to mind. Yet everyone, including actors who think they disagree profoundly about the substantive issues that matter, would dismiss without a second thought (perhaps as "not a legal argument" or as "simply missing the point") an approach appearing to deny them.
>
> These underlying premises concern the historical background of the legal process, the institutions involved in it, and the nature of the intellectual constructs which lawyers, judges, and commentators manipulate as they attempt to convince their audiences.[34]

Critical Legal Theorists argue that between 1885 and 1935 a new form of legal thought emerged and flourished that amounted to a rationalistic restructuring of the legal universe. Mensch calls this "classical legal thought."[35] As American economic and social life was being transformed, the legal elite, including the Supreme Court, joined forces with treatise writers and leaders of the bar to share a view of the "law" that allied the legal profession with science "against both philosophical speculation and the crudities of democratic politics."[36] While acknowledging ideologies like *laissez-faire* economics and the influence of economic interests and structures of political power, Critical Legal Theorists posit that a common ideological consciousness arose during the late nineteenth and early twentieth century between leading academic and practicing lawyers and jurists that cut across divisions in practice specialty and political orientation.[37]

During this classical period, the legal elite transformed its attitude about the set of legal relationships that comprise the American legal system—private citizen to private citizen, private citizen to state, legislature to judiciary, and federal to state government—from seeing them as qualitatively distinct to seeing them as four particular instances of a single general legal relationship. The role of the judiciary, then, "was the application of a single, distinctively legal, analytic apparatus to the job of policing the boundaries of these spheres."[38]

The fact that tribes were outside this legal matrix meant that the Supreme Court either deferred to the political branches or drew from its own limited bank of culturally-biased information about tribes from within the Court's own institutional memory and judicial consciousness, which rarely afforded a realistic picture of tribes or their own indigenous institutions of governance. There is evidence of this ideological consensus in the fact that of the Supreme Court cases involving tribal sovereignty during this historical era there was written dissent in only five cases: *Cherokee Tobacco* (78 (11 Wall.) 616 (1871); *Leavenworth Railroad Company v. United States* (92 U.S. 733 (1876); *Elk v. Wilkins*, (112 U.S. 94 (1884); *Choctaw Nation v. United States*, 119 U.S. 1 (1886); and *Donnelly v. United States*, 228 U.S. 243.

Critical Legal Theory is impressive in that its advocates posit that conflicting decisions are made because they are based on different, and often controversial, moral and political ideas. Neither lawyers nor jurists can provide simple answers to complex political and legal questions because the legal system, like society at large, is unable to reconcile the contradictory instincts people feel when they confront social problems. Rather than deciding which of these conflicting instincts to follow, the "law" seeks to embrace them all. Critical legal theory argues that law is really politics clothed differently and that it obscures the nature of judicial decision when courts and legal commentators present legal issues as if they were "objective" or even "relatively objective" matters of legal reasoning rather than political choices. Finally, a significant strength of this intellectual approach to understanding law is that it seeks a theoretical and practical understanding of the law that places its institutions and individual actors in their social and historical contexts.

B. The "Masking" of Law: Law as Magic

John T. Noonan, Jr., in his telling study, *Persons and Masks of the Law*,[39] offers equally incisive observations about the place, or the lack of place, of "persons," or, for my purposes, "tribes" in the law. His thesis is that people involved in cases in the American legal tradition are often given "masks" that conceal their true character. These masks, as Noonan defines them, are "legal constructs which suppress the humanity of a participant in the process."[40] Noonan's primary example is the case of African/Americans and the institution of slavery. The humanity of blacks was shielded, "masked," in American law behind various descriptions normally reserved for property of one sort or another (real, personal, etc.). Once the "law" had characterized blacks as "property," they could then be sold, bartered, or even killed without the legal system actually confronting the fact that they (African/Americans) were human beings entitled to certain basic liberties.

Noonan explains how "enlightened" individuals like Thomas Jefferson and George Wythe, "though supporting liberty and advocating emancipation of slaves, actually did nothing, even when vested with political power, to end slavery." He argues that they accepted the entrenched legal framework that had codified the institution of slavery. They ignored the humanity of black Americans by placing "masks" or legal constructs on both their own feelings and the slaves, thus magically removing humanity from the legal process.

For Noonan, there are two kinds of masks. There are those that are imposed on others ("property" when applied to slaves), and those that are put on oneself (the "Court" in the mouths of judges, and "the law" according to judges, law professors, and attorneys.)[41] These masks are socially fashioned and are dangerous because they "have been stamped with approval by society's official representative of reason."

Indian Supreme Court decisions, we shall see, are also pocked with such "masks." Tribes have, at various times, been defined by the Court as a "culturally-deficient" set of individuals who were in need of "cultural-improvement," as "domestic-dependent nations," which were to be dependent on the U. S. Government at a time when they were legitimate independent sovereigns subject to no other political power, and as "dependent wards," who were subject to omnipotent paternalistic guardians. The Supreme Court has manufactured or refined other "masks" to justify deep federal or state intrusions into tribal sovereignty: the doctrine, which was later appropriated by federal officials, that the "discovery" of America by the European countries vested an absolute title to the discovering nation, thereby reducing tribal claims to aboriginal lands to those of a mere tenant; the political question doctrine which for nearly a century and a half denied tribes a legal forum for the adjudication of their rights to lands, treaty enforcement, etc.; the theory of congressional and even federal plenary (read: absolute) power over tribes; and the so-called "trust doctrine."[42]

Although crediting the Marxist argument that "masks" are often employed by the ruling class to protect their interest above those of the lower classes, Noonan notes that "law is not something applied to subjects which leaves those applying it unaffected."[43] Legal constructs, he says, are not simply tools of power; they are not acts of "violence." The legal process "aims at compromise, avoidance of conflict, peaceful direction of conduct."[44] Masks cannot be treated "as armament." Instead, they are more aptly conceived as a "set of communications," as "magical ways by which persons are removed from the legal process."[45]

A synthesis of these two approaches will go far towards providing a conceptual framework useful for explaining the Supreme Court's cases that will be examined. Both emphasize the concept of the law as "masks." Both agree that law must be placed in the larger historical and social context. A significant difference, however, is that while CRITS speak of law as primarily a legitimating device utilized by elites situated at the top of the social, political, and economic hierarchy, Noonan posits that the law affects not only those it is used against but those who wield it as well.

The conjunction, therefore, of the basic premises and legal constructs offered by Critical Legal Theory and Noonan's characterization of legal "masks" operating with reciprocal effects will enable us to craft more convincing arguments as to why the Court treated tribes the way it did during this period. Further evidence of the Court operating with a distinctive consciousness is seen in the fact that the judiciary has never voided a single congressional act that diminished or abrogated an inherent or aboriginal tribal right. The Court, in short, until the recent Rehnquist years, has maintained an extremely deferential position to the political branches insofar as Indian status is concerned. But even the most atrocious Rehnquist court decisions,[46] which run counter to current congressional Indian policy emphasizing tribal self-determination, do not pose any threat to the regnant idea that tribes have an inferior political/legal status to the federal government. The disparity today comes in the Court's articulation of the tribal/state relationship, which is a different situation altogether.

While the Court during the late nineteenth and early twentieth centuries exhibited a fairly consistent overall legal consciousness regarding tribes that stressed their allegedly inferior cultural, political, technological, social, and spiritual status in relation to peoples of the West, it is possible to discern at least three types of judicial consciousness[47] that operated during this era, each wielding a distinctive set of "masks" that have been legally fashioned symbolizing the legal process and concealing or disfiguring the humanity of the actors in the legal drama—both the acting

(Supreme Court) and the acted upon (tribes) in the process.

Tribes, it needs to be pointed out, are rarely always passive recipients of what western lawmakers ruled. In the early decades of the United States' existence, tribes were able defenders of their legal and political interests and were excellent enforcers of their rights. However, a bedrock Supreme Court case, *Cherokee Nation v. Georgia*, 30 U.S. (5 Pet.) 1 (1831), effectively denied tribes *qua* tribes the right to file lawsuits as original parties in the Supreme Court. "After mature deliberation," said Chief Justice John Marshall:

> the majority is of opinion that an Indian tribe or nation within the United States is not a foreign state in the sense of the constitution, and cannot maintain an action in the courts of the United States.[48]

C. Types of Legal Consciousness

There are three types[49] of legal consciousness: Constitutional/Treaty Legal, Civilizing/Paternalistic, and Nationalism/Federalism. Each type is accompanied by one or more sets of legal masks. We shall examine these in order.

Constitutional/Treaty. The basic assumption of this legal consciousness is that constitutional or treaty considerations (i.e., ratified agreements) are the only ones relevant for the adjudication of a legal dispute. This consciousness is evident in Supreme Court opinions dealing with tribal sovereignty which generally acknowledged the inherent sovereignty of tribes and their pre- and extra-constitutional aboriginal right of self-government. These decisions largely left tribes free of the constitutional constraints applicable to the states and the federal government, recognizing that since tribes had not been created pursuant to the U.S. Constitution then that document's provisions and clauses were inapplicable to tribes whose sovereignty was and is original.

This consciousness will usually employ the following masks: For the parties: One party (the Congress) is understood as being within the Constitution's purview; the other (tribes) is understood as being outside the American's fundamental political document. However, the two parties are politically connected by treaties (or treaty-type agreements) that are recognized under the Constitution as being the "supreme law of the land." For the legal process: The Court is seen primarily as a legitimator of policies developed by the political branches. This is the orthodox version of the Court as being a body that should exercise self-restraint and function primarily as an interpreter of the Constitution, not as a policy-making entity. In this "model of law" approach[50] the court is seen as an agent for interpreting and applying pre-existing laws: it is bound (although not absolutely) by the doctrine of *stare decisis* (past precedent).

Civilizing/Paternalistic. The basic assumption of this variety of legal consciousness is that law is the most impressive instrument for civilizing indigenous (or primitive) peoples, who were considered culturally inferior. An excellent example of this view is found in a federal district court case, *United States v. Clapox.*[51] This decision involved a determination of the status of federally-created Courts of Indian Offenses, that were developed by the Bureau of Indian Affairs in 1883. These courts, manned by agent-appointed Indians, were charged with enforcing the Code of Federal Regulations which was designed to "civilize" and assimilate Indians by punishing tribal members who engaged in tribal dances, polygamy, traditional healing ceremonies, etc.

As Commissioner of Indian Affairs Hiram Price stated in his annual report of 1883:

> there is no good reason why an Indian should be permitted to indulge in practices which are alike repugnant to common decency and morality; and the preservation of good order on the reservation's demands that some active measures should be taken to discourage and, if possible, put a stop to the demoralizing influence of heathenish rules.[52]

Five years later, an Umatilla woman (identified as "Minnie") was arrested and charged with adultery. She was subsequently freed from jail by several friends who were later caught and charged with her jail-break. When the case reached federal court, the main issue to be addressed involved the status of the Courts of Indian Offenses. Were they constitutional courts organized pursuant to section 1, article 3 of the Constitution, or were they developed under some other authority? In answering this question, the court explicitly capsulized the general view of federal policy-makers of the time regarding Indian culture. The court held that the offenses courts were not constitutional courts but:

> mere educational and disciplinary instrumentalities, by which the government of the United States is endeavoring to improve and elevate the condition of these dependent tribes to whom it sustains the relation of guardian. In fact, said the court, the reservation itself is in the nature of a school, and the Indians are gathered there, under the charge of an agent, for the purpose of acquiring the habits, ideas, and aspirations, which distinguish the civilized from the uncivilized man.[53]

The individuals responsible for Minnie's futile rescue were convicted and charged with "flagrant opposition to the authority of the United States on this reservation," and their actions were deemed "directly subversive of this laudable effort to accustom and advocate these Indians in the habit and knowledge of self-government."[54]

According to most federal policy-makers and Anglo-Americans in general, this alleged tribal cultural "inferiority" was apparent in a number of ways. Whites viewed tribes as being primitive technologically. They invariably classed all tribal-based cultures as hunter/gatherer societies, which were perceived as inferior to the agriculturalist-based society of whites with their domestic industries. Finally, indigenous peoples were purportedly "pagans" or "savages;" in other words, they were without legitimate religious beliefs since they apparently had no knowledge of Jesus Christ or the Christian church.[55]

Some tribes, however, like the Cherokees, Choctaws, Chickasaws, Creeks, and Seminoles (often referred to as the "Five Civilized Tribes"), and the various Pueblo groups, were, at least for the first century or more of U.S/tribal interaction, perceived as being less savage[56] or pagan than other tribes. These tribes, therefore, were for a significant period treated with more leniency by the Supreme Court and the U.S. government's political branches as well. For both the allegedly "wild" tribes and the so-called "civilized" tribes, there was a fundamental belief among most of the important federal policy-makers, including the Court, that Indians could be culturally "elevated" with proper education, training, and spiritual (read: Christian) guidance. Hence, paternalistic policies (e.g., Christian missionaries funded by the federal government, boarding schools, reservations, and the individualization of tribal lands and funds) were developed by the Congress and sanctioned by the Supreme Court to make this cultural transformation occur.

This type of consciousness will usually employ the following masks. For the parties, this mode of legal thought will utilize two different sets of masks for Indian tribes. The first are masks that caricature tribes as "wild," "heathenish," or "savage," (tribes of the Great Plains, the midwest, the Pacific Northwest, and the desert Southwest—esp. Navajo, Apache groups, Tohono O'odham, Utes, etc.), the second set includes masks that portray selected tribes as "civilized," "peaceful," and "hard-working" (the Five Civilized Tribes and the Pueblos are the clearest examples). Gradations of "savagery" were, of course, evident and the Court vacillated in the manner in which it employed these masks. For the Supreme Court, the masks worn posit a view of the Court, and by extension the federal government, as deeply moralistic, Christian, and nearly always above reproach.

For the legal process, law is considered an absolutely essential element in moving Indian persons and tribes from an uncivilized to a civilized state. The question was never about whether this was right or not; it was about whether this cultural transformation would take place gradually or rapidly. Regardless, the paternalism that characterized federal Indian policy during this era, also known, however legally incorrect the depiction was, as the "guardian/ward" relationship, had two faces—it could be benevolent paternalism (viewing Indians as children or as incompetent wards), or it could be malevolent paternalism (viewing Indian lands, resources, and political rights as sources to be unilaterally and forcefully taken or abrogated).[57]

Nationalism/Federalism. This third type of judicial consciousness has as its core the assumption that law is conceived of as a prime mechanism for furthering the political development of the United States as a Nation-State. The process of political development is a topic of great interest to those attempting to shape their society as well as to those attempting to understand the political world. Accordingly, one perspective holds that political development occurs:

> primarily in response to development of the economic and social systems. Because of increases in the elements of modernization, such as greater economic development, urbanization, and social mobilization, there is a need for a more complex and more efficient political system.[58]

Barrington Moore, for example, in his classic study *Social Origins of Dictatorship and Democracy* (1966)[59] attempted to compare the three major roads taken by nation-states from the pre-industrial to the modern world.[60] He treated in detail the struggles of Great Britain, the United States, France, Japan, China, and India to achieve modernity. The United States, according to Moore, like all the major capitalist democracies, passed through a civil war or a period of revolutionary violence in which certain aspects of the old order were destroyed—slavery in America during the U.S. Civil War, 1861–1865. This was necessary, Moore says, because slavery was incompatible with political development along democratic lines. In effect, the destruction of the institution of slavery made it possible for the social, political, and economic struggle to continue within a democratic framework.[61]

After the Civil War, industrial capitalism advanced significantly. Moreover, there were important political changes as well. One of the most crucial development involved the role of the federal government and "big property." This later included the railroads, which received massive grants of land and support, and property in the public domains, which was given to various timber and mining interests. As Moore noted, one of the first actions was "preservation of the Union itself," which meant, as the West filled up after the war, the creation of one of the largest domestic markets in the world. It was also a market protected by the highest tariff to date in the nation's history.[62] As U.S. political development increased in the last quarter of the nineteenth century, several key concepts emerged that would influence the shape and direction of nationalism. These include: political democracy, political stability, political culture, political institutions, political participation, and political integration.[63] While each of these is important, it is political integration that has special significance for the status of tribes in the United States. The term generally refers to the holding together of a political system; however, it has been used in various specific ways. The two types of relevance to our study are national integration and territorial integration.

National integration is the:

> process of bringing together culturally and socially discrete groups into a single territorial unit and of establishing a national identity. This often involves plural societies, with distinct ethnic, religious, linguistic, or other groups and strata.[64]

Territorial integration, on the other hand, is the establishment of "national central authority over subordinate political units or regions. [It] means objective territorial control."[65] The United States has historically had an assimilative political culture in a hierarchical ethnic structure (whites in relation to blacks, Indians, and Asian/Americans), within which there have also been parallel ethnic relations (WASP, Irish, Italians, Jews, etc).

The United States has used various responses to the problem of national integration of indigenous groups: social engineering, assimilation, cultural genocide, partition (segregation), and expulsion.[66] Of these, assimilation, or the effort to induce the merger of a politically subordinate cultural group into the politically dominant cultural group, has been the most persistent response. Assimilation may be viewed on four distinct, though related, levels or dimensions: the cultural, the structural, the biological, and the psychological.[67] Several of the opinions we will examine, particularly on negative tribal sovereignty cases, involve various dimensions of assimilation with the United States Supreme Court insisting that the only sovereigns it can recognize are the federal government and the constituent states.

The Supreme Court's utilization of the "law" was not only as an instrument of "civilization," but was also the West's most vital and effective "instrument of empire building."[68] Hence, some of the cases that came before the Court involved questions relating to the diminished status of tribes, a status that was sometimes even denied any existence whatsoever. Related to this is the theory of federalism in which the Supreme Court, acting as a coordinate branch of the federal government, clearly identified the Congress as the only constitutional source entitled to deal with tribes. This was in direct contrast to what African/Americans were experiencing. There the states had been granted virtually free reign to reassert their dominance over blacks. Tribes, on the other hand, were generally shielded from the states, though the shielding device used by the federal government was effective congressional omnipotence over Indian sovereignty and over Indian civil, political, and property rights.

This consciousness will employ the following masks. For the parties, this mode of thought will use two different kinds of masks. One is the mask worn by U.S. federalizing agents, which thinks of the federal government as the core unit so that other non-federal entities must be either absorbed into it or vanquished by it. The other is the set of masks applied by the Court to tribes. The first applies to tribes that are deemed capable of being Americanized (from an Anglo perspective) and found to be capable of joining the United States as separate, though integrated, political entities.[69] The other is a mask that caricatured most western tribes as wild and uncivilized. Federal policy-makers never had an opportunity to think about bringing western tribes into the constitutional framework. Tribal resistance to western settlers, railroads, and other intrusions precluded this.

For the legal process, law is clearly an agent of national unity. We will see that during this era, the Court rendered a number of decisions indicating a clear intent to dilute the extra-constitutional status of tribes by unilaterally declaring them "wards" of the government and by disavowing their separate, independent status. The assertion of congressional plenary power over tribal lands, resources, and rights is evidence of this nationalizing effort.

These three types, as noted at the onset of this discussion, are ideal types and reflect the broadness of the continuum on which the Supreme Court operated. We will discuss some cases, moreover, which will exhibit more than one consciousness and often more than one set of masks.

This study will proceed by analyzing the most important sovereignty and related cases in which the Court commented on the relationship between congressional power and tribal sovereignty. I will first examine cases in which the Court restrains or inhibits congressional authority over tribal affairs. These cases are generally supportive of tribal sovereignty. Next, I will focus on those cases in which the Court comments negatively on tribal sovereignty. In these cases, the Court either upheld sweeping congressional authority over tribes or took an active policy stance and generated peculiar doctrines on its own that opened the door for virtually unreviewable federal power over tribes. Finally, an assessment of the principles in these apparently conflicting sets of opinions is made.

Table 1-1 illustrates the significance of congressional power and federal exclusivity. In negative tribal sovereignty cases, in which congressional authority is an issue, tribal autonomy is diminished or adversely affected in fifty percent (50 percent) of the cases (12 in all). On the other hand, in positive tribal sovereignty cases, congressional power is the major issue in only twelve percent (12 percent) of the cases (4 in all), though it is alluded to in several other cases.

Broadly speaking, this finding is consistent with the Marshallian principle enunciated in *Worcester*[70] of federal supremacy in the field of Indian affairs. Equally interesting, this table indicates yet another Marshallian doctrine brought forth in *Cherokee Nation*.[71] This doctrine, it will be recalled, held that tribes were domestic-dependent nations, a unilateral reduction in tribal status from their rightful depiction as independent states. In short, tribal autonomy, when confronted head on by congressional power, will be reduced at least fifty percent (50 percent) of the time.

TABLE 1-1
Congressional Power and Federal Authority

			Cases with Congressional Power and Federal Exclusivity	
		No. of Cases	No.	Percent
Legal	Neg. Sov.	24	12	50
Outcome	Pos. Sov.	31	4	12
	Total	55	16	9

Key:
Negative Sovereignty: Decisions that adversely affect tribal sovereignty
Positive Sovereignty: Decisions that affirm tribal sovereignty

Source: Federal Indian Court Case Data Base

Furthermore, the results are more enlightening when we see which tribes are represented in the cases. Table 1-2 graphically depicts the variety of tribes represented in the cases. While a total of 59 tribal individuals or nations appeared before the federal courts, the Five Civilized Tribes (Cherokee, Choctaw, Chickasaw, Creek, and Seminole), so named because these tribes had effectively integrated certain western

TABLE 1-2
Major Tribal Entities Represented in Federal Court Cases[72]

Tribes Represented	No. of Times Appeared	Percent of Times Appeared
A. Civilized Tribes		
Five Civilized Tribes Collectively	6	4
Cherokee	9	6
Cherokee and one other tribe	10	7
Creeks	6	4
Creeks and one other tribe	6	4
Chickasaw	2	1
Chickasaw and one other tribe	12	8
Chocktaw	2	1
Chocktaw and one other tribe	8	5
Seminole	2	1
Seminole and one other tribe	6	4
Total Five Tribes	69	73
B. All Other Tribes		
Sioux (all bands)	11	12
Chippewa (all bands)	8	8.5
Osage	4	4
Shawnee	3	3
Yakima	3	3
Others	9	10
Total Other Tribes	38	40
Total All Tribes	107	103

Source: Federal Indian Court Case Data Base

political institutions with their own, collectively or individually were parties in 69 (73 percent) of the total 107 cases. Other tribes constituted the remaining 38 cases (40 percent).

In nine of the twelve negative cases in which congressional power was at issue, tribes or Indian individuals living in Indian Territory (later Oklahoma) were either indirect or direct parties. This is an interesting finding. It indicates that the Oklahoma Tribes, particularly the Five Civilized Tribes who were involved in seven of these nine cases, had the requisite legal sophistication as well as willingness to challenge the territorial (later state government) and the United States governments when it became evident that their treaty rights were being violated.[73] Conflicts were virtually non-stop since the Indian Territory had enormous amounts of oil and natural gas, in addition to vast acreage.[74]

III. Legal Consciousness and Legal Masks in Positive Tribal Sovereignty Cases

The following section provides an analysis of the most prominent Supreme Court cases that tend to support, although with certain caveats, the generally independent and sovereign character of tribal nations. Two caveats were recognized by the court—the perceived tribal cultural and political "inferiority" and federal guardianship over tribes. These are important and play a critical role in the transformation of legal thought and tribal status by the Supreme Court, which utilized one or sometimes a combination of the first two types of legal consciousness discussed above constitutional/treaty or civilizing/paternalistic.

A. *United States v. Joseph*[75]

Background. Anomalies abound in the field of Indian law probably to a greater degree than in all other areas of law. This should be readily apparent based on the evidence presented in the first part of this paper. The field, however, is made even more exceptional when the Pueblo Indians (actually 22 distinctive tribal entities) of New Mexico are brought into the landscape.

The situation of the Pueblos is unique because of their historical relationship with the Spanish, and later Mexican, governments. The Pueblos had written agreements with the Spanish that unquestionably affirmed Pueblo ownership of their territories. Their recognized land title was also respected by the State of Mexico. Later, the Pueblos' various land grants came within the limits of the United States by the 1848 Treaty of Guadalupe Hidalgo by which Mexico ceded a portion of its territory to the United States.[76]

One of the Hidalgo treaty's provisions specified that Mexican citizens were given the privilege of choosing either Mexican or United States citizenship. Some have argued that the Pueblo Indians, by choosing to remain in their homeland rather than retire to Mexico, implicitly accepted United States citizenship.[77] The federal citizenship status of the Pueblos was implicitly affirmed by the United States Supreme Court in *United States v. Ritchie*[78], though the issue would be revisited later.

Because of their generally accepted, if not expressly noted, enfranchised status, the Pueblos were not considered "Indian Tribes" within the meaning of existing federal statutes. Thus, laws like the 1834 Non-Intercourse Act, which protected tribal lands from white encroachment, were not enforced against Anglo/American or Mexicans who settled on Pueblo land grants.[79]

Decision. By virtually any standard, except the factual one, the *Joseph* decision is extraordinary. The facts are quite simple. Antonio Joseph, a non-Indian, had settled on lands held by the Taos Pueblo Tribe. The Pueblos resented this intrusion and through the United States sought to have Joseph evicted in violation of the Trade & Intercourse Act of 1834. This Act had made it illegal for non-Indians to settle on tribal lands without tribal and federal approval.

The United States, represented by the Solicitor General, suggested that the Pueblos were an Indian tribe despite their high level of "civilization." As a recognized tribe, the government could protect their lands against trespass, insisted the Solicitor. The Solicitor noted in his brief that:

> it would be a cruel mistake to suppose that Indians who show a disposition to become civilized, do not need for their tottering steps special aid and guidance by the Government.[80]

The United States was arguing, in effect, that the Pueblos were inferior and dependent and therefore needed federal guardianship.

The Supreme Court was asked to decide whether the Pueblo authorities had the right to dispose of their lands to outsiders. In other words, was their title complete, or was it one of a reduced right to occupancy alone? Formally, the Court wondered whether the Taos Pueblo was an Indian tribe under the meaning of the Intercourse Act of 1834. Using ethnocentric phraseology the Court, through Justice Samuel Miller, carefully differentiated these "peaceful, industrious, intelligent, honest, and virtuous people" from "wilder" more allegedly "uncivilized" tribes like the Apache, Comanches, and Navajos deemed "nomadic" and as semi-independent groups "left to their own rules and traditions, in whom we have recognized the capacity to make treaties."[81] In the Court's ironic words:

> The Pueblo Indians, if indeed, they can be called Indians, had nothing in common with this class. The degree of civilization which

they had attained centuries before, their willing submission to all the laws of the Mexican Government, . . . and their absorption into the general mass of the population (except that they hold their lands in common), all forbid the idea that they should be classed with the Indian tribes for whom the intercourse acts were made.[82]

The Court refused to expressly address the issue of whether the Pueblos were indeed United States citizens. They stressed that this question should be reserved until it was specifically broached.

Legal Consciousness Exemplified and Legal Masks Employed. This case is replete with evidence indicating that it is the Court's conceptualization of the Pueblo's as a racial and cultural group comparable in many ways with Anglos and clearly distinguishable from their more "savage" indigenous neighbors, along with the Pueblos' preexisting status as a sovereign whose sovereignty had already been acknowledged by Spain and Mexico that enabled the Pueblos to secure this legal victory. Despite the ethnocentric tone in the Court's language, this case is an affirmation of tribal sovereignty because the court acknowledges that the United States has no legal jurisdiction over the Pueblos. In the Court's words, "if he [Joseph] is there with their [Pueblo] consent or license, we know of no injury which the United States suffers by his presence, nor any statute which he violates in that regard."[83] The Supreme Court clearly recognized that the federal government could not involve itself in an internal tribal matter. In addition, the Court somewhat surprisingly asserted that the Pueblos held "their lands by a right superior to that of the United States. Their title dates back to grants made by the government of Spain before the Mexican revolution."[84]

In effect, the Court was operating with elements of the first two types of legal consciousness—Constitutional/Treaty (hereafter, Legal Con I) and Civilizing/Paternalistic (hereafter, Legal Con II). While the Pueblos never negotiated treaties with any European or European-derived nation, there was certainly an understanding that the United States had a constitutional duty to respect Pueblo rights that had previously been affirmed by other western nation-states. There was an element, in short, of a trust relationship that has both legal as well as moral connotations. And while the United States Solicitor General tried to paint the Pueblos as culturally deficient, and, therefore, in need of federal guardianship and military protection, the Court held that their cultural distinctiveness actually precluded the need for federal protection. That distinction according to the Commissioner of Indian Affairs, was:

The Civilized Pueblo and Mission Indians, or those inhabiting towns or villages and engaged in pastoral and agricultural pursuits, noted

> for their intelligence, virtue, sobriety, and industry, and Indians only **in race and as to a few of their customs**; and (b) the wild, nomadic, and savage tribes, not farther advanced in civilization than the hunter state, whose only means of subsistence were the chase and depredations not infrequently committed upon the property of their more civilized and industrious neighbors.[85]

B. *Elk v. Wilkins*[86]

Background. Seven years later the issue left untouched by the Supreme Court in Joseph, Indian citizenship, came roaring to the surface in Elk. In 1879 a federal circuit court in the noted case, *Standing Bear v. Crook*[87] ruled for the first time that an Indian was a "person" under the Habeas Corpus Act and had an inalienable right to expatriate, if he so desired.[88] This decision, however, also did not address the question of citizenship.

The citizenship issue had been debated in Congress since the period preceding the adoption of the Fourteenth Amendment to the Constitution in 1868. In the Senate debates before the submission of the Fourteenth Amendment, section one of the amendment which read, "All persons born in the United States, and subject to the jurisdiction thereof, are citizens of the United States and of the States wherein they reside"[89] was debated at length.

In an intensive and prolonged debate, several Senators expressed their confusion on the subject of tribal status and whether the amendment applied to tribal members. Several legislators sought to amend the provision by inserting after the word "thereof" the words "excluding Indians not taxed." Another group of Senators earnestly stated that the amendment would in no way apply to tribal members because they belonged to independent nations and although born within the territorial limits of the United States were not born within the allegiance of the federal government.[90] The proposition to amend was voted down thirty to ten. Senator Willard Saulsbury (D., Delaware), speaking immediately before the vote, summed up the feelings of the minority when he noted:

> I feel disposed to vote against [this] amendment, because if these negroes are to be made citizens of the United States, I can see no reason in justice or in right why the Indian should not be made citizens.[91]

However, bewilderment persisted on what effect, if any, the Fourteenth Amendment had upon the status of tribes. A second question considered whether Indian treaties were invalidated by the amendment. The Senate Judiciary Committee, chaired by Matthew Carpenter (R., Wisconsin), was called upon to analyze the issue. The Committee issued a detailed eleven-page report on December 14, 1870. Written in part to "fix more clearly in the minds of Congress and the people the true theory of our relations to these unfortunate tribes," the committee elaborately analyzed the historical relationship between tribes and the United States.[92] In fact, Senator Carpenter stated pointedly that such a report was warranted because of the existence of some loose popular notions of "modern date in regard to the power of the President and Senate to exercise the treaty-making power."[93]

Perusing treaties, statutes, and Supreme Court decisions, as well as responding to popular opinion, the committee report forthrightly asserted that the Fourteenth Amendment had no effect on tribal status and that Indian treaties were not annulled. The crystalline nature of the report justifies an extended quotation:

> Volumes of treaties, acts of Congress almost without number, the solemn adjudications of the highest judicial tribunal of the republic, and the universal opinion of our statesman and people, have united to exempt the Indian, being a member of a tribe recognized by, and having treaty relations with, the United States from the operation of our laws, and the jurisdiction of our courts. Whenever we have dealt with them, it has been in their collective capacity as a state, and not with their individual members, except when such members were separated from the tribe to which they belonged; and then we have asserted such jurisdiction as every nation exercises over the subjects of another independent sovereign nation entering its territory and violating its laws. [Thus] to maintain that the United States intended, by a change of its fundamental law, which was not ratified by these tribes, and to which they were neither requested nor permitted to assent, to annul treaties then existing between the United States as one party, and the Indian tribes as the other parties respectively, would be to charge upon the United States repudiation of national obligations, repudiation doubly infamous from the fact that the parties whose claims were thus annulled are too weak to enforce their just rights, and were enjoying the voluntarily assumed guardianship and protection of this Government.[94]

More pertinent to this discussion, however, is the committee's closing comment on detribalized Indians. There it was suggested that "when the members of a tribe are scattered, they are merged in the mass of our people, and become equally subject to the jurisdiction of the United States."[95] The importance of this report was not lost and six days after its release, December 20, 1870, Senator and president *pro tempore*, Henry Anthony (R., Rhode Island), offered a resolution, which was adopted, that 5,000 extra copies of the committee's report be printed "for the use of the Senate."[96]

Here the issue of Indian citizenship lay in abeyance until John Elk stepped forward. Elk, whose tribal affiliation is never given, was a resident of Omaha, Nebraska. He had presented himself to Charles Wilkins, an Omaha registrar, to have his name registered as a qualified voter.[97] Elk maintained that he had separated himself from his tribe and had "completely surrendered himself to the jurisdiction of the United States."[98] In so doing, Elk declared that under the Fourteenth Amendment of the Constitution he was an American citizen and, therefore, was entitled to the right to vote.

A year earlier in *The Civil Rights Cases*,[99] (another suit involving an interpretation of the Fourteenth Amendment), the Supreme Court struck down as unconstitutional the first and second sections of the 1875 Civil Rights Act. The Court ruled that the Fourteenth Amendment did not compel a private citizen to refrain from discriminatory practices. In this case the Court almost matter-of-factly remarked that Congress had "direct and plenary powers of legislation" over a broad range of subjects, including commerce "with the Indian tribes."[100] This restatement was nothing new. But in Elk, tribes were not involved. The issue was the citizenship of a solitary, detribalized Indian.

Before the case went to the Supreme Court, Wilkins filed a general demurrer, which was argued before a two judge panel. Interestingly, one of the judges was Elmer S. Dundy, the same judge who had ruled in Standing Bear that Indians were "persons" with the inherent right of expatriation. In this case, however, Judge Dundy sided with the defendant, Wilkins, and dismissed Elk's petition. Thereupon, Elk, by writ of error, took his case to the Supreme Court.

Decision. In a 7-2 decision,[101] the Supreme Court forcefully put the issue of Indian citizenship to rest, at least temporarily. The majority held:

> Indians born within the territorial limits of the United States, members of, and owing allegiance to, one of the Indian tribes, (an alien, though dependent, power), although in a geographical sense born in the United States, are no more 'born in the United States and subject to the jurisdiction thereof,' within the meaning of the first section of the Fourteenth Amendment, than the children of subjects of any foreign government."[102]

The Court, reaffirming John Marshall's earlier characterization of tribes as distinctive political entities, said that while they were not "strictly speaking, foreign States," they were "alien nations, distinct political communities" with whom the United States "dealt with through treaties and legislation."[103] Moreover, this separate tribal status is evidenced by the Court's statement that general congressional legislation does "not apply to Indians, unless so expressed as to clearly manifest an intention to include them."[104]

Justices John M. Harlan and William B. Woods joined in a stirring dissent, written by Harlan. Harlan vociferously argued along a more historically accurate path. Citing both the 1866 Senate debates on the Fourteenth Amendment and the closing remarks of the 1870 Senate Judiciary report, Harlan asserted that the 1866 Civil Rights Act protected detribalized Indians. Simply put, Harlan noted that "the exclusion of Indians not taxed evinced a purpose to include those subject to taxation in the State of their residence."[105] In his conclusion, Harlan vividly described the sad legal status of non-tribal Indians. He noted that the majority's interpretation of the Fourteenth Amendment had created:

> a despised and rejected class of persons, with no nationality whatever; who, born in our territory, owing no allegiance to any foreign power, and subject, as residents of the States, to all the burdens of government, are yet not members of any political community nor entitled to any of the rights, privileges, or immunities of citizens of the United States.[106]

Having failed to identify Elk's tribal affiliation, however, it is impossible to say whether Elk was "detribalized" as Harlan presumed. But, even if we follow Harlan's assumption and place Elk under state law, clearly Elk would still have to prove his citizenship.

Legal Consciousness Exemplified and Masks Employed. This decision seems to exemplify the Legal Con I, but also has an element of Nationalism/Federalism (hereafter, Legal Con III). The decision on the surface seems to be made on purely constitutional grounds without any recourse to any notion of civilization or to the alleged "superiority" of Anglo civilization. On the other hand, the implicit assumption seems to have been that "once an Indian always an Indian" so that even individualized/detribalized Indians, as such, could not be assimilated into American society. This mode of consciousness would be relying (although implicitly) upon a distinction between civilized individuals and those incapable of being civilized.

During this era, this is a rare case in which the Supreme Court fails to act in accord with the general Indian policy of Congress. By the mid 1880s, Congress and the Bureau of Indian Affairs had explicitly adopted a predatorial assimilative policy of forcing the cultural break up of tribes with the goal of assimilating and incorporating the individualized Indian into the larger American society. Either voluntarily or as a direct result of some unspecified federal policy (we are never told by the Court), Elk found himself away from his tribal homeland. The Court, however, for inexplicable reasons continued to view Elk as a member of a tribe with whom the United States had a political relationship.

The Court refused to concede that an Indian could expatriate from his/her tribe or that the United States could receive such an expatriated person without some positive action from the federal government. The legal mask of conceptualizing tribes as "alien nations" in this case acted as an effective barrier that denied the individuals constituting those nations any opportunity to have and exercise individual rights which the United States or states were bound to respect. "The members of these tribes," said the Court, "owed immediate allegiance to their several tribes, and were not part of the people of the United States."[107] This last statement was evidence of Legal Con III where the Court was asserting that tribes (even anonymous ones) and their members (even detribalized) were incapable of participating in American society and thus were unwanted in the larger picture of American nation-building.

C. *Talton v. Mayes*[108]

Background. In 1892 Senate Bill 1548 was introduced. This would have extended the jurisdiction of the United States Supreme Court to cases brought up from tribal courts. The Senate Committee on Indian Affairs favored the bill despite acknowledging that "the tribal courts are not United States courts in any respect. They are not created by United States laws nor supplied with United States judges, juries, or officers."[109] Still, the committee believed the measure would force the Five Civilized Tribes to understand that they "belong to a country where all laws must grow out of the legitimate powers of the Legislators, conformably to the Constitution of the United States."[110]

The House Judiciary Committee, however, had an opposite view. They submitted an adverse report in which they asserted that:

> all five of these tribes of Indians are civilized and capable of self-government. If intruders settle among them, they should submit to the final decision of the local tribunals.[111]

For the time being the measure was defeated.

Two years later, in *Standley v. Roberts*[112] the Eighth Circuit Court of Appeals held that:

> the judgments of the Courts of these nations, [Five Civilized Tribes] in cases within their jurisdiction, stand on the same footing with those of the courts of the territories of the Union and are entitled to the same faith and credit.[113]

This decision was sustained by the Supreme Court in 1896.[114] Thus, by the time *Talton* was decided there had been a long history of federal respect for the internal sovereignty of the Five Civilized Tribes.[115]

Decision. The principle question in *Talton*, while not involving congressional power *per se*, did involve an important constitutional question. Did that portion of the Fifth Amendment of the Constitution requiring grand jury indictment apply to tribal nations? Justice Edward White, speaking for the majority, stated that the key to this decision depended upon an understanding of where Cherokee powers originated. If Cherokee powers of self-government were considered as "[f]ederal powers created by and springing from the Constitution of the United States," then they were controlled by the Fifth Amendment.[116] On the other hand, if Cherokee sovereignty was original, then the tribe was not subject to the constitutional amendment. The Court gave an indepth analysis of Cherokee treaty law, federal statutory law, and Cherokee legislative history in general, and concluded the following:

> As the powers of local self-government enjoyed by the Cherokee nation existed prior to the Constitution, they are not operated upon by the Fifth Amendment, which, as we have said, had for its sole object to control the powers conferred by the Constitution on the National Government.[117]

Therefore, the crime of murder, if committed by one Cherokee against another is "clearly not an offence against the United States, but an offence against the local laws of the Cherokee nation."[118]

This case was decided on the same day as the infamous *Plessy v. Ferguson*.[119] *Plessy*, which upheld a Louisiana law calling for separate railroad accommodation for whites and blacks, represented the high-water mark of the constitutional sanction of state "Jim Crow" laws. Both cases were 8–1 majorities, with Justice John M. Harlan dissenting in both. In *Plessy*, Harlan enunciated the brilliant and often quoted statement that the "Constitution is color-blind, and neither knows nor tolerates classes among citizens."[120] Harlan, however, did not issue a written dissent in Talton. Despite the similarity in numbers, 8–1, and in dissenter, Harlan, the Court's attitude toward tribes was quite anomalous when compared with its statements on blacks and other racial minorities of this time.

Legal Consciousness Exemplified and Masks Employed. This case has elements of Legal Con I and Legal Con II. On the one hand, it was clearly decided on purely constitutional/treaty grounds. That is to say, the Court could find no evidence whatsoever that tribal powers were subject to the U.S. Constitution because Indian sovereignty sprang from an entirely different well than that of the federal or state government's. The various treaties, federal statutes, and the tribe's own separate legislative system were evidence of this. On the other hand, this is also a Legal Con II case because the Court was very cognizant of the fact that the Five "Civilized" Tribes had legal and political institutions comparable to the Anglo model. These institutions, therefore, were worthy of independent recognition.

More importantly, the civilizing or cultural evidence is even more overwhelming when we consider that since Congress enacted the Major Crimes Act[121] in 1885, the federal government had been exercising criminal jurisdiction over any of seven "major" crimes committed by anyone in Indian Country. The *Talton* ruling directly contradicted this federal law and indicates the racial/cultural consciousness of the court. "Civilized" tribes could try their own criminals, especially if they were tribes that had legal systems loosely modeled after the federal system which the Cherokee institutions were; "uncivilized" tribes could not because they were deemed to "lack" not only the necessary political and legal institutions to administer law and order, but that they were inherently incapable of such administration of impartial justice.[122]

D. *Choate v. Trapp*[123]

Background. The Five Civilized Tribes in Oklahoma, as part of the Indian Removal program implemented between the 1820s and 1840s, had been given fee simple titles to their new homelands in the Indian Territory. This fact, combined with their willingness to synthesize tribal and Anglo institutional patterns, had led to their separate, and oftentimes more courteous, treatment by the United States. However, the inevitable, and often illegal, occupation of Indian Territory by whites by the late nineteenth century culminated in the enactment of a series of agreements and laws which debilitated the tribal groups.[124]

On November 16, 1907 Oklahoma became a state. The State constitution provided that Indian treaty and property rights were to continue unaffected. One important Indian property right was that tribal land was exempted from taxation by virtue of various treaties and federal laws. Nevertheless, Oklahoma's five member congressional delegation, supported "by powerful influences" secured the passage of an Act on May 27, 1908 which removed the restrictions upon the sale of a large class of Indian lands "so that these lands become subject to sale the same as lands of white people."[125] Another section of the act provided that these unrestricted lands were now subject to state taxation.[126]

Oklahoma's tax assessors wasted little time and proceeded to levy taxes on a wide cross-section of tribal members. The state argued that the tax was a legitimate exercise of governmental authority and that the Congress had acted to withdraw its protection of the tribes' tax exempt status by its passage of the 1908 Act. The tribesmen, on the other hand, asserted that this 1908 Act was a violation of the contract they had made with the United States and that their tax exempt status was a property right which could not be divested without due process of law.[127]

The 8,110 Chickasaw and Choctaw plaintiffs lost in Oklahoma's trial court and then in the State Supreme Court. They appealed to the United States Supreme Court. The principal question was whether the Indians had acquired vested rights under the Curtis Act of 1898 which were protected by the Fifth Amendment of the Constitution?[128]

Decision. While some commentators have read Choate as an individual property rights case, the real issue, according to Cohen, was the "plenary power of Congress over tribal affairs."[129] Plenary here is defined as federal power which may preempt state law, not as unlimited or absolute.[130] The Supreme Court, in effect, went far to support a rule which not only limited state efforts to tax Indians, but which also laid limits upon federal efforts to tax Indians as well.[131]

The Court carefully drew a distinction between "tribal property and private property" and affirmed that "Congress, in consideration of the Indians' relinquishment of all claims to the common property, and for other satisfactory reasons" extended vested rights to the tribal individuals.[132] These rights could not be taken without the individual Indian's consent. These passages illustrate the distinctive manner in which tribal sovereignty was applied in this case. As the Court noted:

> After he accepted the patent the Indian could not be heard, either of law or in equity, to assert any claim to the common property. If he is bound [by the agreement], so is the tribe and the Government when the patent is issued.[133]

Congress, therefore, could not impair a vested private property right by law which allowed the land to be taxed, regardless of the so-called "guardianship" power exercised by the Congress over the individual's status.[134]

The day after the decision (May 14) *The New York Times* ran an article entitled "Oklahoma Indians Win: Decision Will Cost the State Millions and May Bankrupt Counties."[135] J. F. McMurray, one of the Indians' attorneys, reported that sixty million acres of Indian lands would be exempted from taxation. This, it was estimated, would result in the loss of about two million dollars a year in tax revenues for the State.[136]

Oklahoma's congressional delegation, enraged at the lost tax revenues, had put together a legislative response. Representative Dick Morgan (R., Okla.) introduced a bill, H.R. 28670 in February 1913, which, if enacted, would have had the United States pay the state twenty million dollars in sixteen annual installments "in lieu of taxes on lands and other property within the State."[137]

Legal Consciousness Exemplified and Legal Masks Employed. This case, like *Talton*, seems also to have been decided on both constitutional/treaty (Legal Con I) grounds and on the basis of Legal Con II. In an important expansion, however, this case adds two additional elements onto the pre-existing extra-constitutional status of tribes and the rights of their members which were derived from this status and to the "civilized" status of the persons involved. The first element is federal legislation, which has added an additional layer of protection to protect tribal members' (this invokes federalism or federal supremacy) individualized rights drawn from a once collective tribal source. The second is the idea of Indians as private property owners, which is a central dynamic in the continued federal effort to "civilize" Indians.

E. *United States v. Sandoval*[138]

Background. A year after the *Choate* decision, congressional power and the status of the Pueblos of New Mexico were again an issue before the Supreme Court. Earlier the *Joseph* decision, which held that the 1834 Non-Intercourse Act was inapplicable to the Pueblos because of their unique legal status which dated back to Spanish times and which afforded them a land title "superior" even to that of the United States, was analyzed.[139]

Federal officials continued to differentiate the Pueblos from other tribes as evidenced by CIA Thomas Morgan's 1891 Annual Report wherein he notes that the "civilized" Pueblo tribes are pastoral, intelligent, industrious, and sober when compared to the "wild, nomadic, and savage tribes, not farther advanced in civilization than the hunter state . . ."[140] Despite their purported cultural dissimilarities from other indigenous groups, however, Commissioner Morgan admitted that "like the individual members of the wild tribes, the Pueblo Indian has no civil status in the eyes of the law."[141]

So long as New Mexico had territorial stature, the Pueblos generally remained a peripheral concern of the federal government. When, however, New Mexico was admitted to statehood in 1912, the subject of intergovernmental relations and Pueblo status cast a long shadow in need of clarification.[142] Congress had provided in New Mexico's Enabling Act[143] that the terms "Indian" and "Indian Country" were to include the Pueblos and their lands. These provisions were incorporated in the state constitution as well.[144]

These provisions were first tested in 1912. In *United States v.*

Sandoval,[145] the defendant, Felipe Sandoval, had been indicted for illegally taking liquor onto the Santa Clara Pueblo village. The District Court had to determine whether the federal statute admitting New Mexico into statehood, which contained a section prohibiting liquor onto Pueblo Territory, was constitutional. The Court said it was not. After reviewing the history of Pueblo related legislation and court precedent, District Judge Pope noted that:

> the effect of the decision may be to break down a safeguard which Congress and the framers of the New Mexico Constitution have attempted to provide for the Pueblo Indians. However, mere desirability of a result can furnish, as against constitutional limitation, no jurisdiction for an assumption of federal power nor for a denial of state jurisdiction.[146]

Decision. Shortly thereafter, the United States appealed to the Supreme Court. Despite a sizeable body of statutory and judicial law which had held that the Pueblos were not federal Indians for purposes of Indian-related legislation, the Supreme Court unanimously reversed the District Court's ruling.[147] The primary question before the Court was the constitutionality of Congress' exertion of protections in the form of liquor prohibitions over the Pueblos. The Court went to extraordinary lengths to illustrate its belief that although the Pueblos were "industrially superior" to other tribes, they still remained, like other tribes, "easy victims to the evils and debasing influence of intoxicants."[148]

Legal Consciousness Exemplified and Legal Masks Employed. In deferring to the congressional power lodged in the Commerce Clause, the Court, in a telling passage indicating the racial undertones of federal Indian law, said:

> As before indicated, by an uniform course of action beginning as early as 1854 . . . the legislature and executive branches of the Government have regarded and treated the Pueblos of New Mexico as dependent communities entitled to its aid and protection, like other Indian tribes, and considering their Indian lineage, isolated and communal life, primitive customs and limited civilization, this assertion of guardianship over them cannot be said to be arbitrary but must be regarded as both authorized and controlling.[149]

United States v. Sandoval contains multiple examples of racist and prejudicial language.[150] For instance, the Court noted that "the people of the Pueblos, although sedentary rather than nomadic in their inclinations, and disposed to peace and industry, are nevertheless Indians in race, customs, and domestic government."[151] The Court went on to assert that the Pueblos always reside in "isolated communities," pursue "primitive modes of life," lean toward "superstition and fetishism," and practice "crude customs inherited from their ancestors." In short, they are "essentially a simple, uninformed, and inferior people."[152]

Read more broadly, however, *Sandoval* merely extended federal protection over the Pueblos and their territory based on long-standing principles dating back to the Northwest Ordinance (1 St. 50,52 (1787)). As Cohen noted, "the effect of the *Sandoval* decision was to spread consternation among the people of New Mexico who held lands to which the Pueblos laid claim."[153] Thus, this case, while not dealing explicitly with tribal sovereignty, does provide a lucid statement on the distinctiveness of these tribal groups and, of more importance, can be read as placing some broad, though ill-defined, constraints on congressional power. As Justice Willis Van Devanter quickly noted, however, this ruling did not mean that Congress could bring "community or body of people within the range of this power [Commerce Clause] by arbitrarily calling them an Indian tribe . . ."[154]

The inherent sovereignty of the Pueblos redulates throughout the text of the Court's opinion. By stripping away the ethnocentric and patently paternalistic language, it is apparent that the Court determined the necessity of legitimating the political relationship between these tribes and the United States to protect them from Anglo settlers who had dramatically encroached upon Pueblo territory. Thus, in a strange sense, both *Joseph* and *Sandoval*, although called upon to answer different questions and, although arriving at conflicting results, actually reinforced Pueblo sovereignty.

This is clearly a Legal Con II case where the aim of the federal government was to protect the Pueblos, as a group, on their journey to "civilization." This cultural development was being hindered, ironically, by the presence of whites who had settled in large numbers among them, selling them liquor and other items considered detrimental to their cultural evolution. This case is similar to *Joseph* in which the aim was to protect purportedly undeveloped tribal groups who were taking their first steps toward civilization. What changed in the intervening years was not the Pueblo people, *per se*, (though surely there was growth and development), but federal policy and the sheer number of whites in Indian Country.

The Pueblos in 1877, having mastered an European language (Spanish), having allowed the construction of Catholic churches in their villages, and in general having less of an inclination toward violent confrontations with the few whites they encountered, had been left alone by the federal government and the Supreme Court, probably because they were believed to be well on their way toward civilizing themselves. By 1913, however, the number of whites had increased dramatically, federal policy was focused on coercive assimilation of all Indians and a general guardian/wardship relationship was said to exist in which tribal people were viewed as utterly dependent groups in need of constant federal tutelage to both protect the Indians from callous and unscrupulous whites and to protect them from themselves. Hence, the masks placed upon the Pueblos by the Supreme Court conceptualized them as "primitives," "inferior peoples," and "dependents," thereby necessitating the use of an unconstrained federal plenary power that was based on benevolent paternalism.

F. *Perrin v. United States*[155]

Background. The study of Indian liquor laws by itself would be a fascinating venture. In fact, liquor was the major issue in roughly 10 percent (12 cases) of the 107 cases comprising my data base. From the various laws enacted during the colonial period prohibiting the sale of liquor to Indians to the 1953 federal statute which finally allowed tribes the right to suspend federal liquor laws by an enactment subject to Interior Department approval,[156] liquor has played an important role in the dynamic relationship of the tribal/federal/state triumvirate.

A year after the *Sandoval* ruling, which had involved the introduction of liquor onto Indian territory, the issue of liquor and tribes was again before the Court. This time, though, the sale had occurred not on tribal land but on land owned by non-Indians in an organized non-Indian municipality, Dante, South Dakota. The key question, once again, was whether Congress had the authority to prohibit liquor sales, even on lands that had previously been ceded by the Yankton Sioux tribe under an 1894 agreement.[157] In the 17th section of that agreement, it was stipulated that no liquor should ever be sold or given away upon any of the lands ceded, nor upon the lands comprising the Yankton Reservation as described in the treaty between the Sioux and the United States of April 19, 1858.[158] Article twelve contained interesting language that tribal annuities would be withheld for one year from any Yankton Sioux found drunk or transporting liquor onto the reservation.[159]

Decision. The State of South Dakota claimed that it possessed jurisdiction since the event took place on private lands. But Justice Van Devanter, stressing a general theme of commerce power utilized as a limitation on state power and a more concentrated theme of federal supremacy over states regarding tribal affairs, held that Congress enjoyed the power to create "measures for their [Indians] protection."[160] Congressional power, stated the Court, "does not admit of any doubt."[161]

Although explicitly deferring to the legislative branch, the Court, for the first time since the 1880s, suggested that Congressional authority, in certain well-defined circumstances, could be constrained:

> As the power is incident only to the presence of the Indians and their status as wards of the Government, it must be conceded that it does not go beyond what is reasonably essential to their protection, and that, to be effective, its exercise must not be purely arbitrary, but founded upon some reasonable basis.[162]

This was a significant and long awaited comment for tribes and their growing number of non-Indian support groups who advocated a greater degree of tribal self-government. The Court, however, because of the political question doctrine and because of its general deference to congressional authority, has rarely invoked the "standard of arbitrariness" as a tool to constrain congressional power. In fact, in a statement immediately below the passage quoted above, the Court said that Congress "is invested with a wide discretion, and its action, unless purely arbitrary, must be accepted and given full effect by the courts."[163] Nevertheless, for the first time in several decades, the Court suggested there were some limits to Congress' exclusive power over the regulation of commerce with Indian tribes. This was a police power which the States could not infringe upon until Congress chose to withdraw the restriction.

Legal Consciousness Exemplified and Legal Masks Employed. This case exemplifies Legal Con II. *Perrin* arose during a time of great flux in federal Indian policy. It was an era in which the Bureau of Indian Affairs was investigated yet again for its gross failure to fulfill the federal government's trust obligations to tribes in an efficient and professional manner.[164] It was also an era in which a growing number of federal policy makers grudgingly came to the reality that tribal cultures should not be physically or intellectually vanquished and that instead the country would be better off if it preserved at least some aspects of indigenous culture. But more importantly, this decade represented a period in which federal legislation focused less on protecting Indians from whites and more on "providing a form of trust for Indian property." Indians, in effect, became viewed as an "attachment to their lands rather than owners."[165] Hence, while *Perrin* was an important victory, administrative agencies like the BIA were left virtually unchecked and remained largely unaccountable to Congress.

III. Legal Consciousness and Legal Masks in Negative Tribal Sovereignty Cases

Now the brace of Supreme Court opinions in this historical era which represent the onerous side of federal Indian policy insofar as they relate to congressional power and tribal sovereignty will be examined. The following cases provide overwhelming evidence supporting a view of the

Court as a body intent on legitimating congressional policies that stripped many tribes of their sovereign as well as vested political and property rights. Since tribes were precluded in 1871 from negotiating additional treaties,[166] though agreements continued to be made, and since many Indians were not federal citizens, they were effectively denied any political remedies for violations of their rights. The tribes and the tribal individual's quest for legal remedies—via the Supreme Court—also proved a fruitless endeavor when the request was for the Court to constrain federal power over tribal sovereignty and tribal property.

These cases, in effect, exemplify a distinctively different type of legal consciousness, what we earlier described as Nationalism/Federalism—Legal Consciousness (Legal Con III). With the first two types of legal consciousness, we have seen that it is possible for tribes to have their sovereignty recognized by the Supreme Court. Regarding Legal Con I, it is possible because of the tribes pre-existing, and, therefore, extra-constitutionally established, rights, which place indigenous groups on a political plane somewhat akin to that between the United States government and foreign powers (treaty-based), but also somewhat like the relationship between the United States government and the states. In fact, Vine Deloria, Jr.[167] and Charles F. Wilkinson[168] have equated the tribal/federal relationship (based on treaties) to the relationship between states and the federal government (based on the 10th Amendment).

With Legal Con II, it is possible for tribal sovereignty to be affirmed since some tribes can be recognized as civilized or an capable of civilization. Thus, the law, as defined and wielded by the Supreme Court, was in some cases deemed inapplicable to those tribes possessing legal systems considered parallel to that of the United States. In those opinions, the Court accorded a measure of respect to the tribe.

In the third type of consciousness, however, the concepts of political development, nation-state, nation-building, nationalism, and national integration are defined by the Court in such a way that there is no room, sometimes not even any acknowledgment, of any other sovereign than that which is the sole expression of national unity (i.e., the federal government and the constituent states). Not surprisingly, in the case of the United States, national identity was defined in western terms. Thus, the stark denial followed by the virtual elimination (usually by cultural and structural assimilation) of tribes as distinctive polities was considered an essential element in the nation-building process occurring in the United States after the Civil War. The goal was the assimilation of tribes, followed by the imposition of a single view of political democracy that everyone in the nation was subjected to—both the dominant and the subordinate groups.

In an enlightened article written in 1934, W.G. Rice braved an attempt to explain the anomalous legal position of American Indians. He noted:

> The law has long been uncertain and its future is uncertain chiefly because the fundamental question of whether destruction of tribal life is to be encouraged is undecided.[169]

There is then, said Rice, "no sure aim either to preserve tribal culture or, on the contrary, to melt it down in the great cauldron of American life."[170] Rice's depiction is not only simplistic, it is also deeply ethnocentric. Nevertheless, the "either-or" scenario he drew was widely accepted almost nonchalantly at the time, and still, unfortunately, represents the thinking of many federal officials today. Of more importance, it was even more pertinent during the late nineteenth century.

Certain scholars and government officials alike have argued at times that it was perfectly permissible for the United States Congress to act without regards for the Constitution in its dealings with tribes precisely because tribes were extra-constitutional. According to Canfield:

> The Constitution was an instrument framed for a nation of independent freemen, who had religious convictions worth protecting . . . to suppose that the framers of the Constitution intended to secure to the Indians the rights and privileges which they valued as Englishmen is to misconceive the spirit of their age, and to impute to it an expansive benevolence which it did not possess.[171]

Kagama and the other cases to be described in this section, typify the nationalism/federalism side of the cultural perspective, with the assimilative twist to which Rice alluded. This held that the destruction of tribal life was both good and necessary to elevate the Indian from his "inferior" position to one slightly below, though certainly not equal, to that of the Anglo majority. It was also, as we will see, determined to be necessary to facilitate the nation-building process.

This form of consciousness (Legal Con III) was also operative to a degree in several of the pro-sovereignty cases discussed above. For example, congressional and administrative reaction to the Elk decision was swift, though ill-focused.[172] Some groups, like the Board of Indian Commissioners reaffirmed the idea it had maintained as an organizational tenet for some time—the solution to the Indian "problem" was unfettered citizenship.[173] Others, however, like Senator Henry Dawes (R., Mass.) and the Commissioner of Indian Affairs (hereafter "CIA"), John Atkins, asserted that citizenship should be a "gradual" process tied to individualized land ownership.[174] Eventually a compromise was reached. The General Allotment Act, also known as the Dawes Severalty Act,[175] enacted on February 8, 1887, contained a provision which extended citizenship to every Indian who received an allotment and to every Indian who separated himself from his tribe and adopted the ways of civilized life.

Federal citizenship, however, would not impair their right "to tribal or other property."[176]

The issues of land allotment, tribal membership, and citizenship raised more problems than they solved. It is, however, beyond the scope of this paper to treat this triangle of issues although they have been ably explored elsewhere.[177] Legal Con III also led to a major assault on the sovereignty of the previously shielded Five Civilized Tribes. The first major threat to their autonomy came in the form of a special Commission, authorized by Congress and headed by Henry Dawes, designed to force these tribes to negotiate agreements with the federal government that called for the allotment of their lands.[178] The Five Tribes (and several others) were excluded from the provisions of the 1887 Dawes Severalty Act because they held fee simple titles to their communally held lands.[179] Not surprisingly, many tribal members and their leaders refused voluntarily to surrender their lands, despite the Commission's persistent efforts.[180]

The patience of certain powerful congressmen and bureaucrats ran low. The House Committee on Indian Affairs issued a report in March 1898, indicating the government's frustration and real interest on the one hand, and the political savvy and determination of the tribes to resist the government's efforts to abrogate their treaties, destroy their tribal governments, and radically reduce their landholdings on the other. It stated:

> It appears that the title to lands in the Indian Territory has been conveyed by patents to the tribes, and cannot be taken from them without their consent. There are about 20,000,000 acres of land thus owned. It is rich in mineral deposits, and contains a large area of splendid farming and grazing land . . . For the last few years the Dawes Commission has been endeavoring to secure agreements with the various tribes, but so far there has been little accomplished. Agreements were made with the commissioners of the several tribes—all, in fact, except the Cherokees—but the Creek agreement was rejected by the tribes when the vote was taken upon it. The Chickasaws rejected the joint agreement with the Choctaws and Chickasaws . . . In view of the fact that it is now impossible to secure agreements with the tribes, and the fact that the title is in the tribes, your committee has provided for the allotment of the exclusive use and occupancy of the surface of the lands of each of the nations.[181]

What the committee "provided for" was a bill, which would become law three months later, entitled the Curtis Act.[182] With this Act, Congress, unilaterally and in direct violation of treaty and statutory law, terminated the legal existence of the Five Civilized Tribes.[183] Political and social conditions among the Five Tribes deteriorated rapidly thereafter. Tribal laws and courts were abolished, tribal members were to be enrolled, and allotment was to proceed quickly.

While some of the positive sovereignty cases recognized that it was possible for tribes to pursue their own paths to civilization, the opinions in this section hold, for the most part, that civilization of the Indians can be obtained only by their Americanization and thus their assimilation into the American melting pot. A good example of how this "Americanization" process was to occur can be seen in the subject of forced labor. Despite the comments of the Supreme Court in *The Slaughter-House Cases* on the illegality of slavery and involuntary servitude,[184] a year later a federal law was enacted which forced all "able-bodied male Indians" to perform labor before they could receive their treaty entitlements.[185] Commissioner Edward Smith put it this way:

> Congress, at its last session, recognizing the propriety that Indians, like other people, should toil for what they have, directed that all annuities should hereafter be paid only in return for some form of labor . . . This eminently wise legislation has been of great avail to the Bureau during the year in enforcing industry.[186]

Twenty-five years later, Commissioner Jones reported that the Indian Bureau regulations continued to give each reservation's Indian agent the authority "not only to encourage, but also to enforce, regular labor among Indians." The agent, moreover, was given great discretion to ascertain whether Indians were actually entitled to their daily rations. He was more interested in determining whether the Indians exhibited the proper "spirit and disposition to work" than with the actual value of the work accomplished.[187] As late as 1913, the Commissioner reported that such a requirement to labor was in the best interest of the Indian.[188] Similar manifestations of this type of legal consciousness can be seen again and again in the Court decisions that denied tribal sovereignty.

A. *United States v. Kagama*[189]

Background. Criminal law represented a major area in which this disagreement on whether to respect or obliterate tribal autonomy transpired. Before the 1880s, relations between tribes and the United States were largely determined either by treaties or by the so-called Indian trade and intercourse acts. These Intercourse Acts, the first passed in 1790, the final and enduring one in 1834, were designed to regulate the general and commercial relations between tribes and Americans.[190] Importantly, the Intercourse Acts extended minimal federal jurisdiction over Indians only in their relation with whites. Internal tribal sovereignty, especially offenses committed by Indians against Indians, was not touched by the laws.[191] According to Prucha, until the mid-1800s there were no federal treaty or statutory constraints on the internal affairs of tribes.[192]

The subject of the imposition of federal criminal jurisdiction over purely internal tribal disputes slowly increased as western expansion inexorably encircled tribal lands with the concomitant rise of a "reservation policy." In fact, Commissioner George Manypenny bluntly stated in 1856 that "the conviction and execution, under criminal laws of all Indians guilty of the murder of Indians, would, it is believed, put a stop to the war parties." Such a policy, the Commissioner observed would "be an act of humanity," with the result being "a most salutary influence" on tribal behavior.[193]

By 1866 the arguments favoring federal jurisdiction were both refined and broadened. Now, it was no longer simply a desire to "make an example" of one Indian for another's benefit. The goal was the inevitable "civilization" of the Indians whether they wanted it or not. Commissioner D. N. Cooley resurrected Manypenny's idea for the imposition of a federal criminal code applicable to reservation Indians. Cooley alleged the following:

> Retaliation is the law of the Indian; and if, in his early approaches to civilization, he is compelled to abandon that law, he looks for a substitute in the white man's law.[194]

After the 1871 treaty-termination amendment,[195] an assortment of congressional lawmakers, federal administrators, private philanthropic organizations, and Christian societies stepped up their desire to see the "Indian Problem" solved by having the tribes dissolved and the Indians forcibly incorporated into American society.[196] In fact, the Board of Indian Commissioners declared in 1871 that until Indians were brought under "the domination of law, so far as regards crimes committed against each other," the government's best efforts to "civilize" the Indians would be handicapped.[197]

Three years later, April 2, 1874, Senator William Buckingham (R., Connecticut) introduced S. 652, which would have conferred "exclusive jurisdiction over Indian reservations upon the United States courts for the punishment of crimes by and against Indians."[198] The bill was not enacted, however. Nevertheless, federal agencies and reform groups continued to push for federal criminal jurisdiction over tribal members.[199]

Some authors contend, arguably, that the "dominant concern" of federal and private individuals and groups desiring the imposition of federal law was "the protection of the individual Indian in his personal and property rights."[200] While this was certainly one of the concerns, it is debatable whether it was the "dominant" one. There is ample evidence which indicates that the primary reason for such an encroachment on tribal autonomy was because the Indian's form of "primitive" justice was, ironically, not considered stern enough for whites, who firmly believed in *lex talionis* (law of retaliation). In the Commissioner's own words, Indian murderers occasionally went "unwhipt of justice."[201] This is not true, of course. In most traditional tribal societies, the primary goal in the resolution of tribal disputes was not to "ascertain guilt and then bestow punishment upon the offender;" rather, it was "simply to mediate the case to everyone's satisfaction."[202]

The issue of Indian-on-Indian crimes finally arrived at the Supreme Court in 1883 in the case of a Sioux leader, Crow Dog, who had been sentenced to death by the First District court of South Dakota for the murder of Chief Spotted Tail. In the landmark case, *Ex Parte Crow Dog*,[203] the Supreme Court held that the United States lacked jurisdiction over crimes committed by one Indian against another. This decision from the nation's highest tribunal was a most dramatic and positive statement on tribal sovereignty and served as the final catalyst necessary to propel the jurisdictional changes viewed as essential by the melange of groups that desired to have Anglo law replace tribal law.[204]

On March 3, 1885, a short year and a half after *Crow Dog*, these groups received their wish when Congress, by an amendment to the general appropriations act, extended federal criminal jurisdiction over "all" Indians for seven major crimes—murder, manslaughter, rape, assault with intent to kill, arson, burglary, and larceny.[205] In reality, however, several tribes, most notably the Five Civilized Tribes, were excluded from this Act's provisions. In fact, as noted above in the *Talton* decision, the Supreme Court recognized in the Five Tribes a continued right to hand down judgments on major crimes. Tribal sovereignty, for most other tribes, had been dealt a swift, though not fatal, blow. Nevertheless, passage of this Act indicated the future direction of much federal legislation. But first the determination had to be made: Was this profound federal intrusion of tribal sovereignty constitutional? This was the question in the *Kagama* case.

Decision. The facts in *Kagama* are simple enough. Two Indians from the Hoopa Valley Reservation in Humboldt County, California, Kagama (alias "Pactah Billy") and Mahawaha (alias "Ben") had been indicted for the murder of another Indian, Iyouse (alias "Ike"). The murder occurred on the reservation. The case arrived at the Supreme Court by certificate of division of opinion.[206] The two principal questions certified were as follows: 1) Was section nine (seven major crimes provision) a constitutional law?, and 2) Did the federal courts have jurisdiction over the case? The court answered both questions in the affirmative.

Disregarding a century of federal legislation, several hundred treaties, and an earlier Supreme Court precedent, the Court began its tortured opinion by noting that the Constitution says little about the tribal-federal relationship.[207] Justice Samuel Miller then described the placement of

Indians in the Enumerative and Commerce clauses, which are the only two clauses that expressly mention Indians. The Court correctly stated that neither of the pertinent constitutional clauses or any other language provided the United States with any legal power "to enact a code of criminal law for the punishment of the worst class of crimes known to civilized life when committed by Indians."[208] The Court then sought to provide some sort of rationale for the constitutional curiosity of their creation of a federal legislative authority over tribes lacking a constitutional source.

The Court, instead of locating a legitimate constitutional basis for its decisions, crafted an ingenious and largely bogus two-pronged explanation—Indian helplessness and land ownership. First, Justice Miller transmuted Marshall's 1831 "analogy" of Indians as "wards" to their federal "guardians" to a principle of law. He said: "These Indian tribes are wards of the nation. They are communities dependent on the United States."[209] Continuing the facade, the Court said that federal power over these "weak" peoples was "necessary to their protection, as well as to the safety of those among whom they dwell." This power, the Court held, "must exist in that government, because it never has existed anywhere else."[210]

Second, the Court misinterpreted the "Doctrine of Discovery," originally enunciated by Chief Justice Marshall, and stated that by its self-declared ownership of the continent the United States had the authority to do as it pleased regarding tribes. "These Indians," said the Court, "are within the geographical limits of the United States." Thus, Justice Miller argued, "the soil and the people within these limits are under the political control of the Government of the United States, or of the States of the Union."[211]

The Court in the span of a few short pages had cleverly and extra-constitutionally found a way to protect the tribes from state jurisdiction, but in so doing had also given both itself and the legislative branch *carte blanche* to exercise whatever power it believed necessary in the best interests of its "helpless wards." Many contemporary Indian law scholars and historians assert that *Kagama* is the fountain of congressional plenary and judicial plenary interpretive power, although the concept "plenary" never appears in the decision.[212] These commentators have pointed out the multitude of untenable errors lodged in the Court's statements.

First, how could Congress legitimately apply its laws to tribes that until that time had not been subject under the Constitution to its legislative jurisdiction?[213] Second, if the Constitution limits the authority of the various branches to enumerated powers, why did the Court cite extra-constitutional reasons for holding a congressional statute to be constitutional?[214] Third, "consent of the governed" is a treasured democratic principle. However, the fact that most Indians were not citizens and were thus unable to vote because they were "in a semi-independent position" seemed irrelevant to the Court. Furthermore, Newton asserts that:

> Concentrating or justifying federal power the Court reinforced earlier precedents abdicating its role in accommodating the legitimate but competing interest raised by the federal government's interference with tribal rights. Such accommodation was left to the political arena—an arena from which Indian were excluded.[215]

Congress' Major Crimes Act presaged an impressive transformation in the relationship between the tribes and the federal government. However, it was restricted legislation, applying only to seven crimes. Furthermore, some scholars have suggested that theoretically tribal courts still may exercise concomitant jurisdiction along with the United States and that, in fact, the Major Crimes Act merely added federal jurisdiction to pre-existing tribal jurisdiction.[216] Finally, while the Act was ostensibly comprehensive, it was noted earlier that the Five Civilized Tribes were in practice exempted from its provisions. With this major exemption in mind, one is compelled to ask: Who actually determines how a law that involves tribal nations is to be applied? The Congress? The President? The Courts? Or, in the case of the Five Tribes, local federal bureaucrats?

Legal Consciousness Exemplified and Legal Masks Employed. Justice Miller's opinion for a unanimous court is a classic example of the Supreme Court functioning as an institution with a mystifying brand of legal consciousness that is purely aberrational. This was aberrational because the Court almost entirely transformed the previously well-defined political relationship between tribes and the United States despite their statement that it was morally their "duty to expound and execute the law as [they] find it."[217]

In this case the Court went far beyond merely expounding and executing. Instead, it exercised a "plenary interpretive power" that very nearly supplanted tribal sovereignty, that completely omitted the doctrine of enumerated powers, and that elevated a simple analogy—a relationship resembling a ward to his guardian—to a newly-created federal and extra-constitutional power to regulate internal tribal affairs—the so-called "guardianship" power.

What accounts, then, for this transformation in the legal consciousness of the Court, which had been asked simply to determine the constitutionality of this legislation? Why did it abruptly and inexplicably invest in Congress an unlimited and unauthorized power not connected to any constitutional provisions? As late as 1883 in *The Civil Rights Cases*,[218] the Court had properly noted that the Commerce Clause gave Congress the exclusive power to deal with tribes. Furthermore, in the case *In Re*

Sah Quah, decided May 8, 1886, two days before *Kagama*, a federal district court following, as it was bound by law to do, Supreme Court precedent, held the following:

> From the organization of the government to the present time, the various Indian tribes of the United States have been treated as free and independent within their respective territories, governed by their tribal laws and customs, in all matters pertaining to their inherent affairs, such as contracts and the manner of their enforcement . . . and the punishment for crimes committed against each other.[219]

Broadly put, the legal transformation occurred to legitimate the unabashed and forced congressional policy of assimilation and acculturation of tribal citizens into American society. As Indian Affairs Commissioner John Oberly noted in his 1888 annual report, the Indian "must be imbued with the exalting egotism of American civilization, so that he will say 'I' instead of 'We,' and 'This is mine,' instead of 'This is ours'."[220]

The Court, in its efforts to legitimate the federal government's policy of Americanization and assimilation of Indians developed the non-constitutional legal sophistry of "wardship" and would coin other "masks" over the next several decades to further the assimilative process but also to "protect" tribal people from state, corporate, and private interests as well. The Court's extra-constitutional principles sent a message to those seeking to intrude into tribal affairs (excepting the federal government) that unconstrained federal authority over Indian affairs would be used "precisely because they [Indians] are [were] outside the protections of the Constitution" and because "it [Congress] needed to be immune from ordinary challenges which might otherwise hamper the wise administration of the affairs of Indians."[221] Unfortunately, the absolute power the Court arrogated to itself and the Congress in *Kagama* set a destructive precedent tribes still confront, for there is no obvious limitation on Congress' presumed plenary power regarding tribal sovereignty "except the moral sensibility of Congress."[222]

Coincidentally or not, on May 10, 1886, the same day tribes were learning of their completely vulnerable position insofar as the protection of any constitutional rights protections were concerned, the Supreme Court in *Santa Clara Company v. Southern Pacific Railroad*, by way of *dictum*, unanimously affirmed that the due process clause of the Fourteenth Amendment protected corporations as "legal persons."[223] In effect, corporate property rights were extended constitutional protections; tribal political and property rights, however, could be quashed and lacked constitutional safeguards.

B. *Cherokee Nation v. Southern Kansas Railway Company*[224]

Background. Congress enacted the General Allotment Act[225] a year after *Kagama*. I have already discussed this act. I also noted that the Act's provisions were inapplicable to the Five Tribes. Nevertheless, a myriad of interests, including the powerful railroad companies, were intent on securing rights-of-way to tribal lands.[226] By the mid-1880s, there were four transcontinental railroad lines—the Union Pacific-Central Pacific, the Atchison, Topeka and Santa Fe, the Southern Pacific, and the Northern Pacific.[227] Each of these lines and many tributary lines coursing throughout the country already passed through various Indian reservations.[228] Although admitting that "railroads are of the first importance in the solution of the Indian problem," the Commissioner of Indian Affairs observed, as early as 1872, that a railroad's right-of-way request would not be considered if it appeared to be a "demand for the disruption of a reservation." The Commissioner noted that "the treaty-rights of the Indians are paramount, and must in all honor and conscience be preserved inviolate."[229]

Despite the railroad lobby's power, securing rights-of-way through tribal lands was sometimes difficult. President Grover Cleveland, on July 7, 1886 vetoed an act that would have granted railroads the right-of-way through a reservation in Montana. The President, while acknowledging the federal government's right of eminent domain if "for the general welfare of the country," said that the Indians had "not given their consent" to the right of way . . . neither have they been consulted regarding it."[230]

Cleveland emphasized that the Act under review posed a serious threat to democratic principles. It is, said Cleveland:

> A new and wide departure from the general tenor of legislation affecting Indian reservations. It ignores the right of the Indians to be consulted as to the disposition of their lands, opens wide the door to any railroad corporation to what, under the treaty covering the greater portion of the reservation, is reserved to the United States alone . . . [and] it invites a general invasion of the Indian country.[231]

In 1889, two of the Five Tribes, the Creeks and Seminoles, bowing to mounting private, state, and congressional pressure to cede their lands, had entered separate agreements with the United States whereby they had collectively ceded some 1,887,796 acres of land, which was soon opened for white settlement. The following year the *Cherokee Nation* stood before the Supreme Court contesting an 1884 congressional law which granted a right of way through Cherokee Territory to the Southern Kansas Railway Company. There were several related questions to be settled: Did

Congress have the authority, by eminent domain, to confiscate Cherokee lands and give them to this company without Cherokee consent and without having paid prior to their confiscation just compensation? Did Congress' passage of the 1884 act violate Cherokee rights, and was the Cherokee Nation sovereign in its own territory? The Court unanimously held that the Cherokees' inherent sovereignty could not prevent the Federal government from exercising its power of eminent domain to take Indian lands.

The Cherokee Nation's attorney had argued that his client's inherent sovereignty, as recognized in treaties, vested exclusively in them the right of eminent domain. In addition, he stressed that in exchange for ceded tribal lands the Cherokees had received from the United States fee simple title to their lands in Indian territory over which they alone exercised jurisdiction and sovereignty."[232] Justice John M. Harlan, however, held that the Cherokees were not "a sovereign state, with no superior within the limits of its territory."[233] Harlan, in rapid succession, appropriated the wardship and dependency phrases raised first in *Cherokee Nation v. Georgia*,[234] and then used again in *United States v. Rogers*,[235] and finally reified in *United States v. Kagama*,[236] and stated that the tribes "peculiar" and "inferior" status deprived them of enforceable rights. Even the fact that the Cherokee Tribe held fee simple title to their territory was "of no consequence" to the Court.[237] Harlan capped off his crushing opinion by using the now entrenched and reified concept of "wardship:"

> It would be very strange if the national government in the execution of its rightful authority could exercise the power of eminent domain in the several States, and could not exercise the same power in a Territory occupied by an Indian nation or tribe, the members of which were wards of the United States, and directly subject to its political control.[238]

Legal Consciousness Exemplified and Legal Masks Employed. As the above quote indicates, the Court, following the aberrant and mystifying ideology voiced in *Kagama*, said in effect that because tribes had the status of "wards," Congress had authority to confiscate even fee simple tribal property previously guaranteed to the tribes by treaty. Because of their fee simple title, the Five Civilized Tribes were, at least until the late 1880s, immune from any forced major land concessions. But the conceptualization of Indians as "wards"[239] requiring "guardianship," enunciated in *Kagama*, had become the regnant perception of most government officials, Christian reformers, and many private citizens. The notion of "guardianship," which had first been broached in the 1831 *Cherokee Nation* case, had revisited the Cherokee Nation in a far more devastating manner. Again, as in *Kagama*, congressional power over tribes is here defined as essentially unlimited. The Cherokee nation was only entitled to just compensation for the lands they were losing. Congress had this "paramount authority" over the Cherokees even though they held these lands "in fee simple under patents from the United States." This was so because the:

> United States may exercise the right of eminent domain, even within the limits of the several States, for purposes necessary to the execution of the powers granted to the general government by the Constitution. Such an authority . . . is essential to the independent existence and perpetuating of the United States, and is not dependent upon the consent of the States.[240]

Here it can be very clearly seen that the Supreme Court is using the law both to strengthen the doctrine of federal supremacy and to perpetuate tribal wardship. Further evidence of this is found in a succeeding passage in which Justice Harlan observes that:

> it would be very strange if the national government, in the execution of its rightful authority could exercise the power of eminent domain in the several States, and could not exercise the same power in a Territory occupied by an Indian nation or tribe, the members of which were wards of the United States and directly subject to its political control.[241]

This combination of nation-building, which denied the Cherokees full sovereign status, synthesized with the assimilative view of the Cherokees as wards completely subject to federal dominion, was enough to seal the loss of Cherokee territory, notwithstanding ratified treaties and even vested fee-simple property title. As the Court maintained, while the Cherokees were a "distinct community" with certain rights as a state recognized in treaties and earlier laws, these documents did not:

> evince any intention, upon the part of the government, to discharge them from their condition of pupilage or dependency, and constitute them a separate, independent, sovereign people, with no superior within its limits.[242]

C. *Stephens v. Cherokee Nation* (1899)[243]

Background. The Five Civilized Tribes, largely because of their distinctive legal, social, and cultural standing, received comparatively more "favorable" treatment by the Congress, various Presidents, and the Supreme Court until the end of the 1880s. Around that period, the Cherokees and Seminoles were compelled into negotiations with the

United States in which they ceded nearly two million acres of land.

Pressure continued to mount against these and the other Five Tribes for additional concessions of lands and rights. In 1891 President Harrison observed that "the relation of the Five Civilized Tribes now occupying the Indian Territory . . . is not, I believe, that best calculated to promote the highest advancement of these Indians." According to Harrison, the fact that there were "within our borders five independent states having no relations, except those growing out of treaties . . . [was] a startling anomaly."[244]

Two years later, Congress authorized the President to appoint a commission whose purpose was to convince these tribes of the benefits of breaking up their communal land holdings and having them converted into individual allotments.[245] Over the next few years, an unbearable amount of pressure was exerted on the Five Tribes intended to press them into entering negotiated agreements where they would cede additional chunks of tribal land in exchange for small, isolated parcels.[246] Four of the Five Tribes resisted, however.[247]

While this was transpiring, the Dawes Commission issued a report on May 7, 1894 which declared that the Five Civilized Tribes separate legal and political status had to be terminated. "It is not only non-American," noted the Commissioners, "but it is radically wrong, and a change is imperatively demanded in the interest of the Indian and white alike, and such change cannot be much longer delayed."[248] Congress later, by way of a provision in the Indian Appropriation Act of 1896, authorized the Dawes Commission to move directly to supplant a key right of self-government—the Commission was empowered to determine who could be enrolled as citizens in the Five Tribes.[249]

A year later, on June 7, 1897, the relentless process to terminate tribal governing authority and replace it with Anglo authority was furthered with the passage of a congressional statute that gave federal courts civil and criminal jurisdiction over the Indian Territory. This transfer of jurisdiction was slated to begin January 1, 1898.[250] Congress then prepared to enact unilateral legislation to complete its dubious mission—the legal dismemberment of the Five Tribes' self-government and the individualization of their lands. The tribes responded by astutely employing every political means at their disposal to head this off. For instance, the Creek and Seminole Nation submitted a petition to the Senate in which they implored that body not to enact such a measure. "We desire," said the tribal politicians, "to call your attention to the fact that under the solemn treaty stipulations the right of unrestricted self-government has been guaranteed to our people."[251]

Despite these and other formidable and constitutionally-based arguments, Congress, on June 28, 1898 enacted the Curtis Act, which effectively gutted what remained of the Five Tribes governing powers in

Indian Territory.[252] Interestingly, the 24-page law was entitled "An Act for the protection of the people of the Indian Territory." The bill was so titled because one of its principal selling points in Congress had been that white residents in Indian Country, who deluged Indians 300,000 to 65,000, allegedly had to deal with tribal officials who purportedly engaged in "unlawful and fraudulent transactions."[253]

Decision. In *Stephens v. Cherokee Nation*, the Supreme Court[254] acquiesced to the congressional trampling of tribal governing rights and upheld the federal legislation under which Congress assumed the tribe's power to determine their own membership rolls. Furthermore, the Court did not question whether the government's usurpation of tribal enrollment was proper, *per se*; it merely restated the delusion of tribes as "wards," first articulated in *Cherokee Nation* (1831), as a justification for the Congress's ousting of tribal jurisdiction regarding membership.[255]

The 7-2 majority, (Justice's Edward White and Joseph McKenna dissented, but only regarding the extent of the Court's jurisdiction) early in the opinion, cited Congress' "plenary power of legislation" regarding tribal citizenship.[256] This is the first case in which the concept "plenary" is explicitly used, although unlike the *Kagama* decision, congressional power is here defined as exclusive and not unlimited because it is "subject . . . to the Constitution of the United States."[257] This constitutional constraint was not present in *Kagama*. In addition, the Court openly deferred to the legislature, and quoting from *Thomas v. Gay*,[258] stated that questions such as Congress' power to supersede a treaty and others "are beyond the sphere of judicial cognizance, and must be met by the political department of the Government."[259]

Hence, this is the first case which combines congressional plenary power, judicial deference, and the political question doctrines. This doctrinal synthesis is a devastating and oppressive alliance which invariably overwhelms tribal sovereignty.[260] Equally interesting is the placement of the political question doctrine in the opinion's text. It is inserted immediately after the Court's statements dealing with the cessation of treaty-making in 1871. The Court said that:

> It is true that the Indian tribes were for many years allowed by the United States to make all laws and regulations [for their own people] . . . [t]he policy of the Government, however, in dealing with the Indian Nations was definitely expressed in a proviso [1871 treaty-termination clause].[261]

The High Court not only legitimated Congress' questionable action of stripping the President of his constitutional authority to negotiate treaties with tribes and of no longer recognizing tribal sovereignty via the treaty process, but had, in employing the political question doctrine, simultaneously precluded tribes from a judicial remedy.

Chief Justice Melville Fuller, near the end of his opinion, concisely asserted why such immense congressional power was necessary and how it would be used:

> We respect that in view of the paramount authority of Congress over the Indian tribes, and of the duties imposed on the Government by their condition of dependency, we cannot say that Congress could not empower the Dawes Commission to determine . . . who were entitled to citizenship . . . [this was] an essential preliminary to effective action in promotion of the best interests of the tribes.[262]

Legal Consciousness Exemplified and Legal Masks Employed. For the Court, the "plenary dependency" of the tribes mandated a "plenary congressional power" to ensure the individual Indian's proper evolution towards citizenship and full assimilation. The "mask" of wardship had been reified to such a point that even the question of tribal citizenship had to be handled by the federal government. After all, such an important determination could not be left in the hands of "incompetent wards."

D. *Lone Wolf v. Hitchcock*[263]

Background. On October 21, 1867 representatives of the Kiowa and Comanche Tribes (the Apache Tribe joined the other tribes by separate treaty)[264] entered into a treaty with the seven member delegation of the congressionally created Indian Peace Commission at Medicine Lodge Creek in Kansas.[265] This multi-purpose treaty required land cessions, established peace, and created reservation boundaries. Moreover, it contained several "civilizing" provisions, including the following: Indian parents agreed to send their children to school, heads of households could select up to 320 acres for farming, and the Indians agreed to remain within the boundaries of their newly-established homelands.

The most relevant provisions, however, are found in Articles 2 and 12, which deal with the establishment and protection of the three million acre reservation. Article 2 reads in pertinent part that the reservation was to be "set apart for the absolute and undisturbed use and occupation of the tribes herein named."[266] The germane section of Article 12 states:

> No treaty for the cession of any portion or part of the reservation herein described, which may be held in common, shall be of any validity or force as against the said Indians, unless executed and signed by at least three-fourths of all the adult male Indians occupy-

ing the same.[267]

Notwithstanding these legal and moral assurances, the fervor to individualize tribal land holdings following the passage of the 1887 General Allotment Act, soon reached the confederated Kiowa, Comanche, and Apache Reservation (KCA reservation).

In 1892 the three-member federal Cherokee Commission (also known as the Jerome Commission), established by Congress in 1889 to engage certain Oklahoma tribes in land cession agreements,[268] concluded an agreement with representatives from the KCA tribes for the allotment of their lands. The remaining "surplus" lands were to be opened for non-Indian settlement. Although a number of Indian signatures were obtained, the three-fourths requirement was not met. Nevertheless, the agreement was sent to Washington, D.C. for ratification by both Houses of Congress.

On October 20, 1893, three-hundred and twenty-three KCA tribal members memorialized the Senate, vociferously arguing that the October 6, 1892 agreement should not be ratified for several reasons: 1) the negotiating sessions were not, as required by law, conducted "in open council nor in the presence or with the knowledge of their [tribal leaders] people and constituents;" 2) after having fraudulently obtained the tribal leaders' signatures, the Jerome Commission then "caused numerous pretended councils of said Indians to be held under the guns of said fort" [Ft. Sill] where additional signatures were gathered "by misrepresentation, threats, and fraud;" and 3) that the government's commissioners then moved to the Indian agency headquarters of Anadarko where "for more than a month . . . it continued its campaign of mendacity, fraud, and coercion until the alleged signatures of four-hundred and fifty-six Indians were claimed to have been obtained."[269] The tribal memorialists then asserted that once the four-hundred and fifty-six signatures were collected "said agreement was, without the loss of an hour, but upon the same day, transmitted to Washington."[270]

Despite the apparent haste with which the agreement had been delivered to the Capitol, the ratification process would not be so quick. In 1898, five years from the date of the agreement's arrival in Washington, and after several previous attempts, a bill was reported out of Committee on the House side favoring enactment of the 1892 agreement. This bill, however, substantially altered the original agreement. The KCA tribes had fought every legislative attempt to approve the agreement. Nevertheless, the House bill was passed on May 16, 1898.[271]

The Senate, however, bowing to pressure from the KCA tribes and their non-Indian advocate group, the Indian Rights Association, adopted a resolution in January, 1899 which directed the Secretary of Interior to determine whether the requisite number of signatures had been obtained.[272] When Secretary Hitchcock responded on January 13, 1900, his findings were startling and confirmed the major contentions of the KCA tribes and their supporters. Hitchcock acknowledged that not only had "less than three-fourths of the adult male adults . . . signed" the agreement, but that the agricultural acreage provided for in the 1892 agreement was inadequate to meet the needs of the Indians.[273]

W. A. Jones, the Commissioner of Indian Affairs, also submitted his equally revealing findings. The Commissioner gave three reasons why he felt the agreement should not be ratified: 1) he first questioned "when, if ever, the Indians [would] receive any compensation for their lands;" 2) he asserted "if the lands are paid for there is no certainty that the Comanche, etc., Indians will ever receive one cent;" and finally 3) he observed that "the agreement, as amended, made no provision for the payment of the interest to the tribes."[274] The Commissioner ended his remarks by suggesting that "the agreement should be rejected by Congress, or that it be ratified with the proposed amendments and submitted to the Indians for their acceptance or rejection."[275] After all, noted Commissioner Jones, "it is certainly a novel proposition in law that one party to an agreement may, without the consent of the other, alter or modify an essential part of such contract." Continuing, he stated, incorrectly it turns out, that "no court of law would uphold or enforce any contract so altered or amended."[276]

However sound these and the KCA tribes' arguments were, it was apparent that Congress intended to ratify the agreement. On June 6, 1900, nearly eight years after the original agreement was signed, Congress amended and ratified the agreement.[277] Three supplementary acts enacted in 1901 expanded the manner in which ceded tribal lands were to be disposed.[278]

Lone Wolf, a well-known Kiowa headman supported by the Indian Rights Association, an influential reform organization, filed suit in the Supreme Court of the District of Columbia[279] on June 6, 1901 to obtain an injunction to prevent implementation of the acts confirming the 1892 agreement.[280] Lone Wolf and his associates lost in the District Court. They then appealed to the District Court of Appeals. Even as this appeal was pending, President McKinley issued a proclamation on July 4, 1901 which declared that the KCA ceded surplus lands were to be opened for settlement on August 6, 1901,[281] well before the case was settled.

The Court of Appeals ruled for the United States. The Court stated that reservation Indians with "assigned lands" had no vested rights but only a right to occupy "at the will of the government." The judges, however, after having crippled tribal treaty and property rights ironically ended their opinion by gratuitously saying that "we shall be greatly gratified if that high tribunal [U.S. Supreme Court] may be able to find a way for affording a remedy for what is alleged to be a grievous wrong to the

Indians."[282]

Decision. The fate of the KCA tribes now lay at the Supreme Court's doorsteps. Their hopes, however, and by implication those of all tribes with treaty-based rights and desirable lands, were crushed. The Supreme Court's unanimous opinion represented a perfect, and for tribes deadly, synthesis of the plenary power (read unlimited, absolute) concept and the political question doctrine. The Court refused, citing the political question doctrine, to consider the tribes assertion of "fraudulent misrepresentation" by government officials. They also would not consider the issue of the Senate's unilateral alteration of the 1892 agreement's provisions.[283]

The only question the Court considered was whether the Act of June 6, 1900 was constitutional. Despite Lone Wolf's compelling treaty and constitutional arguments, the Supreme Court, relying on the so-called "relation of dependency" the tribes reputedly had with the United States, maintained the following:

> [T]o uphold the claim would be to adjudge that the indirect operation of the treaty was to materially limit and qualify the controlling authority of Congress in respect to the care and protection of the Indians, and to deprive Congress, in a possible emergency, when the necessity might be urgent for a partition and disposal of the tribal lands, of all power to act, if the assent of the Indians could not be obtained.[284]

The Court had concocted a bogus set of rationalizations apparently to protect the rights of the white squatters who had already descended upon the KCA lands by prior presidential proclamation in 1901 and to legitimate Congress' treaty abrogation. First, they relied on the so-called "dependent" relationship which, when so defined, gives the United States a status as guardian and protector of the tribes. Second, the Court cleverly created a bogus national security question when it alleged that the United States "in a possible emergency" needed unlimited power to act. No specific "emergency" was ever described. The subject of ratification of the 1892 agreement had been an issue for nearly eleven years. Nevertheless, the combination of these two manufactured factors enabled the Court to fashion an opinion, devoid of any constitutional phrases, which literally extended to Congress omnipotent authority over tribal treaty-based political and property rights.

This decision had enormous implications for tribes. As noted at the outset of this article, tribal political and property rights are treaty-defined, not constitutionally delineated. Tribal people were cognizant that the federal Constitution could not shield their rights. And despite the fact that certain Indian treaties had been violated before, there was still a sense that tribal lands defined by treaty, were not subject to confiscation without tribal consent. However, tribal citizens learned to their utter disbelief that, in essence, they had no treaty rights which were beyond Congress' power of suppression or even confiscation.

Legal Consciousness Exemplified and Legal Masks Employed. Lone Wolf, like *Kagama*, "punctuated" the general judicial trend by constructing deviant analyses not on constitutional but on extra-constitutional grounds. Moreover, the Court continued to rely on a completely mythical and fictitious conceptualization of tribes as "wards" utterly dependent upon their federal "guardians."

Displaying a lucid, if ludicrous, ability to rewrite history, the Court, speaking through Justice White, asserted that "[p]lenary authority over the tribal relations of the Indians has been exercised by Congress from the beginning . . ."[285] But as Deloria notes:

> If there had always been a plenary power . . . then why didn't it simply use that method from the very beginning? Why all the hoopla over treaties and agreements? Why, at that very moment, were a number of treaty and agreement commissions in the field on several reservations asking the tribes to make treaties and agreements with the United States?[286]

The Court, quoting from *Beecher v. Wetherby*,[287] attempted to soften its sanction of Congress's power to bludgeon tribal rights by asserting that the government's actions would be "governed by such considerations of justice as would control a Christian people in their treatment of an ignorant and dependent race."[288] Nevertheless, the Court, returning to its problematic national security argument, sought to buffer Congress's power and insisted that:

> It was never doubted that the power to abrogate existed in Congress, and that in a contingency such power might be availed of from considerations of governmental policy, particularly if consistent with perfect good faith towards the Indians.[289]

The judiciary, acting in this instance, as a true legitimator of congressional policy, "presumed" that Congress had acted in good faith in dealing with the tribes.[290]

Lone Wolf was a devastating blow to tribal sovereignty. Congressional "plenary" power unconstrained by the Constitution was interwoven with the "political question" doctrine and judicial deference to the legislature to form an almost impregnable shield, which could not recognize the possibility that tribal interests and federal interests could conflict. But if there was conflict, then clearly the federal had to outweigh the tribal. Although the Supreme Court had asserted that Congress' action was for a public purpose, one could argue that this was not the case since the land taken was sold to white homesteaders. The 1900 agreement, therefore, "probably would not have been constitutional had the property been held by non-Indian owners."[291]

In short, the Court's refusal to examine congressional enactments violative of treaty property rights was a most oppressive blow. A month after the decision, Senator Orville Platt (R., Connecticut) requested that extra copies of the decision be printed as a Senate document, because "there is a great demand for it."[292] When the Senate could not agree on the number of copies to be printed–five hundred or one thousand–Sen. Matthew Quey (R., Penn.) stepped forward and cogently said one thousand copies were needed. His justification reads as follows:

> I think we had better make the number of additional copies 1,000. It is a very remarkable decision. It is the Dred Scott decision No. 2, except that in this case the victim is red instead of black. It practically inculcates the doctrine that the red man has no rights which the white man is bound to respect, and, that no treaty or contract made with him is binding. Is not that about it?[293]

In the March 29, 1902 edition of *The Outlook* magazine, an article entitled "Have Reservation Indians Any Vested Rights?" appeared. Its author was George Kennan, *The Outlook*'s Washington correspondent. Kennan focused on the federal government's policy of leasing tribal lands on the Standing Rock Sioux Reservation and concluded that Indian lands were not being protected, treaties notwithstanding, and that Indian lands were in fact, being confiscated without tribal consent.[294]

As evidence that this could happen, Kennan quoted from the recent, March 4, 1902 decision rendered by the Court of Appeals of the District of Columbia in the case *Lone Wolf v. Hitchcock*.[295] There, the judges had held that the pertinent provisions of the 1868 treaty between the Kiowa and Comanche and the United States did not give the tribes legally enforceable title to their lands. In the appeal judge's own amazing and prophetic words:

> The treaty of 1868 certainly did not vest in the Indian, either in their individual or tribal capacity, anything more than the right to occupy the lands as against the United States until it was found necessary to make other provisions for them. There was no grant of estates either of freehold or leasehold; only a mere right to occupy and use the land, according to the habits and customs of the Indians; but those rights of the Indians were sacred to them as against every one, until

> Congress made provision for assuming control over the lands, and making other disposition thereof, upon such terms and conditions as Congress should prescribe.[296]

The issue of Congress' power to abrogate non-Indian related treaties had been dealt with by the Federal Courts in several earlier cases.[297] Those cases, at least the one involving Indians, however, are easily distinguished from *Lone Wolf* because they did not specifically involve a deprivation of tribal property rights previously acknowledged under a ratified treaty.[298]

IV. Conclusion: Varieties of Legal Consciousness and Legal Masks

This article opened with an extended discussion of the "peculiar relationship" between American Indian Tribes and the United States Government, especially the Congress. The peculiarity, if we must insist on continued usage of that awkward and belittling term, has more to do with the creative talents of various Supreme Court justices and the development of judicial policies and precedents which simultaneously 1) recognize the vested treaty rights of Indians, 2) legitimate federal supremacy over that of tribal status and states' rights vis-a-vis tribes, 3) legitimate congressional Indian policies designed to assimilate "ward-like" Indians who were believed to be culturally inferior, and 4) develop a set of protective measures for Indian rights exempt from state and even federal agency intrusions if the rights being protected have vested in detribalized individuals. This creative judicial process, exemplified in the assorted types of legal consciousness and sundry masks, officially began with Chief Justice John Marshall and his cohorts in the case *Johnson v. McIntosh* in 1823.[299]

From Marshall's explication and redefinition of the "Doctrine of Discovery," which strangely vested an "absolute" title of historically-held tribal lands to the United States, to the perceptions wielded by most European commentators from the Roman Crusades forward that tribal laws, customs, and institutions were somehow culturally "inferior" to those of western European because they derived from non-Christian peoples,[300] tribal sovereignty has endured, though not unscathed, overwhelming pressure from nearly every direction. At times, it has been enervated by federal court decisions, laws, regulations; at other times, it has been vigorously resuscitated, often by the same set of jurists, and lawmakers, though rarely by the federal bureaucrats.

This article centered on the origin and exercise of congressional and judicial authority as related to tribal sovereignty. What do these apparently inconsistent opinions illustrate? How do we assess the implications of these sometimes disparate judicial comments? These decisions suggest, at least regarding congressional authority when dealing with tribes, that the Court, as one branch of the federal triad, will generally acquiesce or defer to the Indian policies and laws enunciated by the political branches and administered by the bureaucracy. This is especially the case when a state is attempting to challenge the government's exclusive relationship to tribes. It is also clear that the Court, while correctly admitting to Congress' exclusive exercise of power as defined by the Commerce Clause, will also generate, of its own volition, an implicit or implied congressional intent if it will serve the Court's own perception of what is in the "tribal interest."[301]

As federal political, economic, and military power waxed in the late nineteenth century with the corresponding waning of tribal power in these areas, there was a change, sometimes gradual, sometimes abrupt, in the way tribal sovereignty was conceptualized by the Court. In Barsh and Henderson's words, by the time of *Lone Wolf* "[t]ribal domestic sovereignty had been surreptitiously transmogrified, from exclusive to residual, from presumptively inherent to presumptively delegated."[302] The concept "guardianship/wardship" was a principal element in this legal transformation.

In Marshall's *Cherokee Nation* (1831) decision, there was an illusion of tribal wardship, but beginning with *Kagama* (1886) and continuing, albeit inconsistently, throughout the next five decades, wardship had become a delusion. The distinction between the illusion of wardship versus the delusion of wardship is important, for while the two terms are related they are not interchangeable. An illusion is an erroneous concept or belief, applicable to a false impression. It may be based on fancy or on wishful thinking. Marshall used the analogy of "Indians as wards" in 1831 to justify or rationalize the federal government's self-imposed right or power to "protect" Indian tribes, both from states and foreign nations. He said that the relationship between tribes and the United States "resemble[d] that of a ward to his guardian," and that tribes as "domestic-dependent nations," were in a "state of pupilage."[303]

By contrast, a delusion refers to false beliefs held without reservation as a result of self-deception. It is a much stronger term, typically associated with harm. In the Court's legal consciousness, by the last two decades of the nineteenth century and into the first several decades of the twentieth century, tribes were, and according to *Lone Wolf* (1903) "had always been," wards subject to the plenary authority of the federal government, despite ample invalidating evidence. Reified in the Court's consciousness, the justices employed masks like "wardship," "dependency," "savagery," "primitivism," "Christian nation," "civilized tribe," "plenary power," "political question," "Doctrine of Discovery," in vacillating ways to achieve whatever ends they deemed viable. When the Court, for instance, considered that a certain group of Indians was civilized or on the way to being civilized and when it accepted the possibility of there being an

Indian mode of civilization independent of or parallel to the Western model, it tended to look at the interest of the tribe in terms of protecting it from outside interference. Thus, it enhanced tribal sovereignty against the states. On the other hand, when the Court held that to be civilized was to be Americanized or nationalized, it determinedly acted to terminate tribal sovereignty so that detribalized Indians could be gradually or vigorously assimilated into American society.

Since congressional policy favored the individualization of tribal property and funds, it follows that a majority of the few judicial victories for American Indians during this period occurred when the Indian person had been individually allotted either their own section of the tribal estate or a per capita share of the tribal funds. However, not even complete individualization guaranteed that the Court would enforce the rights of the individual. The Court, not the tribe, the individual, nor even Congress, retained plenary discretion to decide whether the right involved was worthy of protection.

Commissioner of Indian Affairs, T. J. Morgan, in his 1891 Annual Report to the president, noted that the United States exercised a "paternal care" and nearly omnipotent control of tribal affairs not by any constitutional grant of authority but by "virtue of the necessities of the situation."[304] Nearly fifty years later, W. G. Rice, a noted lawyer acknowledged that as a result of the commerce clause, the expenditure-for-the-general-welfare power, the government's control of the national domain, and the treaty clause, the U.S. Supreme Court had never held that any congressional regulation of Indians was beyond the reach of national power. "Indeed," said Rice, "the net result is the creation of a new power, a power to regulate Indians."[305]

Rice, interestingly enough, wrote his article a decade after all American Indians had become U.S. citizens by unilateral congressional statute.[306] However, even federal citizenship has not proven an adequate shield of Indian political and property rights because the Supreme Court held in an earlier case involving enfranchised Indian allottee's that congressional power over Indians had both a constitutional (Commerce clause) and an extra-constitutional base (tribal "dependency").[307] Chief Justice Van Devanter said:

> Citizenship is not incompatible with tribal existence or continued guardianship, and so may be conferred without completely emancipating the Indians or placing them beyond the reach of congressional regulations adopted for their protection.[308]

In essence, *Nice* served to seal the status of tribal Indians in perpetual legal and political limbo. Henceforth, tribal members who had secured citizenship were simultaneously recognized as being federal citizens and dependent peoples subject to the overriding authority of congressional power. With this fascinating dichotomous status enshrined in federal law a logical question to ask would be: What exactly does federal citizenship really bestow upon tribal citizens? Ostensibly, U.S. citizenship should mean that the federal government retains no more power to legislate Indian lives or resources than it does the lives or property of any other citizen. In fact, however, the U.S. Supreme Court, speaking for the federal government, has historically asserted, and continues to declare, that the Congress has virtually unlimited plenary authority over the sovereign powers, political affairs, and property rights of tribal nations[309]—and even over the individualized Indians' rights (be they constitutional, property, or civil).

Collective and individual Indians political/legal status will remain problematic until such time as the Supreme Court disavows the use of those types of legal consciousness and miscellaneous legal masks that conceal the true nature of Indians and tribes in their relations with the states and federal government. Legal Con I (Constitutional/Treaty) must become the mode of thought utilized by the Supreme Court when its deals with tribes. This will not happen easily. The Supreme Court, in its articulation of the two other types of consciousness and associated masks, has treated the law as separable from history. But to do this is, according to Noonan, "to suppose that law can be made apart from a knowledge of those acts, apart from experience vicariously apprehended."[310]

Finally, Vine Deloria, Jr. has suggested that the type of history evident in much of federal Indian law is "mythical" and "doctrinally determined" and will be replaced with a more accurate history "only with exceptional difficulty and hardship."[311] This is, in effect, a fictional history pocked with legal masks that have been developed by a more powerful economic and political polity. Each of these individual masks and the legal consciousness that encompasses and perpetuates them, particularly those that disavow humanity or ignore historical reality and constitutionally sanctioned bilateral legal/political documents, must be challenged to discover their actual point of origin. Only then will tribes and the United States begin to return to a consensual relationship, which is the only legitimate basis of a political relationship.

**David Wilkins is Assistant Professor of Political Science and American Indian Studies at the University of Arizona.*

Notes

1. *Cherokee Nation v. Georgia*, 30 U.S. (5 Pet.) 1,16 (1831).

2. Tribal nations are sovereign since they were not created pursuant to the federal Constitution. Thus, the U.S. Bill of Rights does not apply to the acts of tribal governments, and the limits on state and federal power delineated in the U.S. Constitution cannot constrain tribal governing powers. Tribes, for instance, may legally discriminate against non-tribal and non-member Indians in voting solely on the basis of race [Indian Civil Rights Act (82 St. 77 [1968])]; the Fifth Amendment right to indictment by grand jury does not apply to prosecutions in tribal courts [*Talton v. Mayes*, 163 U.S. 376 (1986)]; and as separate sovereigns tribes enjoy sovereign immunity [*Santa Clara Pueblo v. Martinez*, 436 U.S. 49, 56 (1978)].

3. Joseph C. Burke, 1969, "The Cherokee Cases: A Study in Law, Politics, and Morality," *Stanford Law Review*, 21 Feb., pp. 500-531; Vine Deloria, Jr. and Clifford M. Lytle, 1983, *American Indians, American Justice*, Austin, Texas: University of Texas Press; Milner S. Ball, 1987, "Constitution, Court, Indian Tribes," *American Bar Foundation Research Journal*, 1, pp. 1-139; Charles F. Wilkinson, *1987, American Indians, Time, and the Law: Native Societies in a Modern Constitutional Democracy*, New Haven, Connecticut: Yale University Press; and Robert Williams, Jr., 1990, *The American Indian in Western Legal Thought: The Discourses of Conquest,* New York: Oxford University Press. See also *Fletcher v. Peck,* 10 U.S. (6 Cranch.) 87 (1810); *Johnson v. McIntosh,* 21 U.S. (8 Wheat.) 543 (1823); *Worcester v. Georgia,* 31 U.S. (6 Pet.) 515 (1832); and *Mitchell v. United States,* [9 Pet. 711 (1835)].

4. See Burke, 1969, *Ibid.*

5. *Cherokee,* 30 U.S. (5 Pet.) at p. 55.

6. *Worcester* 31 U.S. (6 Pet.)(1832) at p. 515.

7. Vine Deloria, Jr. has forcefully made this argument on several occasions. But see Felix S. Cohen, 1972, *Handbook of Federal Indian Law,* 1991 reprint ed., Albuquerque, New Mexico: University of New Mexico Press, who asserts with minimal proof the Congress' power over tribes in addition to the treaty-making power gives the Congress much broader power over the tribes than over commerce between states. On the previous page (p. 90),

Cohen more accurately noted that Congress has no constitutional power over Indians except what is conferred by the Commerce Clause and other clauses of the Constitution.

8. *Worcester* 31 U.S. 515, 559 (1832).

9. U.S. House, 1834, *Report on Regulating the Indian Department*, House Report No. 474, 23rd Cong., 1st Sess, p. 19.

10. *Ibid.*, at p. 13; emphasis added.

11. Stephen Skowronek, 1982, *Building a New American State*, Cambridge: Cambridge University Press.

12. *Ibid.*, at p. 41.

13. *Johnson* 21 U.S. (8 Wheat.)(1823).

14. 158 Fed. 539, 550 (1912).

15. Comment, 1982, "Federal Plenary Power in Indian Affairs After *Weeks* and *Sioux Nation*," *University of Pennsylvania Law Review*, 131, p. 268.

16. 109 U.S. 3 (1883).

17. 163 U.S. 537 (1896).

18. 16 Wall. 130 (1873).

19. 21 Wall. 162 (1874).

20. 149 U.S. 698 (1893).

21. *Merrion v. Jicarilla Apache Tribe*, 455 U.S. 130 (1982).

22. Daniel L. Rotenberg, 1987, "American States and Indian Tribes: Power Conflicts in the Supreme Court," *Dickinson Law Review*, 92, 81.

23. *Johnson* 21 U.S. (1823) at pp. 543, 572, and 586.

24. My data base consists of one hundred and seven federal court cases, ninety of which are Supreme Court opinions. A list of these cases is available upon request.

25. I begin in 1870 because events were underway in the Supreme Court which would culminate in an 1871 case, *Cherokee Tobacco* [11 Wall. 616 (1871)], which held that a general congressional law in direct violation of a treaty provision was a purely "political question" which the "courts were powerless to remedy." This established the dangerous precedent that if a treaty provision and a congressional law conflicted, the one most recently enacted would rule. The process of treaty making with tribes had been unilaterally terminated by Congress just a few months before this decision [16 St. 544, 566 (1871)]. Theoretically, any congressional statute subsequently enacted could be interpreted by the Courts as superseding any prior treaty provision. Although this case was implicitly overruled in [(224 *U.S. 665 (1912)], Choate v. Trapp,* the Courts have never disavowed the "last-in-time, first-in-right" precedent. I chose 1924 as a terminating date for three reasons: First, the drive for universal Indian citizenship concluded that year with the passage of a law that extended the franchise to all Indians who had not yet received federal citizenship. Second, the difficulties over the Pueblo Indians land problems were resolved with the enactment of the Pueblo Lands Board Law (43 St. 636). Finally, there was some acknowledgement by Congress that certain tribes were entitled and should be authorized to file land claims against the federal government. An outgrowth of these three actions was the emergence of a number of private lobbying groups and pan-Indian interest groups who argued that tribal and individual Indian lands and political rights deserved federal protection. Thus, by the early 1920s it was clear that the United States was more willing to concede, in certain limited areas of law and policy, that tribes did indeed have a right to exist autonomously free from a concerted federal effort to assimilate them into the body politics. We will see this in several of the judicial opinions in part one of this essay, particularly as regards individual Indian property and civil rights.

26. Linda Medcalf, 1978, *Law and Identity: Lawyers, Native Americans, and Legal Practice*, Beverly Hills, California: Sage Publica-

tions, vol. 62, Sage Library of Social Research, p. 15.

27. *Ibid.*

28. *Ibid.*

29. The field of Critical Legal Studies was officially born in 1977 at a conference at the University of Wisconsin of Madison. Its membership is quite eclectic and represents a diverse array of scholars and professionals who run from "the disaffected liberal through the radical feminists to the utopian anarchist" (see Hutchison, [below] at p. 3). The main target, however, of Critical Legal Studies has been to challenge the alleged contrast between politics and the law. Critical legal theorists argue that the two are interconnected, not separated. For a good overview of the field see the following two anthologies: Allen C. Hutchison, ed., 1989, *Critical Legal Studies*, Totowa, New Jersey: Rowman & Littlefield Publishers and David Kairys, ed., 1982, *The Politics of Law: A Progressive Critique,* New York: Pantheon Books.

30. John T. Noonan, Jr., 1976, *Persons and Masks of the Law*, New York: Farrar, Straus, and Giroux.

31. See, e.g., Kairys, ed., 1982, *supra* note 29.

32. Duncan Kennedy, 1980, "Toward an Historical Understanding of Legal Consciousness: The Case of Classical Legal Though in America, 1850-1940," Stephen Spitzer, ed., *Research in Law and Sociology*, Greenwich, Connecticut: JAI Press, p. 4.

33. *Ibid.*, at p. 23.

34. *Ibid.*, at p. 6.

35. Elizabeth Mensch, 1982, "The History of Mainstream Legal Thought," in David Kairys, 1982, *supra* note 29 at pp. 18-39.

36. Kennedy, 1980, *supra* note 32 at p. 4.

37. Robert W. Gordon, 1983, "Legal Thought and Legal Practice in the Age of American Enterprise: 1870-1920," in Gerald L. Geison, ed. *Professions and Professional Ideologies in America*, Chapel Hill,

North Carolina: University of North Carolina Press, p. 72.

38. Kennedy, 1980, *supra* note 32 at p. 5.

39. Noonan, 1976, *supra* note 30.

40. *Ibid.*, at p. 20.

41. Noonan, 1976, *supra* note 30 at p. 21.

42. Nancy Carol Carter, 1976, "Race and Power Politics as Aspects of Federal Guardianship Over American Indians: Land-Related Cases, 1887-1924," *American Indian Law Review*, 4, p. 227.

43. Noonan, 1976 *supra* note 30 at p. 24.

44. *Ibid.*

45. *Ibid.*, at p. 25.

46. See, e.g., *Lyng v. Northwest Indian Cemetery Protection Association*, 485 U.S. 439 (1988); *Cotton Petroleum Corporation v. New Mexico*, 57 U.S.L.W. 4643 (1989); *Brendale v. Confederated Tribes and Bands of Yakima*, 109 S. Ct. 2994 (1989); *Employment Division v. Smith*, 1105 S. Ct. 1595 (1990); *Duro v. Reina* ,110 S. Ct. 2053 (1990); *County of Yakima v. Yakima Nation*, 116 L Ed 2d 687 (1992); and most recently, *South Dakota v. Bourland*, 61 U.S.L.W. 4632 (1993).

47. I am deeply indebted to Michael Green for his critical reading of an earlier draft of this article and for his innovative effort to help me reformulate this discussion of different types of legal consciousness and their relationship to judicial "masks."

48. *Cherokee Nation*, p. 20.

49. These are ideal types, both consciousness and masks. As ideal types neither mode completely describes the decisions or the judges, but they do define a range of perceptions, attitudes, and values. In fact, more than one type of consciousness and more than one masks are operative in some judicial opinions.

50. Joel B. Grossman and Richard S. Wells, 1988, *Constitutional Law and Judicial Policy Making*, 3rd ed., New York: Longman Press, p. 11.

51. 35 Fed. 575 (D.C. Oregon, 1888).

52. 1883, *Annual Report of the Commissioner of Indian Affairs*, p. 11.

53. *Clapox* (1888):577.

54. *Clapox* (1888):579.

55. Francis P. Prucha, 1988, *The Indians in American Society: From the Revolutionary War to the Present*, Berkeley: University of California Press. See especially chapter one entitled, "Paternalism."

56. Judicial evidence of separate treatment for the Five Civilized Tribes is available as early as 1832. In the *Worcester* case, the Chief Justice noted that these tribes were better neighbors than "wild-savage" tribes [31 U.S. (1832) 515, 590]. In addition, noted historian Angie Debo, *And Still The Waters Run: The Betrayal of the Five Civilized Tribes*, Princeton, New Jersey: Princeton University Press, 1973 ed., described how astute the leadership of the Five Tribes was: "The Indian leaders quoted the treaties with such skill and fluency that they invariably out-debated their white opponents, and even the most conservative full-bloods knew their [treaty] terms and insisted upon their fulfillment" (p. 9). Commentators like Harold C. Miner, 1989, in *The Corporation and the Indian: Tribal Sovereignty and Industrial Civilization in Indian Territory, 1869-1907*, reprint ed., Norman, Oklahoma: University of Oklahoma Press ethnocentrically argue, however, that the mixed bloods by being so racially "bleached out" opened the door to Anglo exploitation (p. 211). Rennard Strickland, 1982, in *Fire and the Spirits: Cherokee Law From Clan to Court*, Norman, Oklahoma: University of Oklahoma Press, taking the more typical liberal perspective, posits that the full-bloods were "thrust into a world ready to prey upon their weaknesses" (p. 181).

57. See Prucha, 1988, *supra* note 55 at pp. 10-11.

58. James N. Danziger, 1991, *Understanding the Political World: An Introduction to Political Science*, New York: Longman Press, p. 222.

59. Barrington Moore, 1966, *Social Origins of Dictatorship and Democracy*, Boston: Beacon Press.

60. These are 1) the successful bourgeois revolution which commercializes and modernizes the countryside and assimilates aristocracy and peasantry into the modern economy and democratic polity (Britain, France, and the United States); 2) the conservative revolution in which the bourgeois revolution is either aborted or never takes place and where industrialization is carried out from "above" by a coalition of aristocratic-bourgeois elements in which the bourgeois component is the junior partner (Germany and Japan); and 3) the Communist revolution in those areas in which the middle and urban classes were too weak to constitute even a "junior partner" in the modernization proces and in which a large and alienated peasantry provide the main destructive revolutionary force that overthrew the old order and made the peasants its primary victims (the former Soviet Union and China).

61. See, especially, Moore's *supra* note 59 at chapter three, "The Last American Civil War: The Last Capitalist Revolution," which is his rich and detailed case study of the American example.

62. *Ibid.*, at p. 150.

63. Samuel P. Huntington and Jorge I. Dominguez, 1975, "Political Development," in Fred I. Greenstein and Nelson W. Polsby, eds., *Macropolitical Theory*, vol. 3 of the Handbook of Political Science, Reading, Massachusetts: Addison-Wesley Publishing Co, pp. 1-114.

64. *Ibid.*, at p. 66.

65. *Ibid.*

66. Vincent N. Parillo, 1990, *Strangers to These Shores: Race and Ethnic Relations in the Unites States*, 3rd ed., New York: MacMillan Publishing Company, Chapter 7 "Native Americans."

67. *Ibid.*, at pp. 117-122.

68. Williams, 1990, *supra* note 3 at p. 6.

69. For instance, several early treaties with the Cherokee (7 St. 18) and Delaware Tribes (7 St. 13) contained provisions that would have allowed tribes political representation in the U.S. Congress. Article 6 of the 1778 Delaware Treaty, for example, said that:

> And it is further agreed on between the contracting parties should it for the future be found conducive for the mutual interest of both parties to invite any other tribes who have been friends to the interest of the United States, to join the present confederation, **and to form a state whereof the Delaware nation shall be the head, and have a representation in Congress.**

And as late as the 1905, citizens of the Five Civilized Tribes in Indian Territory made a last ditch effort to create a state government of their own choosing. It was to be known as the "State of Sequoyah," after the Cherokee Indian said to be responsible for developing the Cherokee syllabary. The Indians created a constitution which was submitted to the Indian people in November, 1905. It was overwhelmingly approved by the Indians, and then sent to the U.S. Congress. However, it was never considered by that body. Angie Debo, 1935 ed., *supra* note 56, says that:

> there was never the slightest chance that Congress would consent to the admission of two [Oklahoma Territory and Indian Territory together were admitted as the State of Oklahoma on June 16, 1906] Western, radical, and probably Democratic, states in the place on the map that could be occupied by one (p. 165).

70. *Worcester* 31 U.S. (1832).

71. *Cherokee* 30 U.S. (1831).

72. In the majority of these cases, an individual member of a tribe is a part rather than a tribe. In many cases tribes or tribal members would pair up with tribes or tribal members from one of the other Five Civilized Tribes. "Collectively" means that all Five Tribes were directly involved. According to Debo, 1972 ed., *supra* note 56 p. 5, the phrase "civilized" became a part of the Five Tribes after their forced removal from their Eastern United States homelands to lands in present day Oklahoma. Once they resettled, they made tremendous social changes.

73. See note 56.

74. Miner, 1989, *supra* note 56 at p. 211.

75. 94 U.S. 614 (1877).

76. Keith F. Quail, 1931, "The Tragic Story of Pueblo Indian Land Titles," *The Journal of the Bar Association of the State of Kansas*, 6, 158, November.

77. Anonymous, 1913, "Are the Pueblo Indians of New Mexico Subject to Federal Control?," 77 *Central Law Journal*, 455; Cohen, 1972, *supra* note 7 at p. 383.

78. 58 U.S. (17 How.) 525 (1855).

79. Francis P. Prucha, 1986, *The Great Father: The United States Government and the American Indians*, Lincoln, Nebraska: University of Nebraska Press, p. 274.

80. 24 L.ed. 295, 296 (1877).

81. 94 U.S. 614, 616-617 (1877).

82. *Ibid.*

83. *Ibid.*, at p. 619.

84. *Ibid.*, at p. 618; emphasis added.

85. U.S. Department of the Interior, 1891, *Annual Report of the Commissioner of Indian Affairs*, T. J. Morgan. House Executive Document, no. 1, 52nd Congress, 1st Session, pp. 28-29.

86. 112 U.S. 94 (1884).

87. 25 Fed. Cas. No. 14891. (1879).

88. Interestingly, the same attorneys representing the Federal Government and Standing Bear were also involved in the *Elk* case, only this time with opposite results. Standing Bear had been represented by A. J. Poppleton and John L. Webster. G. M. Lambertson, a U.S. attorney, represented the Federal government. This case has been treated at length by several authors. See, e.g., Thomas H. Tibbs, 1989, *The Ponca Chiefs: An Account of the Trial of Standing Bear*, reprint ed., Lincoln, Nebraska: University of Nebraska Press 1972; G.M. Lambertson, 1886, "Indian Citizenship," *American Law Review* 20, 183, Mar.-Apr.; and James A. Lake, Sr., 1981, "Standing Bear! Who?," *Nebraska Law Review*, 60, 451. Standing Bear's trial was also the subject of a recent public television presentation of the Nebraska ETV Network, 1988, Lincoln: University of Nebraska-Lincoln Television. Even after Judge Dundy's precedent setting ruling, there remained uncertainty about an Indian's legal status. See, e.g., George F. Canfield, 1881, "The Legal Position of the Indian," *American Law Review*, January, pp. 21-37, who said that "an Indian is not a person within the meaning of the Constitution."

89. U.S. Congressional Globe at 2890 (1866).

90. Lambertson, 1886, *supra* note 88 at p. 183.

91. Congressional Globe at 2897 (1866).

92. U.S. Senate, 1871, "The Effect of the Fourteenth Amendment on Indian Tribes," Senate Rep. No. 268, 41st Cong., 3d Sess. at p. 11.

93. *Ibid.*

94. *Ibid.*

95. *Ibid.*

96. Congressional Globe at p. 182 (1870).

97. "*Elk v. Wilkins*," *New York Times*, 3, (November 4, 1884).

98. 112 U.S. 94, 95 (1884).

99. 109 U.S. 3 (1883).

100. *Ibid.*, at p. 18.

101. This case, with a written dissent, is a rarity for the period of this study. While there were dissenting opinions in eighteen out of ninety Supreme Court cases, there were written dissents in only four other cases. These were: *Cherokee Tobacco*, 11 Wall. 616 (1870); *Leavenworth Railroad*, 92 U.S. 733 (1875); *Choctaw Nation v. United States*, 119 U.S. 1 (1886); and *Donnelly v. United States*, 228 U.S. 243 (1912). Grossman and Wells, 1988, *supra* note 50 point out, however, that from 1836 to 1930 while the role of dissent in all Supreme Court cases was not great, with the percentage of written dissenting opinions usually not exceeding twenty-five percent. Nevertheless, five percent (five cases out of ninety) is significantly lower than twenty-five percent, and shows a significant level of judicial ideological consensus regarding tribal status.

102. 112 U.S. 94, 102 (1884).

103. *Ibid.*, at p. 99.

104. *Ibid.*, at p. 100.

105. *Ibid.*, at p. 113.

106. *Ibid.*, at pp. 122-123.

107. *Ibid.*, at p. 99.

108. 163 U.S. 376 (1896).

109. U.S. Senate, 1892, *Jurisdiction of the Supreme Court*, Senate Rep. No. 281, 52d Cong., 1st Sess., 6.

110. *Ibid.*, at p. 8.

111. U.S. House, *1892, Jurisdiction of the Supreme Court of the United States Over the Five Civilized Tribes,* House Report No. 1437, 52d Cong., 1st Sess., at p. 2.

112. 59 Fed. 836 (1894).

113. *Ibid.* at p. 845.

114. 17 Sup. Ct. 999.

115. This prior respect was, however, rapidly dissipating in the face of inexorable pressure by non-Indian settlers and territorial officials to force the federal government to allot the fee-simple lands of the Five Civilized Tribes. Congress responded first by enacting a law which extended the jurisdiction of the federal courts over Indian Country [30 St. 62, 82 (1897)]. Second, and most important, Congress enacted the Curtis Act [30 St. 495 (1898)] which effectively dismembered the tribal governments of the Five Tribes. These tribes did not idly sit by while their legal and political institutions were being dismantled. They frequently memorialized Congress against such violative actions. See, e.g., 1896, *Creek and Seminole Memorial*, S. Doc. No. 190, 54th Cong., 1st Sess., Mar. 26; 1897, *Creek Memorial*, S. Doc. No. 111, 54th Cong., 2d Sess., Feb. 6; 1897, *Chickasaw Nation Memorial*, S. Doc. No. 127, 54th Cong., 2d Sess., Feb. 13, and 1898, *Choctaw Memorial*, S. Doc. No. 274, T Cong., 2nd Sess., May 25.

116. 163 U.S. 376, 382 (1896).

117. *Ibid.*, at p. 384.

118. *Ibid.*, at p. 381.

119. 163 U.S. 537.

120. *Ibid.*, at p. 559.

121. 23 St. 362, 385.

122. But see, *Ex Parte Crow Dog*, [109 U.S. 556 (1883)], which was an earlier exception to this standard argument. *Crow Dog* involved the Lakota (Sioux), a tribal people alleged to be "wild and savage," in contradistinction to the Five Civilized Tribes. Although Crow Dog won in that case, Congress responded shortly thereafter with the Major Crimes Act, discussed earlier, which took away tribal jurisdiction over major crimes, or so it did until the Five Civilized Tribes entered the picture. Even the Five Tribes, however, would ultimately have the power to prosecute their own removed by federal law [Curtis Act, 30 St. 495 and see 34 St. 137 (1988)]. Nevertheless, the legal precedent acknowledging that indigenous sovereign powers do not derive from the United States Constitution is still valid today and is used on occasion to benefit tribes or shield them from state and sometimes federal intrusions.

123. 224 U.S. 665 (1912).

124. Debo, 1973 ed., *supra* note 56.

125. Grant Foreman, 1913, "The U.S. Courts and the Indian," 61, June, p. 578; 35 St. 312 (1908).

126. 35 St. 312 (1908).

127. Foreman, 1913, *supra* note 125 at p. 578.

128. 224 U.S. 665, 671 (1912).

129. Cohen, 1972, *supra* note 7 at p. 265.

130. David E. Engdahl, 1976, "State and Federal Power over Federal Property," *Arizona Law Review*, 18, p. 363.

131. Cohen, 1972, *supra* note 7 at p. 265.

132. 224 U.S. 665, 671, 673 (1912).

133. *Ibid.*, at p. 674.

134. *Ibid.*, at p. 677.

135. "Oklahoma Indians Win: Decision Will Cost the State Millions and May Bankrupt Counties," *New York Times*, 3, (May 14, 1912).

136. *Ibid.*

137. 1913, *Congressional Record* at p. 2716.

138. 231 U.S. 28 (1913).

139. 94 U.S. 614 (1876).

140. U.S. Commissioner of Indian Affairs, 1885, *Annual Report*, 28-29.

141. *Ibid.*

142. Cohen, 1972, *supra* note 7 at p. 389.

143. 36 St. 557 (1912).

144. Commissioner of Indian Affairs, 1912, *Annual Report*, 44.

145. 198 Fed. 539 (1912).

146. 198 Fed. 539, 557 (1912).

147. 231 U.S. 28 (1913).

148. *Ibid.*, at p. 41.

149. *Ibid.*, at p. 47; and see Robert A. Williams, Jr., 1986, "The Algebra of Federal Indian Law: The Hard Trail of Decolonizing and Americanizing the White Man's Indian Jurisprudence," *Wisconsin Law Review* 262, n. 146 emphasis added.

150. Irene K. Harvey, 1982, "Constitutional Law: Congressional Plenary Power Over Indian Affairs—A Doctrine Rooted in Prejudice," *American Indian Law Review*, 10, 120.

151. *Sandoval* 231 U.S. (1914) at p. 39.

152. *Ibid.*

153. Cohen, 1972, *supra* note 7 at p. 389.

154. 231 U.S. 28, 46 (1913).

155. 232 U.S. 478 (1914).

156. 67 St. 586 (1953). For an excellent treatment of liquor laws prior to 1942, see Cohen, *supra* note 7, chap. 17. For more recent laws, see Rennard Strickland, et al., eds., 1982, *Felix S. Cohen's Handbook of Federal Law,* Charlottesville, Virginia: Michie, Bobbs-Merrill Publishers, pp. 305-308. And, see *United States v. Mazurie,* 419 U.S. 544 (1975), which upheld Congress's authority to delegate to tribal governments the authority to regulate the distribution of alcoholic beverages on a reservation.

157. 28 St. 319 (1894).

158. 11 St. 743 (1858); CIA, 1914, *Annual Report* 71.

159. Charles J. Kappler, comp., 1903, *Indian Affairs: Law and Treaties,* 2 vols., Washington, D.C.: Government Printing Office, p. 590.

160. 232 U.S. 478, 485 (1914); see also John R. Schmidhauser, 1958, *The Supreme Court as Final Arbiter in Federal-State Relations: 1789-1957,* Chapel Hill, North Carolina: University of North Carolina Press, p. 147.

161. *Ibid.*, at p. 482.

162. 232 U.S. 478, 486 (1914).

163. *Ibid.*

164. See U.S. House, 1913, *Report in the matter of the Investigation of the Indian Bureau,* Report No. 1279, 62nd Congress, 3rd Session, Wash. DC: Government Printing Office. See also U.S. Senate, 1915, *Investigation of Indian Affairs,* Document No. 984, 63rd Congress, 3rd Session, which was a final report submitted by the Joint Commission to Investigate Indian Affairs established by Congress on June 30, 1913. The report concluded by noting that:

> the problems connected with the Indian Service, involving the activities, relationship, and welfare of 300,000 persons and property aggregating in value

> nearly $1,000,000,000, are among the most serious which confront our Government. No quick or complete solution of these great problems has been found or is discoverable. They require the application of patriotic intelligence, which in the past has been hampered and embarrassed by **selfishness, corruption, and inefficiency.** It is believed that a material reorganization of the service is desirable (p. 10).

165. Vine Deloria, Jr., 1985, "The Distinctive Status of Indian Rights," in Peter Iverson, ed. *The Plains Indians of the Twentieth Century*, Norman, Oklahoma: University of Oklahoma Press, p. 248.

166. 16 St. 544, 566 (1871).

167. See, e.g., his recent article, Vine Deloria, Jr., 1992, "The Application of the Constitution to American Indians," in Oren Lyons and John Mohawk, eds. *Exiled in the Land of the Free: Democracy, Indian Nations, and the U.S. Constitution*, Santa Fe, New Mexico: Clear Light Publishers. Deloria says that:

> a strong analogy exists, therefore, between the status of Indian nations and the states of the union with respect to the Constitution. Under the Tenth Amendment, all powers not delegated to the federal government by the states are reserved to the states and the people respectively. It is standard treaty law that everything not specifically ceded to the United States by an Indian nation in a treaty remains vested in the Indian nation [*United States v. Winans*, 198 U.S. 371, (1905)]. The proper relationship of Indian nations and the Constitution is, therefore, also one of delegated rights and powers with the Indian nations, like the states, reserving and preserving everything not specifically ceded by treaty (p. 315).

168. See, Charles F. Wilkinson's article, 1988, "Indian Tribes and the American Constitution," in Frederick E. Hoxie, ed. *Indians in American History: An Introduction*, Arlington Heights, Illinois: Harlan Davidson, Inc. in which he asserts that:

> the Tenth Amendment reserves to states the sovereign powers not delegated to the United States. The treaties and treaty substitutes reserved to tribes sovereign powers not expressly or impliedly relinquished to the United States (pp. 125-126).

While acknowledging that "in theory," state powers are more "permanent" that tribal powers, Wilkinson goes on to note that "in practice, however, congressional power to encroach on state prerogatives under the commerce clause is largely unfettered, just as there are few constitutional restraints on congressional authority over Indian affairs" (*Ibid.*).

169. W. G. Rice, 1934, "The Position of the American Indian in the Law of the United States," *Journal of Comparative Legislation and International Law*, 16, p. 95.

170. *Ibid.*, at p. 95.

171. Canfield, 1881, *supra* note 88 at p. 27.

172. Prucha, 1986, *supra* note 79 at p. 231.

173. In its "Seventeenth Annual Report" for the year 1885 the Board said:

> For what ought we to hope as the future of the Indian? What should the Indian become? To this there is one answer—and but one. He should become an intelligent citizen of the United States. There is no other "manifest destiny" for any man or any body of men on our domain (U.S. House, 1886, "Seventeenth Annual Report of the Board of Indian Commissioners, the Year 1885," *House Executive Document No. 109*, 49th Congress, 1st Session, Washington, DC: Government Printing Office, p. 17).

174. CIA, 1885, *Annual Report* 7-8.

175. 24 St. 388 (1887).

176. 24 St. 388 at 390.

177. John P. Kinney, 1937, *A Continent Lost—A Civilization Won*, Baltimore, Maryland: Johns Hopkins University Press; D. S. Otis, 1973, *The Dawes Act and the Allotment of Indian Lands*, Norman, Oklahoma: University of Oklahoma Press; and Wilcomb E. Washburn, 1975, *The Assault on Indian Tribalism: The General Allotment Law* (Dawes Act) *of 1887*, Philadelphia, Pennsylvania: J. B. Lippincott.

178. 27 St. 645 (1893).

179. 24 St. 388, 391 (1887); Otis, 1973, *supra* note 177.

180. Foreman, 1913, *supra* note 123 at p. 577.

181. U. S. House, 1898, "Report on the Curtis Bill—Laws for the Indian Territory," *H.R. Rep. No. 593*, 55th Cong., 2d Sess., 2 , emphasis added.

182. 30 St. 497 (1898).

183. Francis P. Prucha, ed., 1975, *Documents of United States Indian Policy*, Lincoln, Nebraska: University of Nebraska Press, p. 197.

184. 16 Wall. 36, 90-91 (1873).

185. 18 St. 146, 176 (1874).

186. Commissioner of Indian Affairs, 1875, *Annual Report* 526.

187. Commissioner of Indian Affairs, 1900, *Annual Report* 8.

188. CIA, 1913, *Annual Report* 13.

189. 118 U.S. 375 (1886).

190. Francis P. Prucha, 1962, *American Indian Policy in the Formative Years*, Lincoln, Nebraska: University of Nebraska Press; Henry Pancoast, 1973, *The Indian Before the Law* (1884) in Francis P. Prucha's, ed., *Americanizing the American Indians*, Cambridge, Massachusetts: Harvard University Press, p. 159.

191. 4 St. 729, 733 (1834).

192. Prucha, 1962, *supra* note 190 at p. 211.

193. CIA, 1856, *Annual Report* 557.

194. CIA, 1866, *Annual Report* 17.

195. 16 St. 544, 566 (1871).

196. Loring B. Priest, 1942, *Uncle Sam's Stepchildren: The Reformation of United States Indian Policy, 1865-1887*, New Brunswick, New Jersey: Rutgers University Press; Henry E. Fritz, 1963, *The Movement for Indian Assimilation, 1860-1890*, Philadelphia, Pennsylvania: University of Pennsylvania Press; and Francis P. Prucha, 1976, *American Indian Policy in Crisis, Christian Reformers and the Indian, 1865-1887*, Norman, Oklahoma: University of Oklahoma Press.

197. BIC, 1871, *Annual Report* 432.

198. *Congressional Record*, at 2718 (1874).

199. See comments of the Commissioners of Indian Affairs in their annual reports for 1876, 1877, 1879, 1882-1884. See also the excellent article by Sidney L. Harring, 1990, "Crow Dog's Case: A Chapter in the Legal History of Tribal Sovereignty," *American Indian Law Review*, 14, 191.

200. Prucha, 1986, *supra* note 79 at p. 229.

201. CIA, 1884, *Annual Report* 10.

202. Deloria and Lytle, 1983, *supra* note 3 at p. 111.

203. 109 U.S. 556 (1883).

204. See, e.g., BIC, 1884, *Annual Report* 5-6; Cong. Rec. 934 (1885).

205. 23 St. 362, 385 (1885).

206. As noted earlier, of the one hundred seven cases constituting my core data base, ninety were Supreme Court decisions. These cases arrived at the Supreme Court by one of four routes: Appeals (thirty-six percent, or forty-two cases); Writ of Error (twenty-seven percent, or thirty-eight cases); Certification (seven percent, or eight cases); and Original Jurisdiction (two percent, or three cases). Certification cases are presented when the justices at the Court of Appeals, district or circuit courts, or the Court of Claims, ask the Supreme Court to rule upon certain stipulated questions of law, "the answers to which arise in a case held under advisement by the lower court and are, presumably, in substantial professional doubt." [Glendon A. Schubert, 1960, *Constitutional Politics*, New York: Holt, Rinehart, and Winston, pp. 89-90]. Although representing only seven percent of the cases (eight in all), interestingly enough, tribal sovereignty was curtailed in each and every case. This indicates that the "novelty" of many Indian law questions precludes, or at least significantly inhibits, a favorable decision in the tribal interest.

207. 118 U.S. 375, 378 (1886).

208. *Ibid.*, at p. 379.

209. *Ibid.*, at p. 383.

210. *Ibid.*, at p. 384.

211. *Ibid.*, at p. 379.

212. Comment, 1982, *supra* note 15 at p. 247; Nell Jessup Newton, 1984, "Federal Power Over Indians: Its Sources, Scope, and Limitations," *University of Pennsylvania Law Review*, 132, pp. 195 and 215; Daniel L. Rottenberg, 1986, "American Indian Tribal Death—A Centennial Remembrance" *University of Miami Law Review*, 41, December, pp. 409 and 418; Rachel San Kronowitz, et al., 1987, "Toward Consent and Cooperation: Reconsidering the Political Status of Indian Nations," *Harvard Civil Rights—Civil Liberties Law Review*, 22, p. 507; and Vine Deloria, Jr., 1988, "Beyond the Pale: American Indians and the Constitution," in Jules Lobel, ed., *A Less Than Perfect Union*, New York: Monthly Review Press, p. 259.

213. Rotenberg, 1986, *Ibid* at p. 87.

214. Deloria, 1988, *supra* note 212 at p. 261.

215. Newton, 1984, *supra* note 212 at pp. 195 and 215.

216. Deloria and Lytle, 1983, *supra* note 3 at p. 171.

217. 118 U.S. 375, 381 (1886).

218. 109 U.S. 3, 18 (1883).

219. 31 Fed. 327, 329 (1886); emphasis added.

220. CIA, 1888, *Annual Report* at p. LXXXIX.

221. Deloria, Jr., 1985, *supra* note 165 at p. 240.

222. *Ibid.*

223. 118 U.S. 394, 396 (1886).

224. 135 U.S. 641 (1890).

225. 24 St. 388 (1887).

226. Railroad companies created by congressional law occupied a special federal niche and thus were often treated liberally by the government. The relationship between railroads, as federal instrumentalities, and tribes, however, was problematic. Unfortunately for tribes, the federal government's interest in railroads often outweighed their interests in protecting treaty-described tribal lands. Prior to 1899, railroad companies had to have special individualized bills introduced in Congress which allowed for the acquirement of rights-of-way through Indian reservations or allotments. These bills were occasionally defeated. This was changed, however, on March 2, 1899 with the Omnibus Railroad Act [30 St. 990 (1899)]. The legislation had been touted by W.A. Jones, Commissioner of Indian Affairs, as a way to not only "preserve and protect the rights and interests of Indians," but also to "secure uniformity in the method of obtaining such rights of way . . . "[H.R. Rep. No. 1896, at 2 (1899)].

Railroad companies and lands were at issue in six other cases. These were: *Leavenworth E.T.C. Railroad Company v. United States*, 92 U.S. 733 (1875); *Utah & Northern Railway Company v. Fisher*, 116 U.S. 28 (1885); *Buttz v. Northern Pacific Railroad*, 119 U.S. 55 (1886); *Missouri, Kansas & Texas Railway Company v. Roberts*, 152 U.S. 114 (1894); *Clairmont v. United States*, 225 U.S. 551 (1912); and *Nadeau v. Union Pacific Railroad*, 253 U.S. 442 (1920).

Besides *Southern Railway*, which I categorized as an anti-sovereignty case, I classed three other cases as involving tribal sovereignty: *Utah*, *Buttz*, and *Missouri*. *Buttz* and *Missouri* are treated as anti-sovereignty cases. Utah, however, is an anomaly, and I classed it as a mixed sovereignty case. In this case, the Territory of Utah had taxed the Railroad's lands which coursed through the Shoshone-Bannock Reservation. The Supreme Court held that the Territory had the right to tax "all matters not interfering with treaty stipulations" which had to be protected [116 U.S. 28, 31 (1885)].

227. John A. Garraty, 1971, *The American Nation*, 2nd ed., New York: Harper & Row, p. 571.

228. See Commissioner Francis A. Walker's 1872 *Annual Report*, which provides an excellent summary of the authorizing legislation and the routes and which describes the tribes affected by the fourteen railroad lines traversing tribal lands [CIA, 1872, *Annual Report*, p. 463].

229. CIA, 1872, *supra* note 228 at p. 469.

230. J. D. Richardson, ed., 1886, *Compilation of the Messages and Papers of the President, 1789-1897*, Washington, D.C.: Government Printing Office, esp. p. 472.

231. *Ibid.*, at p. 473.

232. 135 U.S. 641, 648-649 (1890).

233. *Ibid.*, at p. 654.

234. 30 U.S. (5 Pet.) 1 (1831).

235. 45 U.S. (4 How.) 566 (1846).

236. 118 U.S. 375 (1886).

237. *Ibid.*, at p. 656.

238. *Ibid.*, at p. 657; emphasis added.

239. The concept of "wardship" has been treated by several scholars. Esther B. Strong's, 1941, *Wardship in American Indian Administration: A Political Instrumentality for Social Adjustment*, Ph.D. dissertation, Yale University is an excellent study. See also Cohen, 1972 ed. *supra* note 7 at p. 169, who insightfully describes the legal realities of wardship and the ten different connotations the term had evolved up to the 1940s. Also see Felix S. Cohen, 1960, "Indian Wardship: The Twilight of a Myth," in Lucy Cohen, ed., *The Legal Conscience: Selected Papers of Felix S. Cohen*, New Haven, Connecticut: Yale University Press, p. 328.

240. *Ibid.*, at p. 656.

241. *Ibid.*, at p. 654.

242. *Ibid.*

243. 174 U.S. 445 (1899).

244. 1891, *Messages of the President*, at p. 1698.

245. 27 St. 612, 645 (1893).

246. Debo, 1973 ed., *supra* note 56.

247. See, e.g., Creek rejection of agreement [S. Doc. No. 111 (1897)]; and Chickasaw rejection [S. Doc. No. 127 (1897)]. The Seminole Nation was the only tribe to negotiate a pre-Curtis Act agreement [see H.R. Rep. No. 1504 (1898)]. In that report, Representative John Little (D., Ark.) noted that this "tribe has been the first to accept an agreement looking to the allotment of their lands in severalty and the abolition of their tribal government" (*Ibid.*).

248. U.S. Senate, 1894, *Report of the Dawes Commission*, S. Rep. No. 377, 53rd Cong., 2nd Sess., p. 12.

249. 29 St. 321, 339 (1896).

250. 30 St. 62, 83 (1897).

251. U.S. Senate, 1896, *Memorial of Creek and Seminole Tribes Against Curtis Act*, S. Doc. No. 190, 54th Cong., 1st Sess., p. 1; see also, 1898, *Choctaw Petition*, S. Doc. No. 274, 55th Cong., 2nd Sess.

252. 30 St. 495 (1898).

253. H.R. Rep. No. 593 at p. 1 (1898).

254. 174 U.S. 445 (1899).

255. *Ibid.*, at pp. 445 and 484.

256. *Ibid.*, at p. 478.

257. *Ibid.*

258. 169 U.S. 264, 271 (1898).

259. 174 U.S. 445, 483-484.

260. These three doctrines simultaneously appear in five Supreme Court cases during this study's period: *Stephens v. Cherokee Nation*, 174 U.S. 445 (1899); *Cherokee Nation v. Hitchcock*, 187 U.S. 294 (1902); *Lone Wolf v. Hitchcock*, 187 U.S. 553 (1903); *Matter of Heff*, 197 U.S. 488 (1905); and *Tiger v. Western Investment Company*, 221 U.S. 286 (1911). In four of the five, excluding *Heff*, which did not involve tribal sovereignty, the force of congressional plenary power severely diminished tribal property and political rights.

261. 174 U.S. 445, 483 (1871); emphasis added.

262. 174 U.S. 445, 488.

263. 187 U.S. 553 (1903).

264. 15 St. 589 (1867).

265. 15 St. 581; Kappler, 1903, *supra* note 159 at pp. 754-9.

266. Kappler, 1903, *Ibid.*, at p. 755.

267. *Ibid.*, at p. 758.

268. 25 St. 980 (1892); Kappler, 1903, *Ibid.*, at p. 341.

269. U.S. Senate, 1894, *Memorial of Kiowa, Comanche, and Apache Tribes*, S. Misc. Doc. No. 102, 53rd Cong., 2nd Sess., p. 1.

270. *Ibid.*

271. 187 U.S. 553, 557 (1898).

272. *Ibid.*

273. U.S. Senate, 1900, *Memorial from Kiowa, Comanche, and Apache Indian Tribes: Letter from the Secretary of Interior*, S. Doc. No. 76, 56th Cong., 1st Sess., pp. 1 and 2.

274. *Ibid.*, at pp. 6-7.

275. *Ibid.*

276. *Ibid.*, at pp. 4-5.

277. 31 St. 672 (1900).

277. See Acts of January 4, 1901 (31 St. 727); March 3, 1901 (31 St. 1078); and March 3, 1901 (31 St. 1093).

279. Interestingly, *Lone Wolf* was the second case [the first was *Cherokee Nation v. Hitchcock*, 187 U.S. 294 (1902)] which originated in the federal courts of the District of Columbia. Additional research is necessary to determine why certain Indian cases began there. In all, six of the ninety Supreme Court cases started in the District of Columbia. In five of these cases, [*Cherokee Nation* (1902), *Lone Wolf* (1903), *Quick Bear* (1908), *Garfield* (1908), and *Gritts* (1912)], tribal nations or individual Indians lost. The other

case, which involved a tribe's right to tax whites, was a victory (Morris, 1904). The cases, in chronological order: *Cherokee Nation v. Hitchcock* (1902), *Lone Wolf v. Hitchcock* (1903), *Morris v. Hitchcock* (1904), *Quick Bear v. Leupp* (1908), *Garfield v. Goldsby* (1908), and *Gritts v. Fisher* (1912).

280. Prucha, 1986, *supra* note 79 at p. 269.

281. 184 U.S. 553, 562-3 (1901).

282. 19 App. 315, 332 (1901).

283. 187 U.S. 553, 567-8 (1898).

284. *Ibid.*, at p. 564.

285. *Ibid.*, at p. 565.

286. Vine Deloria, Jr., 1989, "Laws Founded in Justice and Humanity: Reflection on the Content and Character of Federal Indian Law," *Arizona Law Review*, 31, pp. 221-222.

287. 95 U.S. 517, 525 (1877).

288. 187 U.S. 553, 565 (1898).

289. *Ibid.*, at p. 566.

290. *Ibid.*, at p. 568.

291. Comment, 1982, *supra* note 15 at p. 265 and 190.

292. 1903, *Congressional Record* at 2028.

293. *Ibid.*

294. George Kennan, 1902, "Have Reservation Indians Any Vested Rights?," *The Outlook*, 70, March, p. 759; Kennan, 1902, "A New Statement from Mr. Kennan," *The Outlook*, 70, April, p. 956.

295. 19 App. 315 (1902).

296. 19 App. 315, 332; emphasis added.

297. See, in general, *Taylor v. Morton*, 23 Fed. Cas. 784 [C.C.D. Mass. (1855)]; and *The Chinese Exclusion Case*, [130 U.S. 581,600 (1889)]. In Indian law, see *Cherokee Tobacco*, [78 U.S. (11 Wall.) 616 (1870)]. But even in *Cherokee Tobacco*, the case did not "go to the title of property or of personal protection, or decide anything more than to subject all persons, citizens or otherwise, within our national boundaries to the uniform duties and penalties of the revenue laws" [H.R. Rep. No. 98 at 10 (1873)]. The United States Committee on Indian Affairs report continued, "has not wilfully, forcibly violated any treaty made with the Indians, and the doctrine has never had either its legislative, executive, or judicial sanction, that it could, touching their rights of person or of property" (*Ibid.*). The only exception to this rule, and the only time an Indian treaty has been formally abrogated, was the abrogation of the eastern Sioux treaty as a result of a war between that tribe and the United States [12 St. 512, 528 (1862)]; and see Deloria and Lytle, 1983, *supra* note 3 at p. 43.

298. Comment, 1982, *supra* note 15 at p. 245.

299. 21 U.S. (8 Wheat.) 542 (1823).

300. See, e.g., Williams, Jr., 1990, *supra* note 3 which details the origins of this European attitude; for a classic statement on this, see Felix S. Cohen, 1951, "Colonialism: U.S. Style," *The Progressive*, 15, February, pp. 16-18.

301. Vine Deloria, Jr., 1977, "A Better Day for Indians,", New York: The Field Foundation, p. 6; Comment, 1982, *supra* note 15 at p. 268.

302. Russell L. Barsh and James Y. Henderson, 1980, *The Road: Indian Tribes and Political Liberty*, Berkeley, California: University of California Press, p. 95.

303. 30 U.S. (5 Pet.) 1, 17 (1831).

304. CIA, 1891, *Annual Report*, p. 25.

305. Rice, Jr., 1934, *supra* note 169 at p. 81.

306. 43 St. 253 (1924).

307. *United States v. Nice*, 241 U.S. 591 (1916).

308. *Ibid.*, at p. 598.

309. Robert T. Coulter, 1974, "The Denial of Legal Remedies to Indian Nations Under United States Law," *American Indian Journal*, 3, pp. 5-11; Coulter, 1978, "Lack of Redress," *Civil Rights Digest*, 10, Spring, pp. 30-37; Deloria, Jr., 1977, *supra* note 301; Deloria, Jr., 1985, *supra* note 165 at pp. 237-248; Barsh and Henderson, 1980, *supra* note 302; Newton, 1984, *supra* note 212 at pp. 78-95; Carter, 1976, *supra* note 42 at pp. 197-248; and Ball, 1987, *supra* note 3 at pp. 1-139.

310. Noonan, 1976, *supra* note 30 at p. 163.

311. Deloria, Jr., 1989, *supra* note 286 at p. 223.

PLACING NATIVE AMERICANS AT THE CENTER: INDIAN PROPHETIC REVOLTS AND CULTURAL IDENTITY

*William Pencak

I. Cultural Identity and Revitalization Movements

In his 1896 essay "Lessons from the History of Science," philosopher Charles S. Peirce argued for a theory of history that opposed the Social Darwinism favored by the times. Far from having "evolved," history proceeded by "leaps," by "the violent breaking up of habits." He dubbed this "cataclasmine" evolution and insisted that new eras in history, like new concepts in science, emerged following periods of chaos and uncertainty in which old norms had collapsed. Novel systems of thought and society did not develop smoothly out of the past, but rather appeared as imaginative responses to situations of crisis and breakdown in which what people had accepted as the "past" had ceased to be relevant.[1]

Peirce wrote from the perspective of a loser—he had lost his government job, university position, and most of his money—in an age when the winners proclaimed that the "survival of the fittest" meant the survival of the morally, mentally, and physically best. Evolutionary history served to justify those winners who constructed a mythical past that placed them at the apex of a prolonged development. For people who are trampled underneath or fall by the wayside, however, the disruptions and cataclysms that constitute history in its entirety are only too real. The resistance, persistence, and eventual re-emergence of those, like Peirce, who have questioned the equation of the temporarily politically triumphant with justice and progress, most impressively rebukes the powers that be, for in the long run no social or intellectual system endures forever.

The breakdown and reconstitution of Native American societies under the pressure of contact with whites provides powerful evidence of Peirce's hypothesis. The form this frequently took was the Prophetic Revolt, which can be understood using anthropologist Anthony F. C. Wallace's typology.[2] He shows that "revitalization movements" are undertaken by people in troubled times who engage in "a deliberate, organized, conscious effort . . . to construct a more satisfying culture." A period of (I) Steady State is first disturbed by (II-III) Increased Individual Stress leading to a Period of Cultural Distortion. (I will combine II and III as the "Period of Crisis.") Then follows (IV) a Period of Revitalization through following the dreamer, prophet, or Messiah. This Period has five general characteristics:

1.	Nativism	"the elimination of alien persons, customs, values, and/or material."
2.	Revivalism	"the institution of customs, values, and even aspects of nature which are thought to have been in the mazeway [mental image] of previous generations but are not now present." This usually occurs through the formation of new moral and legal codes based on old traditions.
3.	Vitalism	"the importation of alien elements into the mazeway," frequently borrowed or adapted from the culture against which the revolt occurs.
4.	Millennarianism	"an apocalyptic world transformation engineered by the supernatural."
5.	Messianism	"the participation of a divine savior in human flesh" (the Prophet) in the transformation.

In the Steady State, the Native American nations were characterized by political relationships which, while shifting, usually maintained the integrity of the societies concerned. Authority was decentralized, shared between men and women, and based upon respect earned by leaders through personal character and exploits. Hunting and/or agriculture was the foundation of life. Property relations were unimportant: material goods that could not be immediately used functioned as gifts that were passed around to demonstrate esteem or loyalty. Human beings were embedded in a chain of being extending from the Great Spirit or Master of Life through other spirits, such as those of ancestors, evil spirits, and a living Nature, including the sky, sun, wind, earth, plants, and animals. The existences of all of these were mutually dependent and worthy of respect. Law was traditional, unwritten, and embodied in stories and community consensus.

In the Period of Crisis, the symbolic universe constructed during the Steady State became meaningless. Contact with the Europeans turned the earth and nature into commodities through the trade in fur, liquor, guns, clothing, and other items. Game was depleted; disease and war killed large percentages of Indian populations. Alcoholism, the decline of social authority, internal strife, and depression were common. White man's law consisted of scraps of paper that confined Indians physically but gave them few enforceable rights against whites who abused them or invaded their territory. Alternatives of false assimilation to white ways, in the hope of retaining some autonomy, and resistance, which could lead to annihilation, offered themselves as desperate strategies for peoples condemned to extermination or to exile on reservations where they could pose no obstacle to white expansion.

The Revitalization Movements then arose. Prophets were frequently, though not always, personal degenerates who had been "born again" following traumatic experiences, through journeys to Heaven and revelations from God. Their personal development thus recapitulated the paths they hoped their peoples would follow. God promised the Indians that a renewed, game-filled paradise on earth and in Heaven would be theirs if they gave up drinking, sorcery, and promiscuity, and practiced peace and brotherhood among themselves. New or traditional dances and rituals received much attention; many stressed reverence for nature. The prophets demanded symbolic destruction of white civilization by rejecting European clothing, weapons, animals, and agriculture. Nevertheless, all combined Indian and Christian cosmologies in creative new ways. Prophets were directly influenced by previous prophets, and both African/American and white religions, usually pacifist or deviant sects (like Mormons or Quakers) who were themselves rebelling against the conventions of white society. Some Indian revivals were pacifistic and preached patient waiting for the Great Spirit. Others urged unification of the Indian nations, creating a previously non-existent Pan-Indian consciousness and solidarity out of peoples demoralized and fractured through pressure on their lands, as preparation for a militant crusade.

II. Native American Revitalization Movements

Although for clarity I treat the Indian prophets separately, it should be stressed that several of them greatly influenced each other. Neolin and Pontiac owed much to Papoohoon and Wagemond; the Shawnees were in contact with the Muskogees and Cherokees even before the American Revolution. As historian Gregory Dowd has shown, the "middle ground" from the Appalachians to the Mississippi was one of tribal dissolution, combination, and recombination in the eighteenth century, with many attempts to unite Native Americans against either British/American colonists (the Indians first allied with the French, then the English) or against all whites. When Tenskwatawa vowed in 1810 to "follow in the footsteps of the Great Pontiac," he was articulating his indebtedness to a prophetic tradition that had in fact come to constitute a major element shaping Indian history.[3]

A. Neolin (1760-1765)[4]

Once European settlement began in the seventeenth century, the Leni Lenape (Delaware) were progressively displaced westward. By the mid-eighteenth century they lived in northern and western Pennsylvania and the Ohio Valley. In the "middle ground" where Indians and whites interacted with considerable autonomy before the War of 1812, Native Americans began to question the possibility of coexistence with whites as early as the 1730s. In 1737, missionary Conrad Weiser reported an anonymous prophet who accounted for famine and the disappearance of game as follows:

> You kill the animals for the sake of skins, which you give for strong liquors, and drown your senses, and carry on a dreadful debauchery . . . If you will do good, and cease from your sins, I will bring the animals back; if not, I will destroy you from the end of the earth.

Nevertheless, instead of interpreting this message as a call for reform, the Shawnees and Onondagas who heard it simply resigned themselves to their sorry fate: "Rum will kill us, and leave the land clear for the Europeans without strife or purchase."

Not all Native Americans despaired. Under the influence of Quakers and Moravian missionaries, a number became "praying Indians," some of whom were rewarded for their efforts by the Paxton Boys' Massacre of

1764. Another group under Papoohoon lived on the upper Susquehanna and practiced a strict pacifism obviously derived from the missionaries. They remained separate from whites and claimed to adhere to traditional customs. A third community was Wagemond's community at Asinsing on the Chemung River. He read from a picture book that placed the whites in Hell with their rum and the Indians in Heaven with the Sun, a traditional symbol of the Deity. In addition, he also introduced new ceremonial dances and attacked the widespread sorcery Indians resorted to in response to white contact. These two traits came to typify prophetic movements.

However, it was Neolin who brought together a large number of Delaware and others. He provided the ideology for what white historians call the "Conspiracy" of Pontiac. Around 1760, Neolin began traveling among villages telling of a vision from God. He called upon the people to "return to that former happy state, in which we lived in peace and plenty." The way to do this was "to put off entirely from yourselves the customs which you have adopted since the white people came." He rejected the path of racial coexistence that had become traditional in the "middle ground," and preached that God was angry because the original inhabitants were:

> looking upon a people of a different color from our own, who had come across a great lake, as if they were a part of ourselves . . . while they were not only taking our country from us, but this, our avenue to Heaven leading us into the beautiful regions which were destined for us.

Neolin squarely attributed the Indians' demise to the penetration of European trade networks. He demanded his followers give up rum, "which the whites have forced upon us for the sake of increasing their gains and diminishing our numbers." Trading of furs for firearms was just as bad: "Do not sell your brothers what I have put on earth for food. Become good and you shall receive your needs." Becoming good meant doing away with guns (modified by the more practical Pontiac), making medicine with evil spirits, and chasing after women. Neolin produced a map of the universe that he would symbolically "sell" for one buckskin or two doeskins. On it, the Indians' traditional path to Heaven had been blocked by the whites, forcing them to take a more circuitous route that required adoption of the Prophet's moral code. If Indians accepted their sins and amended their ways, Neolin promised that God would drive the whites from their land and restore both their lands on this earth and the way to paradise. Neolin underlined the problem of subsistence caused by white traders and settlers by placing images of fat turkey and deer in Heaven, emaciated ones in Hell. The whites and sinning Indians in Hell would be dehumanized. They would be turned into dogs and horses, two kinds of tame and subservient animals. Neolin in fact referred to British soldiers as "dogs in red coats."

For all Neolin's efforts to renounce white influence, its impact on his prophecy was pronounced. Traditionally, Indians had blamed catastrophes on either witchcraft or on their failure to perform rituals rather than on their moral shortcomings. The transition from performance of specified rites to moral responsibility for a society's failures can be observed in the development of various religions, notably Biblical Judaism and Christianity. Further, the new emphasis on Heaven for Indians and Hell for Europeans (and their Indian followers) was clearly a reverse borrowing of a Christian distinction.

Neolin's and Pontiac's revolt was the most successful of the violent rebellions against British North Americans. Following the French and Indian War, the British had hoped to stop sending gifts to the Indians to appease them, and to reduce them to submission instead. The fierce resistance after the French surrendered stunned them. It led to a continuation of the mixture of presents, negotiation, accommodation, and threats that had characterized the French policy for which the Indians nostalgically longed. It also cemented loyalty to the British, who sought to keep their American colonists from provoking new Indian wars by excluding trans-Appalachian settlement with the Proclamation of 1763. Pontiac and Neolin effectively united enough Native Americans in the Old Northwest to buy many of them nearly a half-century of troubled independence.

B. Handsome Lake (1799-1815)[5]

During the American Revolution, the lands of the Iroquois, many of whom remained loyal to the British, were overrun by the Sullivan Expedition of 1779. By the end of the century, they had lost over half their population and suffered from drunkenness, depression, internal strife, and loss of game. They were confined to small reservations in Northern Pennsylvania and Western New York dubbed by anthropologist Anthony Wallace "slums in the wilderness." Prophets appeared to offer alternative ways of life to those espoused by the Confederation's two leaders. Joseph Brant had changed his name, become an Anglican, and urged his people to become thoroughly Europeanized. Red Jacket rejected Christianity and favored continued communal living with hunting as the basis of subsistence. White revivalists, participants in what is known to history as the Second Great Awakening, and Quaker missionaries, such as Henry Simmons, whom the Iroquois respected and who gave his approval to Handsome Lake, added to the confusion.

The brother of the important chief Cornplanter, Handsome Lake was an elderly drunkard of little reputation until he recovered from near death in 1799 and began recounting his visions. In the first, three angels sent by the Creator ordered him to preach, upon pain of damnation, that his people must give up whiskey, witchcraft, and abortion, and resume their traditional Strawberry Festival. On a second "Sky Journey" Handsome Lake fell into a seven-hour trance in which a guide led him through Heaven and Hell and revealed the constitution of the universe. Ascending through the Milky Way, Handsome Lake saw the human race travelling toward various fates. A hideous fat woman represented preoccupation with material things. A jail, handcuffs, a whip, and a hangman's rope stood for those who took the white man's path rather than Handsome Lake's. There was a church, but no Indians could enter, symbolizing the fact the white man's religion was not for them. Two huge drops of liquid threatened the destruction of the earth if Handsome Lake could not save it by attracting followers. George Washington appeared, supposedly a good man who protected Indian lands. Jesus, still bearing the wounds of his crucifixion, told Handsome Lake that "you are more successful than I for some believe in you but none in me." Handsome Lake here voiced the frequent Indian complaint that the whites' grasping, murderous behavior showed that they did not believe in their own religion. Jesus continued: "Now tell your people that they will become lost when they follow the ways of the white man."

Handsome Lake then saw the judges of human souls from the hereafter. Everyone was given three chances to repent and follow the "Good Way" or "Gaiwiio." If not, they were condemned to a Hell where in Dante-like fashion people received the just deserts of their excesses (a promiscuous woman had to fornicate with red-hot male organs, for example). Heaven, on the other hand, was a natural paradise teeming with game where Handsome Lake met his dog and deceased relatives. In his third vision, Handsome Lake was ordered to travel from village to village teaching his doctrine, to write it in a book, to revive some ancient Iroquois ceremonies, such as the annual sacrifice of a white dog, and to insist that the people not sell their land.

Iroquois culture taught that if visions were authentic they ought to be acted upon. For an initial period of about twenty years the Iroquois argued over whether the Gaiwiio was genuine. But by 1818, assisted by similar visions from other prophets, the nation accepted the Way of Handsome Lake. It is still followed by many Iroquois, was written down in 1845, and forms the basis of Iroquois religion.

Handsome Lake's "Good Way" endured because it reconciled two essential elements. It gave the Iroquois an identity based on their own traditions, which enabled them to survive as islands in a white sea. Yet it also incorporated enough practical wisdom from the whites to facilitate that survival. The Indians rejected Christianity—on no less an authority than Jesus himself! They gave up drinking and sorcery, confessed their sins, and entered Heaven or Hell based on moral performance. (In their zeal, Handsome Lake and his followers executed a large number of real or suspected witches.) The Iroquois kept some of their old festivals, but adopted some of the whites' methods. Men began to farm as well as women. In addition, they began to use the plow, to abandon hunting, and to send their children to white schools. Handsome Lake rebuffed appeals by Tenskwatawa to join the confederation against the United States in 1810. The patrilineal and monogamous family became the rule. Trading with whites was allowed, but land could not be alienated. This last prohibition was so effective that despite great pressure from the 1820s to 1840s, when the Iroquois began to experience heavy settlement in their region, most of them resisted enticing offers of land and cash made to induce them to move. Unlike the violent prophetic revolts that usually ended in disaster, Handsome Lake took a defeated and demoralized people and restored their pride by creatively fusing white and Indian culture. He thereby led them in what Wallace has termed "the Iroquois Renaissance."

C. Tenskwatawa (1805-1812)[6]

The Shawnee from 1795-1805 resembled the Delaware at the end of the French and Indian War and the Iroquois at the end of the American Revolution. Defeated by General Anthony Wayne at the Battle of Fallen Timbers in 1794, they ceded most of their lands to the Americans the next year and moved westward. Drinking, depletion of game, famine, and disorder afflicted them over the next decade. Prophets and chiefs urged them to stop drinking and quarreling among themselves.

In 1805, Lalawethika ("Rattler" or "Noisemaker"), a despised and drunkard shaman of no repute, fell into a trance. He did not awake until his funeral was being prepared. He then told of how two men had carried him to the Spirit World. It was the Indians' traditional view of Heaven, "a rich fertile country abounding in game, fish, pleasant hunting grounds, and fine corn fields." Only good Indians would attain paradise; those who did evil had to first undergo a gruesome purgatory in which the punishment fit the crime (drunkards had molten lead poured down their throats). Tenskwatawa's code resembled Handsome Lake's sufficiently to suggest some influence.

Renamed Tenskwatawa, or "the Open Door," the prophet began to preach the transformation his followers had to achieve. Along with abstinence from liquor, converts had to refrain from violence against other Indians, respect each other's belongings, treat their wives and children gently, preserve marital fidelity, perform new dances and reject old ones, spurn witchcraft (again a purge against sorcerers, most of whom had taken English names, was conducted), and accept symbolic prayer sticks.

Most significantly, Tenskwatawa demanded that all elements of white civilization and any form of contact with whites be eliminated. Indians should only wear breech cloths or animal skins. They had to shave their heads except for scalplocks, kill all their cattle, horses, hogs, and even dogs, destroy all their European goods, and even refuse to speak to Europeans. As historian Richard White notes, Tenskwatawa set up the dichotomies of Indian/manly/free as opposed to white/womanly/tame: the whites were attempting to relegate the Indians to the status of slaves, as they had their animals, or to that of women. The prophet and his followers reduced the traditional influence of women in Shawnee society and stifled some female prophets who had also claimed divine authority. Expounding a fierce anti-Americanism, Tenskwatawa called the Americans the "scum of the great water" because he thought that they had been produced by the frothing of the evil serpent that dwelled in the ocean. Indians, on the other hand, were created by God as a separate race, and all of them should join his movement and abandon tribal loyalty.

Of course, Tenskwatawa was not as free from dependence on the whites as he claimed. When his doctrine spread through the Old Northwest like wildfire in the winter of 1805-1806, it caused large numbers of Indians to gather in the new villages he set up, first at Greenville, Ohio, then at Prophetstown at the junction of the Wabash and Tippecanoe Rivers in Indiana. The concentrated population caused severe food shortages, which Tenskwatawa remedied by begging food from Shakers and nearby United States authorities, whom he convinced of his peaceful intentions.

Challenged by skeptics to demonstrate that the Master of Life had indeed empowered him, he learned from the Shakers of an eclipse of the sun on June 16, 1806. On that day, he convinced his followers that he had indeed blotted the sun from the sky and then restored it. Practical survival dictated that men take up the untraditional role and farm as well as hunt in the Prophet's villages. Even more sensibly, while only bows and arrows could be used for hunting, one could use the whites' firearms against them. As the War of 1812 approached and the prospect of British assistance to the Pan-Indian federation loomed, it turned out only the Americans were the scum of the sea monster: the British, French, and Spanish joined the Indians as children of the Master of Life.

Tenskwatawa's clever fusion of Indian tradition with religious imagery, morality, and material assistance from the whites failed. While his brother Tecumseh visited the Southeastern nations, persuading only the Muskogees to revolt, the Prophet was compelled by overeager followers to launch an attack on an expedition headed by William Henry Harrison, who insisted that Indian criminals be surrendered to the whites for justice. (Tecumseh was furious that his brother did not wait for British aid which in fact soon came.) At the Battle of Tippecanoe in November, 1811, Tenskwatawa promised his followers that a great rain would dampen the powder and guns of the whites and that the attacking Indians would become invisible in the dark. The failure of his magic lost Tenskwatawa all credibility; he wandered in the United States and Canada until his death in 1836, in Kansas where George Catlin painted his portrait. Only after Tippecanoe did Tecumseh assume leadership of the federation, which died with him at the Battle of the Thames the next year. If Tenskwatawa united more people than any other Indian prophet, he dissipated his influence through a premature attack and the promise of a miracle he could not perform.

D. Muskogee (Creek) (1811-1814)[7]

Following the American Revolution, the Muskogees—themselves a newly formed confederacy from various displaced peoples—suffered the same debilitation as the other nations east of the Mississippi. Although some prophets appeared before 1811, the visit of Tecumseh seeking recruits for his pan-Indian confederation triggered the "Red Stick" movement. The Muskogees borrowed heavily from Tenskwatawa. They killed chiefs, destroyed villages that refused to massacre livestock, abandoned agricultural settlements for the woods, resumed a life of hunting and gathering, adapted Shawnee dances, and spurned European clothes and goods to symbolize their initiation into a world excluding whites.

Although Tecumseh was undoubtedly the main catalyst, other factors contributed to the Muskogee movement. The spectacular "New Madrid" earthquake of 1811 confirmed the prophets' claim that God was angry and an apocalypse was near. The neighboring Cherokees also had several prophets who urged their brethren to put aside white clothes and ways. However, this nation was also undergoing a revitalization movement of a different form—the Cherokees were prospering through capitalist agriculture, including some slave plantations, and they were firmly controlled by chiefs who believed they could successfully assimilate to white society. The Cherokees boasted democratic tribal councils, a written constitution, and a police force: many had embraced Christianity, white names, and white dress. Still, a minority of the Cherokees who felt left out of this assimilationist movement either through poverty or guilt at abandoning tradition burned their possessions and resumed old dances and rituals. This Cherokee revival petered out after the prophet Tsali predicted incorrectly that a hailstorm would destroy the old world and the whites, restoring a paradise of game and natural splendor for the Indians.

Another source of the Muskogee revival was the religion of African/Americans. Escaping slaves tried to reach Muskogee territory, where they could easily become free. Many intermarried with the Indians and added European artisanal skills to the Muskogees' considerable repertoire. They also brought their emotionally charged Christianity, which said that God was on the side of the poor and oppressed. He would punish the wicked slaveowners and lead his suffering people to the Promised Land.

During the War of 1812, the Muskogees revolted. After successfully wiping out members of the tribe who would not join them, they believed they were invincible. The prophets told them their red sticks and magic would ward off the whites' guns. As a result, eight hundred out of one thousand Muskogee warriors were killed at the Battle of Tohopeka on March 27, 1814. Like the Cherokees, who trusted the white man's assimilationist rhetoric and who were considerably more civilized than the frontiersmen who took their lands, the remaining Muskogees were removed across the Mississippi to Indian territory in Oklahoma in the 1830s.

E. Smoholla (1855-1880s)[8]

Smoholla was a shaman of the small group of Wanapum Indians. His people, along with the Yakima and Nez Perces, lived in the present state of Washington. By the late 1850s, following a treaty guaranteeing them possession of their reservations—on which the whites promptly encroached—these Indians were in the same state of demoralization as the eastern nations who formed a receptive audience for the prophets. Smoholla fought a duel with a rival shaman in which he was left for dead. His body drifted down a river, but he miraculously recovered and traveled throughout the Southwest and Mexico. He then returned to tell of how he had died and come to life again to preach his message. Falling into deep trances, he spoke of how he had wandered through the stars. The Great Spirit told him he had created the peoples of the earth in order of quality—Indians first, then French, English, Americans, and Negroes last. The earth belonged to the Indians, the only people of purely divine stock, and the only ones who reverenced it. Reflecting traditional Indian cosmology that the earth was a living being to be honored, Smoholla preached against planting, as the Plains Indians traditionally had. Hunting and gathering, the traditional subsistence of the Northwest peoples, alone did not defile the earth. Smoholla, who had been educated by Catholic missionaries, introduced processions to a House of Prayer on Sundays. These processions were preceded by a banner and featured a cross, bells, and choral singing. Festivals he sponsored honored berrypicking and salmon fishing, acceptable forms of obtaining food. During these dances, celebrants would work themselves into a frenzy and receive visions.

Smoholla spread his cult among the various peoples of the Northwest. The most notable participants were Chief Joseph and the Nez Perces. Their revolt of 1877, however, was precipitated by Americans murdering their people and throwing them off their land, after which they retaliated and attempted to escape to Canada. In general, Smoholla's followers were non-violent and persisted until the 1880s.

F. Wodziwob (1869) and Wovoka (1885-1890)[9]

A Paviotso Indian who lived on the border of California and Nevada, Wodziwob experienced a vision in 1869. The Indians' ancestors would return to earth with a great explosion, a cataclysm would shake the world, white Americans would vanish, and the Indians would inherit their wealth. Believers performed a ritual consisting of songs and dances leading to a trance state. Many California Indians followed Wodziwob, as did some Mormons who viewed the Native Americans as the Ten Lost Tribes of Israel. They accepted founder Joseph Smith's vision that the

Messiah would return in 1890 and regarded Wodziwob's prophecies as confirmation. The Ghost Dance gathered momentum after 1885 when a Paiute ranch hand named Jack Wilson, whose father was a disciple of Wodziwob, experienced a trance and dream similar to the cult's founder. The participants then began to wear the Ghost Dance shirt decorated with feathers, symbols, and bones.

The late 1880s were terrible times for the western Indians. There were severe winters and widespread famine. The buffalo disappeared. Efforts were made by the Bureau of Indian Affairs to obliterate their culture and turn them into subsistence farmers. The Ghost Dance spread rapidly throughout the West. Now calling himself Wovoka, Wilson insisted that Indians coexist peacefully with whites until the final catastrophe and even permitted them to wear European/American clothing. The movement's popularity and anti-white rhetoric, however, greatly disturbed the United States Indian agents and army, and the Ghost Dance was outlawed and suppressed. However, many prophets confirmed Wovoka's vision, including Sitting Bull on the Pine Ridge Reservation for the Sioux in South Dakota. There, in 1890, over three hundred Ghost Dancers were massacred by Indian police who feared they might turn violent; it is possible some of the dancers may have been arming for a struggle.

The persistence of the Ghost Dance and the Wounded Knee massacre in Native American memory was dramatically illustrated in 1973. Angered at a corrupt and unresponsive "tribal" chairman, the Sioux on Pine Ridge occupied Wounded Knee for three months until starved out by a siege. The Sioux sought to call attention to the grievances of reservation Indians in general in addition to their particular ills. They were bullied and sometimes killed with impunity when they ventured into nearby white communities; they were miseducated in dreadful schools that sought to expunge their culture; and they were offered little opportunity for employment or self-betterment. At Wounded Knee, the protestors established an "independent Ogalala nation" run on cooperative principles.

Interviews with participants show graphically that the 1973 occupation was indeed a revitalization movement heavily indebted to previous Indian uprisings. "We're trying to regain what we had in the past, being human beings and being involved in society," stated one Sioux Vietnam veteran. A seventy-seven-year-old tribal elder said, "This whole reservation was in total darkness. And somewhere, these young men started the American Indian Movement. And they came to our reservation and they turned that light on inside."

Wallace Black Elk, a shaman, reintroduced the peyote smoking ceremony, which had been the major rite of the Native American Church. This both preceded and succeeded the Ghost Dance, which communities of non-assimilationist Indians preserved throughout the twentieth century as an underground movement. Besides the pipe-smoking ceremony that induced visions, this religion called for abstinence from alcohol, family and community loyalty, selflessness, Indian unity, and the rejection of white ways. It replaced Christianity, although the influence was obvious. Jesus had been killed and abandoned by the whites; however, he protected those Indians who were loyal to his true religion.

Black Elk explained the peyote ceremony:

> This sacred pipe was carved and the Great Spirit put all his knowledge and power in it and gave it to the red nation. And its sacred altar is the Western Hemisphere.

After emphasizing the need for people to respect nature and live in harmony with her and with each other, Black Elk predicted an apocalypse and the ultimate restoration of a cooperative social order:

> We are going back home now. We are tired of going this way with science and technology. This way we're going to blow our heads off. Their [white] philosophy is just like a dead end street. It's going to come to an end.

It will be replaced by "the tree of life, the tree will bloom, it will flower again, and all the people will rejoin and come back to the sacred road, the red road." Through their protest, the Wounded Knee community hoped to point the way to a juster, more human society:

> The white people have to surrender their arms to the Great Spirit. They have to be sorry for what they have done, murdered their own Jesus Christ. Totally murdered him . . . They just fight each other and stumble over each other to get ahead no matter whether it's your brother or sister.

Black Elk's commentary on the difference between Indian and white law is especially astute. The Indian possesses "sacred rules" from the Great Spirit, "unwritten spiritual laws." Even though the whites "put everything in a file or a book," it is all a ploy—as were the treaties the Indians trusted—"to channel and funnel all the money into his [the white man's] belly." "These people don't believe in God. They just believe in material things." Black Elk's point that the whites do not even believe their own laws and religion is a telling one with which I will end this essay.

G. Chilam Balam and the Mayans (sixteenth century to present)[10]

An even more persistent example of how the messages of Indian prophets speak to the problems of subsequent times is the endurance of Mayan belief in *The Book of Chilam Balam*. A compendium of pre- and post-conquest prophecies, these writings were collected between the sixteenth and eighteenth centuries. Meanwhile the Spanish engaged in a slow, piecemeal conquest of the Mayan city-states marked by much bloodshed and resistance. "These are millennial words for the examination of the Mayan people who may know how they were born and settled the land," *The Book* proclaims. "Then came the arrival of Christianity . . . And his [Christ's] word will be everywhere and inflict pain on the born and engendered children, Christianizing us and then treating us like animals." The Mayans were puzzled that after they accepted a Christ of divine love, the God who conquered their gods, they still suffered brutal treatment at the hands of the whites who claimed to represent Him. They longed for the old days:

> Poor are our books to make it come back; . . . poor are our books to unite the parts in the land. [But] if one is clever, if one is strong . . because of the madness of the time . . . Thus will be the termination of the rulers, the two-faced people by our Father who is God . . . So God will be given the achievement of a flood for the second time . . . So then will descend our father who is Jesus Christ . . . Succeeding in redeeming us with His holy blood. And that will be the descent of a great storm, being given the right to Heavenly truth.

The apocalypse seemed to come in 1847. At that time, the wealthy creoles of the Yucatan rebelled against Mexico and tried to form an independent country. They were surprised to find that in the resulting turmoil the masses of Mayan Indians, some only recently conquered and cruelly reduced to serfdom, in turn revolted against them. *The Book of Chilam Balam* was at the center of the Mayans' ideology, as their spokesmen stressed:

> We poor Indians are aware of what the whites are doing to injure us,

> of how many evils they commit against us, even to our children and harmless women . . . They have given just causes for the reprisals of the Indians . . . The whites think that these things are all ended, but never. It is written in the *Book of Chilam Balam*, and so even has said Jesus Christ, our Lord on earth and beyond, that if the whites will become peaceful, so shall we become peaceful.

In the depths of the Yucatan forests, the Mayan rebels established the Kingdom of the Cruzob, or People of the Cross. Much of the priests' powers came from ventriloquists who made a cross appear to speak. Identifying themselves with the Itzu King, who Chilam Balam promised would redeem them from the Dzulob or whites, their political movement, based on a mix of Mayan and Christian elements, endured until 1901, when a major Mexican armed force suppressed them. However, as late as 1959, when Nelson Reed visited Mayan territory to write his book, *The Caste War of Yucatan*, he had a hard time convincing some of the people that he was not the "red man" come from the British to help them drive out their overlords as Chilam Balam had predicted. "The Cross Sleeps," Reed concluded, but the prophecies of Chilam Balam, which inspired rebellions for several centuries, still live in the breasts of Yucatecs dreaming of a better past and future.

Besides inviting comparisons with each other, the Native American Prophetic revolts suggest comparisons with the evolution of European and American nationalism.[11] The current widsom of a long and complex historiographical argument is that "peoples" and "nations" only began to perceive themselves as such in the period from the late eighteenth to the early twentieth century—exactly contemporaneous with the North American Indians. The causes of this "revitalization" were similar as well: a shock in the form of outside disruptions to traditional orders was required. These was provided by the revolutions in France and the United States and the Napoleonic invasions in Spain, Germany, and Russia. This inspired peoples who had hitherto thought of themselves as inhabitants of a village, city, or at best a province to unite, give themselves a world-historical, frequently religiously-based mission, idolize "prophets" like Napoleon, George Washington, and Bismarck, and create a national tradition anchored in a mythical, culturally shared past. Furthermore, nationalism requires an enemy of the "chosen" people—an "Other" who will be described as not quite human and an obstacle to the good life and world the elect are seeking to construct. In turning the tables on their white oppressors, Native Americans joined white nationalists in building group solidarity through purging alien elements. That we do not usually view the Native American Prophetic revolts in the context of nineteenth-century nationalism stems from the practice of regarding small or non-white nations as "tribes" unless they actually succeed in establishing themselves as nation-states.[12] As we examine the nationalist turmoil in the former Soviet Union and Yugoslavia in 1994, the tragedy in committing this category-mistake should be obvious.

III. Placing Native Americans At the Center: Alternative Worlds At the Periphery

For no other group in United States history has the response to the dominant society been so starkly presented as a matter of life and death as it has for the country's original inhabitants. However, African/Americans, women, immigrants, reformers, and Utopians all criticized the greed, selfishness, and violence of America and have constructed alternative cultures, even if their movements did not usually develop the prophetic, messianic aspects of the Native Americans. Unlike the Indians, they could not fight back as independent military powers. Instead, they turned their relative powerlessness into a badge of moral superiority, using the very religious and communal principles trumpeted by the larger society to justify itself. They were then able to use their alternative communities—one might almost call them "nations within a nation"—as bases to launch moral if not military attacks against a United States that failed to live up to its own professed beliefs in liberty, equality, and justice.

If we move Native Americans from the margin of United States history to its center, their sufferings and responses may serve as the model for a cogent rewriting of the nation's past. American history may be viewed as a struggle between the culture of commercial expansion and political power and the cultures of resistance raised against it by the apparently powerless. That such alternative "nations" are no longer hidden from history, presented solely as victims, or totally disenfranchised today constitutes the monument of their struggle, and proof that the struggle continues. In such a context, the Native American Prophets and their ideas remain on the stage of history as symbols of the aspirations of the oppressed, available for inspiration and instruction in the future. Let us now turn to other groups who forged their own cultural identities in reaction to the dominant paradigm.

A. African/Americans[13]

Recent scholarship has demonstrated the extraordinary importance of religion, family, and communal solidarity in sustaining slaves who had been taken from numerous nations in Africa. In America, as a result of the slavery imposed upon them by their masters, they took on a common identity based upon race. They rejected the Christianity of their masters which told them to be obedient and look for their reward in Heaven. Frequently in secret, they held meetings in which emotionally charged singing, dancing, and preaching would go on for hours, sometimes for an entire night. Modelled both on the camp meetings of Baptists and Methodists and on African ceremonies, the African/Americans created an alternative religion. Their spirituals stressed the Old Testament, such as Moses's deliverance of his people from the bondage of Egypt. A theme emphasized in many songs was passing over a river (the Jordan or the Ohio) to a Promised Land. African/American Christianity continued to be a powerful force after the Civil War liberated the slaves, enabling "former slaves to affirm that they had trusted in the Lord and that the Lord had delivered them," in the words of historian Albert J. Raboteau. "Like the children of Israel of old, they had lived through Egypt and Exodus and the experience had constituted them a peculiar, chosen people." They forged a distinctive, underground culture where the whites had only seen a racial distinction useful for defining slave labor.

The Civil Rights movement of the twentieth century has drawn on this heritage. One need think only of Martin Luther King, Jr.'s speech in 1963 at the Lincoln Memorial, in which he compared himself with Moses come to the mountain, having glimpsed the Promised Land of racial equality and human dignity. However, the integrationist attitude of King and the African/American Christian ministers did not suit all African/Americans. Some who argued true equality and dignity were impossible in white America turned to Islam, another religion that began as the revolt of oppressed people and is currently the principal faith of Western Asia and Africa. Black Muslims—the Nation of Islam—rejected white American culture, schools, and sometimes dress and names. They sought to create a territorial black nation within America instead.

The African/American family and community were other sources of strength for the slaves. Herbert Gutman has argued convincingly that slaves went to tremendous lengths to keep their families together and to instill respect for aunts, uncles, cousins, grandparents, and other kinfolk. Slaves maintained solidarity in the face of a system that did not recognize marriage, could compel prostitution, and threatened families with separation—by Gutman's estimates, one-third were broken up. The strength of the African/American family became evident when thousands of African/Americans wandered the South in search of separated loved ones during and after the Civil War.

Given the presence of a white majority, slave rebellion was rare. However, the most famous, Nat Turner's Virginia Rebellion of 1831, shared many of the characteristics of Indian prophetic revolts. Born in 1800, Turner was strongly influenced by his parents and a religious grandmother, who convinced the precocious child that he was destined for great things. As he grew up, Turner lived an austere life, devoting much time to prayer and fasting. Both African/Americans and whites told him he was too smart to be a slave. In 1825, he experienced a vision in which "white spirits and black thunder rolled in the Heavens and the blood flowed in streams." He saw the Savior and the Holy Ghost, was made perfect, and saw signs in the Heavens that indicated that the Day of Judgment was at hand. Turner believed himself God's chosen instrument against the slaveowners, who were the creatures of Satan. Turner's rebellion was nipped in the bud, however, after his band had killed fifty-five whites. Ironically, his last stand occurred when he tried to capture a town named Jerusalem.

B. Women[14]

Women, like African/Americans, proclaimed the moral superiority of the world into which men had thrust them. The center of their culture was the "Home." This, the "woman's sphere" of domesticity, chastity, and religiosity, also provided the base from which women could move into the public world of men and counter-attack them with their own principles. Middle- and upper-class women in the nineteenth century, relegated to the home "for their own protection" from a chaotic and immoral world of politics and commerce, were supposed to be the guardians of virtue. As such they were entrusted with the education of the young; the separation of home and workplace made it difficult for fathers to share in childrearing. Motherhood became the noblest vocation in Victorian society, as Catherine Beecher, the foremost nineteenth-century advocate of the "Cult of True Womanhood" proclaimed:

> Are you not only a housekeeper, but a *mother*? Oh, sacred and beautiful name! . . . You are training young minds whose plastic

> texture will receive and retain every impression you make, who will imitate your feelings, tastes, habits, and opinions, and who will transmit what they receive from you to their children, to pass again to the next generation, and then to the next, until a *whole nation* will have received its character and destiny from your hands! No imperial queen ever stood in a more sublime and responsible position.

If women were indeed morally better than men, then they could leave the home to reform society at large. They formed thousands of associations dedicated to ending drunkenness and even drinking (the Women's Christian Temperance Union), prostitution (the New York Female Moral Reform Society), and the exploitation of labor (the National Child Labor Committee and Women's Trade Union League). Women were important in agitating for the end of slavery, in educating freed slaves, improving sanitary life in the cities, and founding settlement houses, hospitals, colleges, schools, and charitable societies. As scholar Ann Douglas has written:

> Between 1820 and 1875, in the midst of the transformation of the American economy into the most powerfully aggressive capitalist system in the world, American culture seemed bent on establishing a perpetual Mother's Day. As the secular activities of American life were demonstrating their utter supremacy, religion became the message of America's official and conventional cultural life.

Women could "become aggressive, even angry, in the name of various holy causes."

The women's movement also split into separatist and assimilationist factions, as have the Indians and the African/Americans. Many women, glorying in their moral influence, opposed suffrage; others used their superior moral position as an argument for it. In the late twentieth century, the women's liberation movement has taken great pains to stress that women want more than equal work with equal pay in male society; they hope to bring a more caring and less belligerent attitude to foreign and domestic problems. "Women are not more moral than men," Gloria Steinem has noted:

> We are only uncorrupted by power. But we do not want to imitate men, to join this country as it is, and I think our participation will change it. Perhaps women-elected leaders—and there will be many of

them—will not be so likely to dominate black people or yellow people or men . . . After all, we won't have our masculinity to prove.

C. Immigrants[15]

Social historians have recently shown that the "melting pot," in which newcomers assimilated into American society, never existed for most immigrants. Second and third generation descendants of immigrants ultimately Americanized, but the foreign-born themselves generally lived (and still live) in ghettoes. They faced a society which, as it has for Indians, African/Americans, and women, demanded cultural assimilation without granting equal economic or political opportunity or respect for the groups' distinctiveness. So immigrants turned the tables. They tried to advance economically and politically, as through urban political machines and labor unions. They thereby not only preserved but intensified their feelings of ethnic identification. This process began with the Irish Catholics, who began to arrive in large numbers from the 1820s through the 1840s. They remained in their own urban neighborhoods, stood steadfastly by their own religion, built parochial schools to resist Protestant conversion efforts, and took over Tammany Hall. Interestingly, this self-segregation only occurred after a vigorous debate within the Irish/American community itself, in which more liberal Catholics, who wanted to cooperate with Protestant-dominated public schools, churches, and charities and send the urban poor to farms, were defeated.

"Ethnic" or "national" consciousness, as we know it, was not so much imported to America as created there. In Europe, the church and state inspired little popular affection, dominated as they were by oppressive upper classes who had evicted millions of peasants from their farms as agriculture became commercialized in the nineteenth century. Confronted by discrimination in the United States, the immigrants used church and community to affirm their identity. Institutions, such as immigrant theater, festivals, newspapers, stores, charitable societies, and political organizations, contributed to the shaping of people proud as never before to be Polish or Italian. Just as the prophetic Native American revolts united displaced Indians from previously distinct or hostile nations and gave them a Pan-Indian consciousness, displacement from Europe and prejudice in America molded immigrants from different villages and regions into strong ethnic groups.

Placing the church and parochial school at the community's center emphasized solidarity and religion at the expense of individualism, economic aggrandizement, and social mobility. Immigrants contributed precious earnings to build churches that catered to a particular nationality. Prospective immigrant families would pool resources and send over usually a strong young male representative, who in turn would scrimp and save to pay the passage of the rest of the family. Families remained together, living in the same neighborhood and sometimes the same building. Efforts were made to keep mothers at home rather than to maximize income. Responding to "scientific" theories of race, which denied their equality along with Indians, Asians, and African/Americans, nineteenth and early twentieth century immigrants similarly resisted assimilation through the creation of independent cultures.

D. Reformers[16]

As historian David J. Rothman has noted, beginning around 1820, American reformers sought to alleviate the ills of urbanization, expansion, and industrialization (that is, the growth of the world-system) by isolating groups of people in protected, "total" environments where they would be subject to benevolent influences. Somehow, the creation of moral, religious, and disciplined people was supposed to fit them for survival in the very cutthroat, amoral world against which they had been institutionalized. The home was one such institution for women; new types of schools and prisons were others.

In early America, children had gone to school erratically, when they were not needed for planting and harvesting. Few attended more than a couple of years. The schoolhouse was decidedly secondary to the family as the prime source of education, as most men followed in their fathers' footsteps as farmers while women learned from their mothers. However, the Common School movement begun in Massachusetts by Horace Mann in the 1820s envisioned protracted and uniform education for all children.

Mann's purpose was several-fold. First, Massachusetts industrialized early, and thus was "exposed, far beyond any other state in the Union, to the fatal extremes of overgrown wealth and desperate poverty." "Nothing but universal education," he argued, "can counterwork this tendency to the domination of capital and the servility of labor." While providing social mobility for the children of the poor, "moral" education would also instill in them a respect for law and society and counteract "the unrestrained passions of men [which] are not only homicidal but suicidal." Education would save the nation. The next generation would redeem the present:

> Education has never yet been brought to bear with one hundredth part of its potential force upon the natures of children and, through them, upon the character of men, and the race.

He predicted that "far beyond any other earthly instrumentality, it is comprehensive and decisive."

Early educational theorists stressed discipline, religion, and morality, not the free development of the child's potential. According to Noah Webster, the prime qualification for a schoolmaster was "unblemished reputation." "The only practicable method to reform mankind is to begin with children, to banish, if possible, from their company every low-bred, drunken, immoral character." Schools would teach "strict subordination:" "the rod is often necessary in school especially after the children have been accustomed to disobedience and licentious behavior at home." The school would thus replace the imperiled family as the primary source of education and create an alternative world in which children would not repeat the sins of their fathers. The prominent role of New Englanders, women, and clergymen in early educational reforms—all of whom looked askance at Jacksonian America and longed for a Puritanical moral order—marks yet another resemblance to Indian prophets, immigrants, and African/Americans who sought through new methods to recapture an imagined golden past.

It is no coincidence that the new type of prisons, now dubbed for the first time "reformatories" or "penitentiaries," arose at the same time as schools. Earlier, people were rarely confined in jail for long periods; punishments consisted of fines, whippings, or death. The idea that incarceration could make a new person out of a criminal through diligent labor and education—provided by ministers and other approved figures—arose in the nineteenth century. Once again, salvation was to come by segregating a group from the greater world and instilling in it a new morality. The schools and prisons of the nineteenth century reformers were the equivalent of the Indian prophets' calls for separation and abstinence. That the larger society supported such alternative worlds in its own midst suggests that it, too, was dissatisfied on a profound level with individualism and commerce as the basis of the moral order.

E. Utopian Reformers[17]

Native Americans were not alone in supplying prophets who urged people to leave behind the corruptions of society, form new communities, practice new moral codes, and await the end of the present world in anticipation of a better one. Nineteenth century America teemed with Utopian communities of which the Shakers, Ephrata Cloisters, Oneida Community, Millerites, Robert Owen's New Harmony, and the Mormons are perhaps the most famous examples. These widely divergent communities shared three major characteristics: a) Charismatic founders: The Shakers' Mother Ann Lee and Mormon Joseph Smith both claimed to have received visions from God of the structure of the true church. Oneida's John Humphrey Noyes, Ephrata's Conrad Beisel, and William Miller all claimed authority based on careful study of the scriptures. Robert Owen was a secular industrialist, but his socialist experiment depended solely on his personal presence. b) Unusual sexual and living arrangements: The Shakers practiced total abstinence from sex and complete sexual equality; the Ephrata community encouraged celibacy and, as with the Shakers, men and women lived and participated in worship separately; Oneida "Perfectionists" believed every man and woman in the community was mutually married. The Mormons practiced polygamy. c) Communal Attitudes toward Property: Ephrata, the Shakers, and Oneida held their goods in common. They encouraged trading with the outside world (Shaker furniture and Oneida Silver were of very high quality and profitability) but pooled the surplus, which they usually spent on charity and reinvestment in the community. The Mormons, too, during their early years, practiced a form of state socialism directed by their elders. Owen's socialist project hoped to show that industry could run smoothly if workers were treated well and given a sense of communal responsibility in lieu of the motives of profits and fear. As the Millerites anticipated the immediate end of the world, first in 1843 and then in 1844, property was not an issue with them, although many used up their resources as quickly as possible.

Historian Alice Felt Tyler has documented many such separatist cults in nineteenth-century America. Especially noteworthy is woman's role in most of these: some sects denied monogamy, others adopted communal living arrangements, and nearly all showed dissatisfaction with the one-mother-per-home domestic cult that was itself a form of separatism. Similarly, most sects practiced frugality, sharing of resources, charity, and simplicity, rejecting the individualism and greed of the larger society. Finally, most claimed divine, Christian inspiration but insisted Christ had given the cult's founder a new mandate.

It would seem that given the similarities of Indian, African/American, women, immigrant, reformist, and Utopian protests against American individualism, expansion, commercial life, and politics, they would have been more successful. The reason, of course, that they were not, is the same reason America has lacked a powerful socialist movement. The different groups were either not aware of each other's protests or shared the greater society's disdain for other groups. Christian women, for instance, could find little in common between themselves and Indian prophets, immigrant groups mistrusted each other as much as they did the WASP establishment, and Utopians wanted to get away from it all, not unite for social change. Divide and conquer has worked quite well for an American social order that paradoxically celebrates pluralism as one of the foundations of its national identity.

IV. Placing Native Americans At The Center: Alternative Worlds At the Core

The most telling indictment of a world order based upon individualism, self-aggrandizement, and political power in nineteenth-century America came not from minorities who articulated rival cultural orders. It came from the two closest approximations of an aristocracy, from the establishment itself of nineteenth-century America—the Southern plantation owners and the Northern industrialists. They too repulsed the world they created, inflicted on others, and profited from so greatly, to escape into alternative cultures based on nostalgia and civility.

No group in pre-Civil War America benefitted so much from exploiting others as the Southern plantation owners.[18] Using African/American slaves, they sold cotton to the North and to England from which they purchased commodities to support an extravagant life. However, they created an ideology that the planter was the victim, of other groups, not their beneficiary. "The pro-slavery argument" insisted that the planter cared for and civilized his slaves far more than the Northern and British industrialists did their workers. Then "Yankee" sharp dealers cheated him out of his legitimate profits—this, rather than high living, caused his debts. Denying materialism and the industrial order (without which his cotton would have had little value), the Southern commercial agriculturalist recast himself as a cavalier, the world's last survivor of a better, aristocratic world that denied the false modern dream of equality. As one of the South's foremost apologists, George Fitzhugh, wrote in his *Sociology for the South*:

There is but one remedy for this evil [of workers competing for

> scarce jobs], so inherent in free society, and that is, to identify the interests of the weak and the strong, the poor and the rich. Domestic slavery does this far better than any other institution . . . High civilization and domestic slavery did not merely co-exist, they were cause and effect . . . Greece and Rome were indebted to this institution alone for the taste, the leisure, and the means to cultivate their heads and their hearts; had they been tied down to Yankee notions of thrift, they might have produced a Franklin, with his "penny saved is a penny earned;" they might have had utilitarian philosophers and invented the spinning jenny, but they never would have produced a poet, an orator, a sculptor, or an architect; they would never have uttered a lofty sentiment, achieved a glorious feat in war, or created a single work of art . . . Domestic slavery in the Southern States has produced the same results . . . The master . . . is lofty and independent in his sentiments, generous, affectionate, brave, and eloquent; he is superior to the Northerner in everything but the art of thrift.

Given this mentality, the Civil War took on the qualities of a prophetic revolt against "the atheistical and fanatical heresies that have so sadly corrupted Northern society." The Confederacy, on the other hand, believed itself "commissioned by God to contend for and illustrate great principles, intimately connected with the progress of humanity." Southern preachers cast Abraham Lincoln as the King of Egypt and Jefferson Davis as Moses, much as their slaves had done to them. As defeat loomed, desperate divines invoked the possibility of miraculous deliverance in tones as extreme as any Indian prophet:

> Let the North march out her million men . . . and bring up the very gates of hell in all their strength . . . A righteous and angry God would fire upon the aliens terrible thunder that angel ears never heard, and . . . if necessary to our deliverance, shake the very earth from under their feet.

Southerners have more in common with the African/Americans and Indians they drove to prophetic revolt than they would like to think. They, too, still remain inspired by memories of heroic resistance. Confederate flags still fly as state flags and private emblems, and not just in the South. Northerners also use them to recall an imagined past as a talisman to combat racial integration and its unpleasant by-products for many whites. The Ku Klux Klan, originally intended to frighten African/Americans with "the ghosts of the Confederacy," was in many respects the successful guerrilla aftermath of the Civil War that wore down the Northern occupation and Reconstruction governments and gave the South control of its racial affairs for almost a century. It is still functioning. Robert E. Lee is a national hero of at least equal stature to Ulysses S. Grant. The South has defined its role in the Civil War for many Americans, not as a war for slavery and wealth, but as the struggle for the Constitutional right to secede, and for a civilization now "Gone With the Wind."

After the Civil War, the Northern industrial barons also began a flight from modernity.[19] Insulating themselves from cradle to grave against the pressures of industrialization and competition that they inflicted on others, they sent their children to prep schools and exclusive colleges, joined urban men's, women's, and country clubs, lived in elite neighborhoods, vacationed in private resorts, and, when they died, were buried in beautiful tombs in garden cemeteries created for that purpose. The architecture of the late nineteenth century suggests escape to an imagined, stable past; the models for colleges at this time, the great churches on Fifth Avenue in New York, the castles on the Hudson, and the seaside villas in Newport were predominantly medieval or Renaissance in style. (Sometimes the buildings themselves were dismantled in Europe and reassembled here, as were great collections of art.) They created, in other words, a paradoxical form of ethnicity based on class, which overlapped considerably with the elite's emphasis on its Anglo/Saxon or "Nordic" ancestry. In a less selfish vein, the "Gospel of Wealth" preached by Andrew Carnegie and practiced by many of his fellows commanded philanthropy on a scale equal to the new industrial order to justify its existence. Mere expansion of the gross national product and the inevitable increase in wealth rang hollow even for businessmen themselves.

It is an awful judgment on a society that was ostensibly devoted to competition and that looked to the private sector to achieve the good life through commerce and industry, when those who benefitted the most from it lacked the courage of their convictions. They seem to have acquired their wealth primarily to escape into nostalgic worlds defined by familial and community values, much like the worlds of rebellion and protest constructed against them. If they refused to live in their own world, why should anyone else have embraced it?

The myth of assimilation dies hard. Native Americans were never offered the possibility of genuine assimilation. Indeed, even in 1994 women, African/Americans, Chicanos, Native Americans, and immigrants still fight for equality. They must do so as distinct groups in order to obtain some of the rights that assimilation, had it occurred, would have already guaranteed. "Liberty and justice for all" is not so much a legal norm as the opportunity for different groups to compete (unequally) on a number of battlefields—legal, political, social, and economic—using a variety of strategies—force, moral suasion, rational argument, political or economic pressure—to get the best deal they can. To put it another way, national, racial, ethnic, or sexual identity can only be understood as defensive constructions against the demonizing, and, subsequently demonized, "Other." The competing legitimacy of various groups is mediated by law in some contexts; in others it destroys or enslaves entire peoples. For all the cosmopolitan influence of international commerce, enlightenment rhetoric, and religious principle to bring about the unity of humankind, the evidence suggests that these beget and intensify national or group identity as reactions against their accompanying injustices. The Native American quest to forge a culture that offered the possibility of communal and self-worth in a hostile new world thus stands as an extreme, though compelling, paradigm not only for the United States, but for a modern world whose facile pronouncements of universal prosperity and brotherhood have moved in tandem with an army of destructive parochialisms.

In the United States, women, African/Americans, immigrants, and reformers have created alternative communities, but many of these have proven temporary or may not last because of the desire to be integrated into the mainstream. Largely because of the genocide inflicted on them, Native Americans have been far less attracted to the dominant society. As a result, as historian/philosopher Michel de Certeau wrote:

> At a time when the idea and effectiveness of Western democracy are everywhere undermined by the expansion of cultural and economic technocracy, and are in the process of slowly disintegrating along with what had been that system's condition of possibility (differences between local units and the autonomy of their sociopolitical representations); at a time when micro-experiments and explorations in self-management are attempting to compensate for the evolution toward centralization by creating the diversity of local democracies—it is the same Indian communities which were oppressed and eclipsed by the Western "democracies" that are now proving to be the only ones capable of offering modes of self-management based on a multi-centennial history. It is as though the opportunity for a socio-

political renewal of western societies were emerging along its fringes, precisely where it has been the most oppressive, out of what Western societies have held in contempt, combated, and believed they had subjugated.

De Certeau finds that traditional values derived from Native Americans offer three major alternatives to the world of the modern West: the creation of autonomous, relatively egalitarian and non-authoritarian communities; respect for the environment; and a tolerance of cultural pluralism, for Native Americans are intelligent enough to realize the West cannot simply decide to model new customs exactly on theirs. This French philosopher/historian suggests that we join with the Native Americans who have been awakening in both North and South America beginning in the 1970s. We too should realize that by respecting their rights and their way of life, we are not only correcting injustice but taking what may be the only path to salvation for a society which has tried, unsuccessfully, for five centuries, to destroy them. The Native American communities of our era thus stand before the whole world at the beginning of a new millennium much as their prophets stood before their peoples in earlier times. The Native Americans are a collective prophet, inviting a world corrupted by greed, pleasure-seeking, destruction of the environment, loss of political and spiritual freedom, and violence to regenerate itself by following the example of a despised "Other." Ironically, the West was destroying itself in the effort to annihilate peoples who are now reappearing in history as the true guardians of morality, liberty, and the earth.[20]

**William Pencak is Professor of History at Penn State University.*

Notes

A brief version of this paper was presented as a comment at the first annual meeting of the World History Association at Drexel University, Philadelphia, June 25, 1992 and a more extensive version at the International Conference on "Others in Discourse: The Rhetoric and Politics of Exclusion," at Victoria University, Toronto, May 9, 1993. The author thanks Lynda Norene Shaffer of Tufts University for suggesting the topic and some of the sources cited below, and for many helpful suggestions.

1. See my discussion, William Pencak, 1991, "Charles S. Peirce, Historian and Semiotician," *Semiotica*, 83, pp. 311-332.

2. Anthony F. C. Wallace, 1956, "Revitalization Movements," *American Anthropologist*, 58, pp. 264-281, esp. p. 267.

3. Gregory Evans Dowd, 1992, *A Spirited Resistance: The North American Indian Struggle for Unity, 1745-1815*, Baltimore and London: Johns Hopkins University Press, quotation at p. xv.

4. *Ibid.*, at pp. 31-40; Richard White, 1990, *The Middle Ground: Indians, Empires, and Republics in the Great Lakes Region, 1650-1815*, Cambridge: Cambridge University Press, pp. 269-271 and pp. 279-285; Charles E. Hunter, 1971, "The Delaware Nativist Revival of the Mid-Eighteenth Century," *Ethnohistory*, 18, pp. 39-49; and statement of John Heckewelder, in Edward H. Spicer, 1969, *A Short History of the Indians of the United States*, New York: Van Nostrand, pp. 52-54 and pp. 251-253.

5. Anthony F. C. Wallace, 1970, *The Death and Rebirth of the Seneca*, New York: Alfred A. Knopf, esp. pp. 239-253 for Handsome Lake and pp. 321-337 for Iroquois survival. See also Spicer, 1969, *supra* note 4 at pp. 47-52 and 256-261 and Vittorio Lanternari, 1963, *Religions of the Oppressed*, trans. Lisa Sergio, New York: Alfred A. Knopf, pp. 101-107.

6. White, 1990, *supra* note 4 at pp. 501-517; Spicer, 1992, *supra* note 4 at pp. 54-56 and 266-269; Dowd, 1992, *supra* note 3 at pp. 123-147; R. David Edmunds, 1983, *The Shawnee Prophet*, Lincoln: University of Nebraska Press, esp. pp. 33-38 and 110-111.

7. Dowd, 1992, *supra* note 3 at pp. 148-173; Joel W. Martin, 1991, *Sacred Revolt: The Muskogees' Struggle for a New World*, Boston: Beacon Press, esp. pp. 73-74, 124, and 129-147. For the Cherokees, see Dowd, 1992, *supra* note 3 at pp. 173-190; William G. McLoughlin, 1984, *The Cherokee Ghost Dance: Essays on the Southern Indians, 1789-1861,* Mercer: Mercer University Press, pp. 3-37 and 111-151.

8. Spicer, 1969, *supra* note 4 at pp. 88-90 and 275-276; Lanternari, 1963, *supra* note 5 at pp. 110-113.

9. Spicer, 1969, *supra* note 4 at pp. 88-92 and 280-283; Lanternari, 1963, *supra* note 5 at pp. 113-116 and 128-132; *Ibid.*, at pp. 63-100 for the Native American Church; Benjamin R. Kracht, 1992, "The Kiowa Ghost Dance, 1894-1916: An Unheralded Revitalization Movement," *Ethnohistory*, 39, pp. 452-477. For the occupa-

tion of Wounded Knee in 1973, see, 1973, *Voices from Wounded Knee 1973,* Akwesasne Notes: Mohawk Indian Reservation, esp. pp. 59, 65, and 103-107.

10. I am indebted to Patrice Olsen of Penn State University for calling my attention to Munro S. Edmonson's, 1986, *Heaven Born Merida and Its Destiny: The Book of Chilam Balam of Chumayel,* Austin: University of Texas Press, esp. pp. 153, 241, 127, and 167. For its application later, see Nelson Reed, 1964, *The Caste War of Yucatan,* Stanford: Stanford University Press, esp. pp. 39 and 48-49.

11. See especially H. Lorkovic, 1993, "Culture Conflicts and Types of Nationalism," *History of European Ideas*, 16, pp. 241-245; Caroline C. Ford, 1993, "Which Nation? Language, Identity, and Republican Politics in Post-Revolutionary France," *Ibid.*, 16, at pp. 31-46; Jost Halfmann, 1992, "From Defeat to Demise: German Nationalism at the End of the Twentieth Century," *Ibid.*, 15, at pp. 817-825; Emiliana P. Noether, 1993, "The Intellectual Dimension of Italian Nationalism: An Overview," *Ibid.*, 16, at pp. 779-784. I am indebted to Michael K. Green for these references.

12. Michael K. Green kindly called my attention to this point, as discussed by Walker Connor, 1991, "From Tribe to Nation," *Ibid.*, 13, pp. at 5-18.

13. Albert J. Raboteau, 1978, *Slave Religion: The "Invisible Institution" in the Antebellum South*, New York: Oxford University Press, quotation at p. 320; Herbert Gutman, 1976, *The Black Family in Slavery and Freedom, 1750-1950,* New York: Pantheon; John W. Blassingame, 1979, *The Slave Community: Plantation Life in the Antebellum South*, 2nd. ed., New York: Oxford University Press; Herbert Aptheker, ed., 1966, *Nat Turner's Slave Rebellion*, New York: Humanities Press, esp. pp. 132-147; Maurice Cranston, ed., 1969, *Prophetic Politics: Critical Interpretations of the Revolutionary Impulse,* New York: Simon and Schuster, essay by George Feaver, "Black Power," pp. 139-175, esp. pp. 142 and 149-154.

14. Barbara Welter, 1966, "The Cult of True Womanhood," *American Quarterly*, 18, pp. 151-174; Ann Firor Scott, *Making the Invisible Woman Visible,* Urbana and Chicago: University of Illinois Press,

esp. pp. 149-158; Ann Douglas, 1977, *The Feminization of American Culture*, New York: Alfred A. Knopf, esp. pp. 1-13; Lori D. Ginzberg, 1990, *Women and the Work of Benevolence: Morality, Politics, and Class in the Nineteenth Century United States*, New Haven: Yale University Press; testimony of Gloria Steinem on the Equal Rights Amendment, reprinted in David J. Rothman and Sheila M. Rothman, 1975, *Sources of the American Social Tradition*, Volume II, New York: Basic Books, pp. 271-273; Catherine Beecher, "Miss Beecher's Domestic Book," excerpted in Gerda Lerner, ed., 1977, *The Female Experience: An American Documentary*, Indianapolis: Bobbs-Merrill, pp. 121-124.

15. Randall M. Miller and Thomas D. Marzek, eds., 1977, *Immigrants and Religion in Urban America*, Philadelphia: Temple University Press; Leonard R. Riforgiato, "Bishop John Timon, Archbishop John Hughes, and Irish Colonization: A Clash of Episcopal Visions of the Future of the Irish Catholic Church in America," in William Pencak, Selma Berrol, and Randall M. Miller, eds., 1991, *Immigration to New York*, Philadelphia: The Balch Institute Press, pp. 27-55; Rudolph J. Vecoli, 1964, "The Contadini in Chicago: A Critique of The Uprooted," *Journal of American History* 51, pp. 404-417.

16. David J. Rothman, 1971, *The Discovery of the Asylum*, Boston: Beacon Press; Horace Mann, *Twentieth Annual (1848) Report to the Massachusetts Board of Education*; and Noah Webster, *On the Education of Youth in America*, both excerpted in David J. Rothman and Sheila M. Rothman, 1975, *Sources of the American Social Tradition*, Volume I, New York: Basic Books, pp. 165-172.

17. Alice Felt Tyler, 1964, *Freedom's Ferment: Phases of American Social History from the Colonial Period to the Outbreak of the Civil War*, Minneapolis: University of Minnesota Press: Shakers, pp.140-164; Ephrata, pp. 111-115; Oneida, pp. 184-195; New Harmony, pp. 196-206; Millerites, pp. 69-78; Mormons, pp. 88-106.

18. Eric McKitrick, ed., 1963, *Slavery Defended: The Views of the Old South*, Englewood Cliffs: Prentice Hall, esp. pp. 34-44; James W. Silver, 1957, *Confederate Morale and Church Propaganda*, Tuscaloosa: Confederate Publishing Company, esp. pp. 14, 24, and 28.

19. E. Digby Baltzell, 1964, "The Social Insulation of the Traditional Elite," from *The Protestant Establishment*, New York: Random House, esp. pp. 109-142. To include one other major group: predominantly middle-class white males formed fraternal organizations whether military (Grand Army of the Republic, United Confederate Veterans), occupational (The Knights of Labor, the Patrons of Husbandry or Grange), racial (The Knights of the Ku Klux Klan), or purely social (Knights of Pythias, Masons, Imperial Order of Red Men) by the thousands. As the names of some of them indicate, these associations looked backward to the imagined chivalry of a past age, and preached a camaraderie denied by the competitive world of capitalism. See Balthasar H. Meyer, 1901, "Fraternal Beneficial Societies in the United States," *American Journal of Sociology*, 6, pp. 646-661; Stuart McConnell, 1991, *Glorious Contentment: The Grand Army of the Republic, 1865-1900*, Chapel Hill: University of North Carolina Press, esp. pp. 85-89 and 103-107.

20. Michel de Certeau, 1986, *Heterologies: Discourse on the Other*, Minneapolis: University of Minnesota Press, ch. 16, "The Politics of Silence: The Long March of the Indians." For the contemporary Indian awakening, the inspiring book by Ronald Wright, 1993, *Stolen Continents: The "New World" Through Indian Eyes*, Toronto: Penguin Books is highly recommended.

HISTORICAL NARRATIVES OF NATIONHOOD AND THE SEMIOTIC CONSTRUCTION OF SOCIAL IDENTITY: A NATIVE AMERICAN PERSPECTIVE

*Donald A. Grinde, Jr.

I. NATIONALISM, SOCIAL IDENTITY, AND THE TRIBAL PERSPECTIVE

A basic human and intellectual right is the ability to have one's own historical identity. However, this is a right that has been denied to indigenous people because they exist largely in a cultural and historical limbo overlaid by nation-states that dominate them. These nation-states often have historical inventions that rationalize the existence of the dominant society, and this history often marginalizes the history, culture, language, and thought of indigenous people.

Modern national social identities are linked so closely to historical narratives and ideologies because colonialism and nationalism require a mythic historical structure that unifies a diverse people across a wide geographic expanse. Such a mythic structure motivates not only the political but also the economic and social structures. Through progressive ideologies and "presentist" analysis, such devices explain how things got to be the way they are today in a positive and unifying manner. Negative aspects in the mythic structure become impediments (for example, political, social, and economic issues of race, class, and gender exploitation) to progress that will be "solved" through better education, material progress, and "reform." This process rationalizes the irrational because it assumes that irrational forces like prejudice, economic exploitation, crime in the streets, and sexism can be conquered through educational and material venues. The idea is to fight the irrational with the rational. Conversely, most Non-Western societies and tribal peoples believe that one fights the irrational with the irrational. For instance, the rise of a new social identity (Nazism) in Germany during 1930s and the "rational" path to the Jewish holocaust has been greatly emphasized in historical narratives. However, tribal people see such a historical paroxysm in group psychological terms in which national hysteria is fueled not only by economic frustrations and ethnic tensions but also by 1) a lack of balance between the irrational or instinctive drives and rational impulse and 2) a lack of balance between scientific detailed observation and intuition. In essence, the mythic social identity invented by German nationalism lost its psychological checks and balances with regards to unifying qualities and devoured itself when the national ideological invention began to couch all acts in rational terms thus denying the irrational forces at work in the fashioning and functioning of social identities in a modern nation-state. With this insight in mind, one can say that national historians configure and reconfigure the history of their nation every generation (one could even argue every ten years now) in order to create a viable historical ideology that keeps the rational and irrational forces of human society balanced so that limited social cohesion can occur. The process of creating these national historical identities is largely a selective process whereby certain events and facts are included or excluded according to the current needs of the prevailing power structures and the external historical forces (Cold War, etc.) impinging on a given society. Thus, members of the ruling group(s) and their supporters must see themselves in these historical narratives (one may style them as externally generated identities) or such inventions become dysfunctional and responses to certain important stimuli (patriotic appeals, etc.) will not occur in a politically appropriate manner.

At the same time, these historical narratives (and I am including media creations) must change to interface with the changing internal identity formations that occur with the family and community (for instance, the rise of suburbia and two income families). If the external national social identity developed through a nation's historical narratives (academic and media-generated) has difficulty linking with the changing internal identities in a society, then nationalism as a political and mythic construct starts to fail. No one can rationalize the course of internal identity formation even when we have powerful forces that shape it like the media. It is driven by irrational and rational forces that bewilder and perplex the "rational" creators of a nation's external identity. However, its course must be regularized and explained in a "rational" overlay, or social, economic, and political linkages and controls break down. In such a process, the mythic qualities of historical "reasoning" are used to explain and interpret the unpredictable. Plumbing the role of history in social identity formation is not so much a critique of its "mythic" qualities as it is a realization of how history is linked to nationalism and is not very hospitable to indigenous peoples.

American Indians in the United States and in other parts of the Americas definitely are prisoners of these constantly changing historical narratives and thus must be "represented" in American history so that national identity formation is not sullied with another culture. Thus, Native peoples "contribute" to American history but remain powerless throughout the narrative because of their "present" status in the society. To admit to Native power and influence three hundred years ago would mean that the historical narrative and consequent social identity would have to explain how Indians lost their power (genocide and ethnocide); this process of explanation allegedly lowers the self-esteem of the dominant group in power and attacks the historical ideological invention that brings the nation together. Indeed, one could argue that the internal and external identities of Native Americans are psychologically abused and even sacrificed because the emergence and elucidation of their identity is too threatening to the external historical and internal identity formations of the dominant group.

With these insights in mind, it becomes obvious that American Indian historical inventions are so important that normal professional standards for the research and writing of history are relaxed in the United States and the rest of the Americas. According to modern historical standards, research historians of American Indian need not know the language, culture, and values of the society they study. Often historians of the American Indian claim that their ignorance makes for objectivity. Some academic historians in positions of power maintain that today's surviving American Indian groups have little or no culture, language, and spirituality left. Moreover, these scholars maintain that what does survive among contemporary American Indians is so distorted that one need not be unduly concerned about communicating with contemporary American Indian groups when studying them!

In a very real sense, indigenous people from all over the world feel trapped in the logic and discourse of Western civilization, which seems to only examine and comprehend the intellectual origins and conceptual constructs of empire. Western academics in anthropology, history, and related social sciences seem to have created a theoretical place that exists as a "rational" explanation for the "other." This intellectual artifice exists in a space adjacent to the history and culture of the "same," i.e. of the dominant society. In essence, this adjacent space exists between the experience of Western society and the experience of the "other." At the same time, the adjacent intellectual space is considered "theoretically" independent of ongoing contemporary "same" and "other" societies. Within this created space, a process of devaluing also occurs. For example, when Jesus Christ walks on water this is treated as "religion," but, when Coyote steals fire in the Navajo Indian spiritual tradition, it is invariably characterized by the dominant society's discourse as "legend," or, worst yet, "folklore." Since such academic/historical artifices are imposed from without, they are largely devoid of Native voices, or, if there is a Native voice at all, it is usually characterized as "deprived" and consequently marginalized. Such an artifice also works against the development of multiple perspectives and identities in the discourse.

In another way, Michel Foucault describes the construction of these academic "truths" as a socio-political construct like many others in a colonial society produced "by multiple forms of constraint." Foucault elaborates on his perceptions of this intellectual process in the following terms:

> Each society has its own regime of truth, its "general politics" of truth: That is, the types of discourse which it accepts and makes function as true; the mechanisms and instances which enable one to distinguish true and false statements, the means by which each is sanctioned, the techniques and procedures accorded value in the acquisition of truth, the status of those who are charged with saying what is true.[1]

Thus, at this historical moment, indigenous peoples find themselves imprisoned by the rhetoric and scholarly inventions of empire and by the semiotics system that it develops in order to project a national identity. Much of the tensions surrounding Ethnic Studies and multiculturalism in the university are a product of the academic tradition that rationalized and "legalized" the construction of nation-states. Thus, these realities invented over the last two centuries now stand in the way of the emergence of conditions that would foster a meaningful discourse about historical and cultural identity. Since 1492, three global forces, have, in the attempt to create national identities, suppressed, but ultimately failed, to displace ethnicity as the crucible of collective identity—capitalism, colonialism, and communism. Each produced its own "regime of truth" that broke down ethnic and tribal identities and conceptually imprisoned indigenous people within its own historical invention.

There is no doubt that capitalism had global ambitions from the start with its domination of town over country, its construction of national markets, and its expansion of commerce. These factors were coupled with a division of labor that eventually replaced the feudal matrix of estate, locality, and region. With the advent of industrial capitalism, these forces became even more pronounced, which triggered a trend toward cultural homogeneity that encouraged the emergence of nationalism. The resulting amalgamation that was created in the course of global capitalist expansion involved a deculturalization of which language and ethnicity are vibrant reminders. In some cases genocide was complete; all that remains are artifacts of voices past.[2]

Of course, colonialism, the second factor, is closely related to capitalism. The long distance trade established between Europe and the distant corners of the world increasingly brought disparate peoples into contact, a process usually requiring the creation of empires. However, the integration of peripheral areas into the global economy implied huge political ramifications. The colonial structures fashioned in the wake of conquest provided the nexus between center and periphery. Also, colonial governments functioned as embryonic nation-states, which dominated and rationalized the various indigenous populations around the globe. In Europe the nation-state emerged as a result of five centuries of conquest, while the colonial administrations attempted to replicate nation-states, which dominated the various populations within those structures. Essentially, the colonial regimes established around the world were centralizing mechanisms imposed from great distances by people of an entirely different culture and phenotype over peoples who were no more eager than their European counterparts to trade tribe, locality, or region for state.[3]

Like capitalism and colonialism, communism is a cosmopolitan ideology committed to a materialist, albeit radically redefined, notion of progress. Communism, like capitalism in its liberal political form, subscribed to the principle of self-determination. In reality, communist centralization suffocated ethnonationalist urges and attempted to create a national identity among a variety of peoples.

While sexism resorts to myth rooted in biology and religion to justify the continued domination of women by men, nationalism relies on the invention of a common historical experience. In order for a contemporary nation to exist and command the fidelity of its citizenry, it must feed the illusion that the multifaceted population within its boundaries is essentially uniform in spirit and purpose. This myth, though, may operate the most seductively of all. What is supposedly represented as a common historical experience is, in reality, a phantasy that serves the hegemonic purposes of not just the dominant class and gender but the ethnic group in power as well. For example, *Annuit coeptis* and *e pluribus unum* adorn American money: "out of many one people." The list of such unifying phrases and symbols is virtually endless in the modern world.[4]

Just as socialism seeks redress from class oppression and feminism from sexual domination, tribalism calls into question the ethnic distribution of power within the nation-state. Not all tribalist expressions should be defended, especially those of the xenophobic variety that deny the basic rights of other ethnic groups. Generally speaking, however, tribalism, thus understood is an extremely important manifestation of a much larger movement toward decentralization whereby people attempt to gain greater control over their lives. This essay does not intend to defend or condemn tribalism or to advocate the legitimacy of horizontal as opposed to vertical struggles. Nor is it suggested here that ethnicity supplant class as the primary theoretical tool of scholars and activists. Rather, both groups will need to rethink such fundamental categories as state formation and revolutionary change with ethnicity not at the periphery but at the center of analysis.[5]

Although the nation-state is a relatively new political invention, nationalist ideology espouses the nation-state as the normative type of social organization, a condition toward which the species has evolved and for which its citizens must stand vigilant if regression is to be averted. Consequently, nationalism is in essence ethnocidal, which is not to say that ethnic groups need be annihilated.[6] By ethnocide, the author means a process whereby the national center comes to impinge upon the political, economic, and cultural sovereignty of the group. As an alleged agent of civilization, the nation breaks down particularism and integrates relatively autonomous areas into large complex units. Together the spread of bureaucracy and the market create a national quilt, which the intelligentsia later normalizes or "naturalizes"—to use the aptly chosen terminology of immigration authorities in the United States and other countries.[7]

Today many scholars are unable to see the nation-state for what it really is, the ideological caprice of a ruling class whose shattering is a necessary part of the struggle for human liberation worldwide. Currently, the principle challenge to the national "idea" comes not from orthodox Marxism of the socialist or communist variety but instead from tribalism of all political persuasions—left, right, and center. However irrational in view of the movement toward integration on an ever larger scale, tribalism addresses easily identifiable sources of oppression and provides a clear identity in an age of multinationalism, neocolonialism, and centralization. It serves little purpose to denounce this particular separatist cause as counter-revolutionary or that ethnic movement as fascist. These political forces are deeply rooted in communities with limited or no alternatives to the present, and they are here to stay. What is necessary at this critical turning point in world history is to stop the carnage of ethnic conflict, to examine the legitimate concerns of ethnic minorities from the perspective of genuine national self-determination, and to temper the resulting decentralization with internationalism (or, to be more precise, with multinationalism). As nationalist ideology increasingly loses its ability to explain and represent the "objective" world, some sort of cultural transformation toward a global identity will have to develop that can effectively address all patterns of domination—nationality, class, gender, and ecosystem. Our twentieth-century minds must begin to accommodate the twenty-first century reality that is already upon us. A hint of what the ideological alternative might be can be seen today in what was once Yugoslavia and the Soviet Union.[8]

II. American National Identity and the Illusion of Unity: Historical Narratives of Nationhood

In spite of an overwhelming body of evidence from which even they cannot completely escape, scholars like Schlesinger argue the same old liberal themes—The genius of America is its capacity to forge a single nation from pieces of remarkably diverse racial, religious, and ethnic origins.[9] Schlesinger, however, always smoothes out the rough edges of American history in the interests of ideological domination and conformity, and he reserves his harshest comments for "ethnic ideologues," cultural separatists who:

> call on the republic to think in terms not of the individual but of group identity and to move the polity from individual rights to group rights. They have made a certain progress in transforming the United States into a more segregated society.[10]

These fragmentationists, who would stir up the melting pot or compensate for past injustice and neglect, conduct much of their mean-spiritedness on college campuses, challenging the canon that the Schlesingers and others have sworn to uphold. Gradations exist among the old guard for sure. Schlesinger, for example, is somewhat more sympathetic to cultural pluralism than the more orthodox defenders of Western civilization. He at least acknowledges that the "ethnic upsurge" has made the public aware of the contribution of women and minorities to American history. Ultimately, however, there is very little that distinguishes "the closing of the American mind" from the "disuniting of America." Schlesinger is still at war with the sixties, a generational conflict that has situated the liberals and the conservatives clearly on the defensive. Rather than bow out gracefully, old line liberals have opted for confrontation and *ad hominem* arguments.[11] In referring to the current cult of ethnicity as an unprecedented "upsurge," Schlesinger seeks to resuscitate the doctrines of liberalism, but he ultimately breathes little life into them.

The history of the tribal people of the world is vital to a realistic comprehension of what has been and what is presently happening. Yet, concepts of tribes and tribalisms are imprisoned within the discourses of nation-states. Many commentators observing the factional violence in Yugoslavia and the 1992 riots in Los Angeles referred to the bloodletting and crowd behavior as "tribal." Arthur M. Schlesinger, Jr. used the terms "ethnicity" and "tribalism" synonymously in his recent discourse.[12] In Schlesinger's and other Euroamericans' scholarly eyes, Native Americans are still perceived as tribes but also are identified as an ethnic group. The same confusion beclouds the representation of African societies. To further muddy the waters, modernization has in part "detribalized" communities with the consequent effect that peoples like the Pushtuns of Pakistan or the Kurds and Azerbaijanies of Asia cannot be easily classified as either a tribe or ethnic group by those who wish to engage in such categorizations. Since much of the distinction made between tribe and ethnic group stems from certain biases (i.e., the people of European stock form ethnic groups whereas Indians and Africans constitute tribes), there is really little need to distinguish the "mini-nationalisms" of the former from the microcosmic categories of the latter. Both concepts are basically biological categories emphasizing some sort of identity that challenges macro- or micro-nationalism, whether of the "liberal" or "communist" variety.

Numerous scholars have recently addressed the question of these "mini-nationalism." In the view of many social scientists, one of the most compelling social phenomena these past twenty years has been the recrudescence of ethnic diversity. Whether an "ethnic revival" has occurred is highly questionable, when ethnic conflict is viewed from a less Eurocentric perspective. Actually, tribalism and the tribal perspective is merely on the rise again after having been suppressed by the forces of empire, nationalism, and domination for several centuries.[13]

The truly fascinating dimension about ethnicity in America lies not simply in its multifaceted aspects but in the diversity of policy responses. One can see in the great sweep of American history the entire spectrum of strategies adopted by other plural societies in an attempt to create national identity. There never was one ethnic policy or approach that could "forge a single nation;" the "melting pot" may have been the ideal of those that rationalized colonial domination, but the United States has always been a multicultural society.[14]

America's oldest and most consistent ethnic policy is not Schlesinger's idealized assimilation but genocide, the physical annihilation of the vast majority of the aboriginal inhabitants. One finds almost no mention of the dilemma of the American Indian in Schlesinger's essay, an example of the kind of silence and elision that has prompted activists and scholars to challenge the Columbus Quincentennial. Controversy about the "discovery" of America abounds not only because of the millions of Indians who died directly and indirectly from the arrival of the Europeans but also because genocide was incomplete. Several hundreds of thousands of their descendants remain and find the little sovereignty left them is still subject to corporate greed and government duplicity. Where do the American Indians fit into the melting pot? Sadly enough as soup bones. To deal honestly with this past is too painful. Americans apparently prefer the guilt-free gloss epitomized by Ronald Reagan's remarks at the opening of his presidential library, which portrayed the United States as both an empty continent and the Promised Land.[15]

America's second oldest experiment in cultural diversity was segregation (apartheid). From the days of slavery to Jim Crow and the present ghettoization, African/Americans have been excluded from the "dream" that most presumably still want (separation is often a marginal movement within the community). No liberal historian, like Schlesinger, should ignore the courageous and consistent effort by Afro-Americans to make White America honor its most fundamental commitments. The Rodney King videotape blatantly showed what most Americans would prefer to deny and confirmed what every black American knows—that there have always been at least two Americas, one for whites and one for African/Americans. This basic and inescapable truth, in addition to corporate investment, is what links the United States with South Africa. To those who might recoil in horror from such an analogy, it should be recalled that lynching was a part of the American landscape just thirty years ago. Despite the progress realized by the Black elite these past several decades, African/Americans regardless of income and success frequently find themselves police suspects merely because of their skin color. White flight transformed urban America into deindustrialized ghettoes not so entirely different from the townships of South Africa. Nearly forty years after *Brown v. the Board of Education*, American society remains separate and unequal, a *de facto* segregation that for demographic reasons South Africa cannot afford.[16]

America developed a third ethnic strategy for the millions who chose to come here, although application has varied according to port of embarkation. Those of non-European origin have often arrived as coolie laborers, a pejorative affixed to Chinese immigrants but one that equally applies to millions of people of Central American and Caribbean origin as well. Due partly to culture and partly to "nativist" reaction, these ethnic groups live in the United States but have not easily assimilated. At various times in the past, segregation was *de jure* as well as *de facto*. California, the state with the largest Asian/American population, prohibited Asian immigrants from owning land and intermarrying with whites until 1948. Japanese/Americans found themselves in concentration camps during World War II, a national disgrace only recently redressed. There is evidence of late to suggest that "Asian/American" assimilation is gathering speed. Income levels, education, and now intermarriage suggest that a significant number of Americans of Japanese, Chinese, Korean, Filipino, and Vietnamese descent are supplementing a melting pot recipe that until recently consisted entirely of European condiments. Whether the currency of personal achievement can buy acceptance, however, remains to be seen. The current backlash against "Asian/American" success suggests that congenital racism and economic uncertainty impede complete acceptance.[17]

III. Historical Narratives and Native American Identity

Because of the process of nation-state building on the American continents, American Indians in the United States and in other parts of the Americas have had their historical and cultural identities created for them. Indeed, American Indian historical inventions are so important that normal professional standards for history are relaxed in the United States. According to modern historical standards, a research historian of American Indian history need not know the language, culture, and values of the society that he/she studies. Often historians of the American Indian claim that their ignorance makes for objectivity. Some academic historians in positions of power maintain that today's surviving American Indian groups have little or no culture, language, or spirituality left. Moreover, these scholars assert that what does survive among contemporary American Indians is so distorted that one need not be unduly concerned about communicating with contemporary American Indian groups when studying them!

Given this historical and professional predicament, what ought those who study indigenous people (and particularly American Indians who happen to be historians) do? Often they try to point out that what passes for the history of American Indians is more an exercise in the study and elucidation of the process of nation-state or empire building. American Indians openly posit the idea that a usable past for the people that lived through the colonizing process may be too difficult to achieve within the current structures of academe.[18] At the risk of being condemned as an "essentialist," many Native American scholars, such as I, maintain that until American Indian scholars develop an independent voice and discourse, this separate and adjacent reality created by Western thought to comprehend the "other" will keep Native American historical identity in thraldom. It is not that the dominant society's discourse is "wrong," but rather it is decidedly "incomplete" when compared to the historical discourses of the dominant colonial powers. In essence, until there are more native voices involved in the process of creating and inventing a usable past for American Indian people, there will not be a sufficient and appropriate historical discourse that can be internalized and utilized by America's native peoples.[19]

The Columbian Quincentenary has launched a great deal of discussion and re-evaluation of the nature of World history in the last five hundred years. Much of the academic discourse focuses on the Columbian Biological and Cultural Exchange and/or the impact of European colonization in the Americas. Non-Indians have usually opted to look at the Columbian Exchange in the broadest possible sense, often avoiding debate about Columbus and the dearth of historical records surrounding much of the initial contact. New publications, museum exhibits, and new paradigms in World history have been discussed. Without a doubt, the discourse on the legacy of 1492 encompasses many issues important to

Twentieth Century peoples (the environment, the educational canons, "multiculturalism," and "political correctness.") However, these activities are almost all Eurocentric in nature, and Native voices are muted or virtually non-existent in this discourse. Moreover, an independent Native American historical perspective has not been a hallmark of the Columbian Quincentenary. While Native American scholars speak, they are largely excluded from mainstream historical discussions on Columbus and Native American history in general.[20]

Indeed, the Columbian Quincentenary is a dramatic example of the lack of balance in history today. Discussions of the impact of 1492 are concerned with the "understanding" of Columbus' world, but there is little attention paid to the Native American world of 1492. When the historical gaze is shifted to the Americas, there is always a preponderance of Non-Indians "experts" who often work diligently to exclude independent Native American viewpoints on the Columbian legacy and Native American prehistory and history. Such exercises in Eurocentric scholarly dominance usually masquerade as "objectivity" and "standards" in scholarship and credentialing. Often, Native American historians are excluded from the discourse because of their alleged inherent or "native" bias. Under these conditions, a practical and usable past for Native Americans has not developed. The American Indian past that has been developed by Non-Indians has utility in the Eurocentric legal system (treaty rights and land tenure) and perpetuates the myth of the "veracity" of dominant European paradigms over the "primitive" indigenous peoples of the Americas.[21] In the 1950s, a few American historians like Bernard DeVoto complained that American historians largely ignored American Indians in spite of the fact that:

> well into the nineteenth century the Indians were one of the principal determinants of historical events . . . American historians have made shockingly little effort to understand . . . Indians and disastrously little effort to understand how . . . [they] affected white men and their societies.[22]

DeVoto's observation about American Indian history remained virtually unheeded until the 1970s when it became a component of "minority" history. However, very little scholarship by Native Americans had made its way into the mainstream at that time.

The process of reclaiming a viable American Indian history by and for Native Americans has been an important component in the discourse of

Native American scholars. In 1964 in the first issue of the *Indian Historian*, Rupert Costo (Cahuilla) asserted that:

> In the past, Indians have had good reason to distrust and even scorn the professional researcher. Too often have they interpreted . . . Indian history [and] misrepresented their way of life. It becomes necessary now to correct the record, to write the history as it should be written [and] to interpret correctly the aboriginal past . . . There is a great and rich store of information still locked in the hearts and minds of Indians all over the nation . . . Friends of the Indian may join in our great work, helping but not leading, aiding but not pushing, taking part but not taking over.[23]

A decade later in 1975, Jack Forbes observed that American history is overly Eurocentric and thus presents to the American people historical scholarship and textbooks that assume that everything begins in Europe. Forbes points out that such a bias is self-evident since "the history of Overseas Europeans [colonists] is the central or only theme" in American history. Forbes believes that although these scholars have assimilated some American Indian ways, they often ignore such traditions when they study the dynamics of American colonial history.[24] This process not only alienates American history from American Indians but from the American people.

Eurocentric academic "standards" of review about the history of American Indians not only distort but also damns American Indians. For instance in 1984, Isabel T. Kelsay's *Joseph Brant, 1743-1807* stereotyped all Mohawk Indians in this manner:

> Harmless, good hearted creatures generally, their one great vice was drink. Male and female, old and young, they all craved rum; it was their greatest pleasure and when really thirsty any of them would give anything he possessed for a dram of "that Darling Water."[25]

This mainstream, university press book, refereed by "reputable" scholars with "standards" clearly contains unsubstantiated and blatant stereotyping of Native Americans (Kelsay provides the reader with no documentation for these assertions). One could compare Kelsay's stereotype of the drunken Indian to an assessment by the South Carolina colonial physician, David Ramsay, who observed that the majority of the Euroamerican population abused "spirituous liquors" and that "drunkenness may be called an endemic vice of Carolina."[26]

A few pages later, Kelsay mixes sexism and racism when she smears Mohawk women by again presenting the reader with an undocumented stereotype of Margaret Brant:

> She was young in years though perhaps not very handsome, for Indian women lost their looks early.[27]

One can easily say, "tongue in cheek," that Kelsay ignores the earlier stereotype of "Indians" by Ponce De Leon who found it difficult to believe that the Indians he met were as old as they claimed and then attributed such youthfulness to a fabled "Fountain of Youth." Kelsay's generalizations about Mohawks are sometimes strange and contradictory when she observes:

> The time was when . . . [the Mohawks] would have thought a dog the finest kind of meat, but now they had a taste for beef and pork and mutton, and many of them tried to keep poultry and a few scrawny cattle . . .
>
> In a very real sense these Indians were, except in name, no longer the same people. But for all their changing of life, they had not yet achieved the status of even the lowest sort of whites . . .
>
> [I]n outward appearance the two Mohawk villages looked not very different from settlements on any new frontier . . .
>
> And there would be white people passing along the road who would cast envious glances at these decent little houses.[28]

Such generalizations about the "traits" and "status" of American Indians are regrettably still with us, and they make the reclaiming of a viable American Indian history for Native Americans all the more difficult.

Aside from the language of domination, nationalism, and empire that is both overt and covert in its applications, there are other obstacles to the development of a usable past for Native peoples. For example, the contemporary multicultural approach with regards to Native Americans is fraught with pitfalls. First, most narratives in the past and today take the colonial viewpoint as the "norm," i.e., historical and contemporary discourses on Native American history often implicitly and explicitly assume that Western civilization is the standard by which all peoples and cultures should be measured. Kelsay's pronouncement about the Mohawks not yet having "achieved the status of even the lowest sort of whites" is a clear example of this multicultural approach. Such statements support the contention that the dominant society is superior, and American Indians are denigrated and taught to conform or engage in self-censorship. Kelsay's further denigration of the physical attributes of Indian women ("Indian women lost their looks early") just reinforces the fact that not only are colonial lifestyles superior, but also Non-white women are clearly less beautiful. The fact that Kelsay can make such assertions without documentation in a scholarly refereed work makes it clear that the "New" Indian history is largely cosmetic and mostly a reconfiguration of old themes of dominance and power relationships. The result is that American Indians are taught to be inferior in such new multicultural histories.

Secondly, many scholars use the "color blind" approach. Essentially, this approach postulates that noticing and elucidating differences promotes prejudice so such differences must be downgraded. A few years ago James Axtell observed in *The European and the Indian* that:

> historians need not feel unduly sensitive about their lack of personal research among contemporary tribal cultures. Often the descendants of their historical subjects no longer survive, or, if they do, have lost much of their historical cultural context.[29]

Thus, he postulates a scholarly world that is virtually devoid of Native voices. In fact, Axtell fears the emergence of American Indian scholars into history and observes that there is an "Indian threat" to contemporary historical scholarship and fears that Non-Indians will accept the "genetic fallacy" that American Indians are the only people capable of understanding their history.[30] Underneath the "color blind" argument is the assumption that the mythological "objective" American Indian history can only be achieved through Caucasian eyes. Indeed, the argument that "we are all the same" really means that we are all Eurocentric, or we ought to be.

Another colonial version of the multicultural approach is the "cultural forms and ceremonies" approach. In this approach, Native peoples are treated as "unique" through the representation of ceremonies, traditional values, and material culture, while the dominant society is portrayed in a more realistic, day-to-day basis. By not picturing American Indians in their daily lives historically, such an approach reinforces stereotypes and "separateness." While this may appear naive, this is the most common approach today in dealing with "diversity" in the classroom and often in historical writing. In the *New England Frontier*, Alden T. Vaughn concludes that:

> My assessment of the early Puritan attitudes and actions [towards American Indians] was on the whole favorable, arguing that until 1675 the New Englanders generally respected the Indians (though not Indian culture) and tried sincerely to win them to English ways and beliefs.[31]

This evaluation of Puritan attitudes, while ignoring or downgrading American Indian attitudes and values, often masquerades as an objective approach. With the dearth of written sources and the consequent lack of analysis of American Indian life by Non-Indians, many Native American people have concluded that Native American history as it is now practiced is not for them and will not be for them until Native sources and scholars are included prominently. The anthropologist, William N. Fenton, has attacked this viewpoint stating:

> The outside observer who is trained can often isolate the patterns that guide behavior that seldom if ever rise to a conscious level among participants . . . Advocates of ethnic chauvinism [stating] that Indian societies are best learned and taught by Indians to Indians may not be aware that in the extreme they are advocating the kind of racism . . . of the nineteenth century . . . [32]

Wilbur Jacobs has observed that while Fenton's point is well taken, one should realize that "Indians have their own version of what happened in the past." Jacobs further advises us that we will better served by a "synthesis of both white and native American ethnohistory."[33] In essence, we need mutual respect and cooperation between both American Indians and Non-Indians in order to achieve a better and more balanced view of American Indian history.

In the process of reclaiming Native American History for Native Americans, we should be conscious of the ways that American Indians have been treated in the history books in the past. Virgil Vogel states that historians have used four methods in the past to foster an erroneous view of Native American History. First, Vogel states that historians often refuse to deal with the history of American Indians, and they are thus *obliterated* as valid themes in the American experience. Second, Vogel believes that Native peoples are often *disembodied* and made parts of the flora and fauna in order to justify the moral right of the "Civilizing

Europeans" to usurp American Indian resources. Third, some historians have implied or claimed that American Indians were deficient and thus a genetically and culturally inferior people. This mode of interpretation can be characterized as *defamation*. Fourth, the Native American is denied his crucial and pivotal role in World and North American history through *disparagement*. In the process of disparagement, historians believe that assimilation is a one-way street with Indians receiving the benefits of European Civilization while Europeans have little to learn from Native Americans.[34] Too many historians have assumed that conquest has rationalized superiority in all areas relating to culture, intellect, and technology.

These analyses of historical narratives dovetail with Foucault's theories about scholarship. He asserts that all "truth" is centered in rational discourse focused primarily in the sciences and academic institutions. He points our that such widely supported truths are central to economic production and political power. Moreover, such inventions (social identities) styled as "truths" are produced by great economic and political apparatuses (the media, army, and university), according to Foucault. In the production of such "truths," many forms of knowledge are subjected, excluded, or denied, and those who are assigned a lower status (like indigenous peoples) find their discourses devalued, discounted, and/or invalidated.[35] For indigenous peoples like Native Americans, the historical process of rationalizing the contemporary power structure means that their voice is often not wanted and is not validated. I suspect that most American historians are not fully conscious of the structures that they function within since it would require the realization that professional historical narratives of nation states must sacrifice their "objective" professional standards to conform to the necessities of creating an external national social identity that has utility for the economic and political power structures.

Often, Native scholars like Vine Deloria, Jr. have expressed concern that American Indian insights concerning land, politics, and community are buried under the white man's fantasies about power and death. Indeed, Deloria believes that a reappraisal of the history of mankind by Euroamericans "in terms of a universe that is alive and not dead is asking too much of the American people."[36] Given these kinds of intellectual inventions within the groves of academe, is it any wonder that American Indian leaders and people are very circumspect about the benefits of scholarship and "history" if it is generated through the theoretical constructs of anthropology or even history?

IV. Native American Historical Narratives and Identity: The Need for an Autonomous Voice

With a scholarly discourse so checkered, how are Indigenous peoples, and, especially Native Americans in the United States, going to reclaim, develop, and nurture a past that is useful to them as a people in the educational, legal, and scholarly realms? First of all, the structural and institutional barriers that are present in American universities need to be addressed. These may range from Eurocentric scholarship that masquerades behind objectivity but really reinforces "white supremacy" at any cost. In addition, we should realize that discourses on "objectivity" and "standards" *vis-a-vis* Native American history and scholarship necessarily support Eurocentrism in academia. Moreover, when those in power in the scholarly world talk of "native" biases in the writing of history and deplore the lack of trained American Indians, they are often, in fact, creating barriers to full fledged Native American participation in academic discourse. Indeed, one scholar has commented that while surveying the historical literature about American Indians he was surprised to find that terms such as "heathen," "savages," and "civilized" Europeans were still present in today's scholarly discourses. Moreover, the stereotypes persisted in spite of the existence of scholars "supposedly emancipated from the religious and racial superstitions of the past."[37] In essence, stereotypical terminologies in academic discourse often unconsciously perpetuate the values and vindications of empire while professing to be "enlightened."

Having realized these factors in the scholarly world today, how do Native Americans move to reclaim their history. First of all, it is absolutely necessary to create autonomous American Indian Studies programs that teach and publish Native American history from a Native perspective. The purpose of such autonomous programs is not so much to challenge the aforementioned problems and power structures within the academy but to serve the pressing educational, cultural, and psychological needs of contemporary Native Americans. In order to serve the historical needs of Native people, there should also be American Indian publications (journals and book presses) that make alternative Native American perspectives accessible to a wide audience. Only in these ways will Native American scholars be "free" to do research and express their ideas about their history in a manner that will create a truly co-equal discourse between Indian and Non-Indian. Native American historians will then feel freer to create a usable and personally identifiable past for Native American people as well. A strong and independent Native voice will intellectually enrich us all.

**Donald A. Grinde, Jr. is Professor of History at California Polytechnic State University, San Luis Obispo.*

Notes

1. Quoted from "Truth and Power," Paul Rabinow, ed., 1984, *The Foucault Reader*, New York: Pantheon Books, p. 73.

2. See John Rex, 1970, *Race Relations in Sociological Theory*, New York: Schocken Books, pp. 75-76 and Malcolm X, 1965, *Malcolm X Speaks*, New York: Grove Press, p. 168.

3. See Mederic-Louis-Elie Moreau de Saint-Mery, "Whites in a Slave Society, 1797," in L. Comitas and D. Lowenthal, eds., 1973, *Slaves, Free Men, Citizens*, Garden City, New York: Doubleday, p. 55, for a contemporary description of this colonial process.

4. M. G. Smith, 1965, *The Plural Society in the British West Indies*, Berkeley: University of California Press, pp. 83-86.

5. See J. S. Furnivall, 1956, *Colonial Policy and Practice*, New York: New York University Press, p. 307. I also wish to thank my colleague, Thomas August, Lecturer at Cal Poly, for his insights and ideas about these themes during our many conversations about Modern World History.

6. See Frantz Fanon, 1967, *Black Skin, White Masks*, New York: Grove Press, pp. 60 and 211 for a perceptive analysis of these concerns about ethnocide.

7. Smith, 1965, *supra* 4 at p. 86. For an excellent discussion of these ideas in a Native American context, see Jack D. Forbes, 1979, *A World Ruled By Cannibals*, Davis, California: DQ University Press, particularly Chapter VI.

8. See M. Annette Jaimes, "Introduction" and Rebecca L. Robbins, "Self-Determination and Subordination: The Past, Present and Future of American Indian Governance," in M. Annette Jaimes, ed., 1992, *The State of Native America; Genocide, Colonization and Resistance*, Boston: South End Press for a deeper analysis of these problems in a Native American context.

9. Arthur M. Schlesinger, Jr., 1991, *The Disuniting of America*, Knoxville: New Agenda, p. 80.

10. *Ibid.*, at p. 78.

11. In addition to Schlesinger, 1991, *Ibid.*, see also E. D. Hirsch, 1987, *Cultural Literacy: What Every American Needs to Know*, New York: Houghton Mifflin, and Dinesh D'Souza, 1991, *Illiberal Education: The Politics of Race and Sex on Campus*, New York: Free Press.

12. Schlesinger, 1991, *Ibid.*, p. 21.

13. For a psychological analysis of these trends, see Frantz Fanon, 1968, *The Wretched of the Earth*, New York: Grove Press, pp. 54-57.

14. Robert Blauner, 1972, *Racial Oppression in America*, New York: Harper and Row, pp. 83-84.

15. See John Mohawk, 1992, "Looking for Columbus: Thoughts on the Past, Present and Future of Humanity," in Jaimes, ed., 1992, *supra* note 8.

16. Blauner, 1972, *supra* note 14 at p. 62.

17. See Thomas Sowell, 1981, *Ethnic America: A History*, New York: Basic Books, pp. 175-176; for a different point of view see, H. L. Kitano, 1969, *Japanese Americans*, Englewood Cliffs, New Jersey: Prentice-Hall.

18. For a good example of an attempt to address the history of Native Americans from an American Indian perspective, see Jaimes, ed., 1992, *supra* note 8.

19. For an excellent discourse on these problems, see an interview with Michel Foucault in *Nouvel Observateur*, March 12, 1977, p. 93.

20. The struggle continues as nation-states continue to subdue and dominate indigenous peoples around the globe. See Bernard Nietschmann, 1987, "The Third World War," *Cultural Survival Quarterly*, Fall, XI, 3.

21. Roxanne Dunbar Ortiz, 1984, *Indians of the Americas: Human Rights and Self-Determination*, London: Zed Press, pp. 27-70.

22. Quoted from Bernard DeVoto's introduction to Joseph K. Howard, 1992, *Strange Empire*, New York: Morrow, p. 8.

23. Rupert Costo, 1964, "Indian Journal to Study History and Development of Native Races," *Indian Historian*, Vol. 1, No. 1, October, p. i.

24. Jack Forbes, 1975, "Americanism is the Answer," *Akwesasne Notes*, 6, p. 37.

25. Isabel T. Kelsay, 1984, *Joseph Brant*, Syracuse: Syracuse University Press, pp. 40-41.

26. David Ramsay, 1809, *History of South Carolina*, Charleston: David Longworth, Vol. 2, p. 391.

27. *Ibid.*, at p. 44.

28. *Ibid.*, at p. 49.

29. James Axtell, 1981, *The European and the Indian: Essays in the Ethnohistory of Colonial American*, Oxford: Oxford University Press, p. 10.

30. James Axtell to William Fenton, September 10, 1975 in William N. Fenton Papers, MSS Collection #20, Correspondence Box 1979-82, American Philosophical Society, Philadelphia, Pennsylvania.

31. Alden T. Vaughn, 1979, *New England Frontier: Puritans and Indians, 1620-1675*, New York: Norton, p. v.

32. See Wilbur R. Jacobs, 1975, "Native American History: How it Illuminates Our Past," *American Historical Review*, Vol. 80, No. 3, June, p. 598.

33. *Ibid.*

34. Virgil Vogel, "The Indian in American History," *Akwesasne Notes*, II, 6, pp. 22-23.

35. Michel Foucault, 1977, *Language, Counter-Memory, Practice: Selected Essays and Interviews*, Ithaca: Cornell University Press, p. 207.

36. Vine Deloria, Jr., "Some Thoughts," *Akwesasne Notes*, IV, 4, p. 31.

37. For a discussion of some of the real problems involving the stereotyping of Native people in the writing of American Indian history, see Neal Salisbury, "American Indians and American Indian History," in Calvin Martin, ed., 1987, *The American Indian and the Problem of History*, New York: Oxford University Press, p. 46.

INDIGENOUS PEOPLES
AND THE
CULTURAL POLITICS OF KNOWLEDGE

*Laurie Anne Whitt

I. Introduction: Some Exhibits

An exhibit, in a court of law, is anything other than oral testimony that is placed before the fact-finder to be admitted as evidence in a case. I open this paper with four exhibits, best marked for identification as diverse instances of cultural imperialism—a form of oppression exerted by a dominant society upon other cultures that, whether or not conscious and intentional, (i) has the result of assimilating, or securing the subordinated status of, those cultures, and (ii) is usually characterized by economic profitability.[1]

Exhibit One. In 1991, at a large gathering in California, a leading figure of the New Age movement announced to the assembled audience that he intended to patent the sweat lodge ceremony since native people were no longer performing it correctly.[2] Several years later, at a meeting of Indian support groups in Geneva, the young Europeans in attendance were informed of the passing of a much respected Muskogee-Creek medicine man, widely known for his defense of the rights of American Indians to retain control of their own spiritual ceremonies. Upon learning of his death "they were heard to openly rejoice."[3]

Exhibit Two. This exhibit documents the activities of "gene hunters"—scientists hired by global corporations to enter the territories of indigenous peoples, and seek out plants with specific properties that can be patented and controlled. This practice is described by its critics as "gene robbery"[4] and "legalized theft."[5] A current example is *tiki uba*, a plant used by the Uru-eu-wau-wau Indians of Brazil in a preparation that acts as an anti-coagulant.[6] Reportedly, a large US-based chemical company is attempting to patent these properties of the plant.[7] The Uru-eu-wau -wau, protesting this commercialization of their knowledge, are challenging that company's right to patent their traditional medicines.[8]

Exhibit Three. This exhibit is an article by American biologist Daniel Jantzen. "Biologists," Jantzen declares, "are the representatives of the natural world . . . [and] are in charge of the future of tropical ecology."[9] They alone have the knowledge and "a clear mandate" to determine who is to populate "the tropical nature that humanity has corralled."[10] He urges his colleagues to extend their proper territorial claims, advising them that if they "want a tropics in which to biologize, they are going to have to buy it with care, energy, effort, strategy, tactics, time, and cash."[11]

Exhibit Four. This exhibit covers a controversy in Kansas over the skeletal remains of one hundred and forty-six Smoky Hill River people that were transformed into a tourist site known as the "Salina Burial Pit," visited by thousands each year. Cultural descendants of these people—including the Pawnee, Wichita, Mandan, Arikara, and Hidatsa—protested this as a racist violation of common human decency. Some scientists and historians however, maintain that such human remains are vital for research and education. According to one of them:

> It's an issue all over the United States . . . a real clash between science and religion . . . There is a concerted effort by American Indians to shut down archaeology all over the country.[12]

Walter Echo-Hawk, a lawyer with the Native American Rights Fund, sees it differently:

> There appears to be a loophole in legal protections and social policies that tends to permit disparate treatment of dead bodies and graves based on race . . . If you desecrate an Indian grave, you get a Ph.D. But if you desecrate a white grave, you wind up sitting in prison.[13]

This essay addresses three contextual features that these exhibits share: 1) the conflict between knowledge systems and value systems within contemporary dominant and indigenous cultures; 2) how the fact of oppression and the particular relations of power that hold between these cultures figures in this; and 3) how certain cultural practices (such as those attested to in the exhibits) are thereby enabled, rendered possible, even probable. To prevent my discussion from foundering in the abstract, I periodically revisit two concrete issues raised by the exhibits: the "marketing" of indigenous spirituality and the cultural politics of science.

Let me begin with a comment on terminology. Most often I contrast "dominant" (or less often, "Western") with "indigenous" knowledge systems. Such terms might seem rarefied and problematic generalities. By "dominant" knowledge system,[14] I have in mind a fairly specific but enormously influential strain of the Western intellectual heritage—the value-neutral ideology of scientific knowledge that most often wears the label of "positivism." While purportedly dead as a movement, the spirit of positivism continues to haunt much of Western science and philosophy.[15] Moreover, given the existence of some five thousand distinct indigenous nations worldwide, reference to an "indigenous" knowledge system—even if one confined its scope to Native North America as I tend to do here—is empirically tenuous at best. Nevertheless, as José Barreiro notes:

> Native peoples of the Americas exhibit both cultural diversity and philosophical consistency . . . the . . . principles that guide the Native cultures bear a remarkable resemblance to one another.[16]

Concrete diversity does not preclude commonality or community, and increasingly there are political reasons to acknowledge this.

> Indianness . . . is reinforced by the common experience of almost five centuries of [Eurocentric] domination . . . The differences between these diverse peoples (or ethnic groups) have been accentuated by the colonizers as part of the strategy of domination.[17]

The characterizations of indigenous knowledge and value systems presented here are intended to be neither definitive nor complete. At best, they capture in a tentative net some features of the cognitive and evaluative systems typical of a number of indigenous cultures.

II. The Commodification of Indigenous Spirituality

> . . . those who would violate the trust and confidence . . . placed in them when we share some of our secrets . . . don't have the slightest sense of [respect]. Even worse are those who take this information and misuse or abuse it for their own purposes, marketing it in some

way or another, turning our spirituality into a commodity in books or movies or classes or "ceremonials."[18]

A series of voices from Native America have been raised recently in eloquent, powerful critiques of some deeply disturbing aspects of contemporary Western culture. The phenomena being contested are diverse, and include literary, artistic, scholarly, and commercial products consumed in the markets of popular culture as well as in those of the cultural elite. The critics too have been diverse. Among them are writers, intellectuals, activists, and spiritual leaders, such as, Vine Deloria, Oren Lyons, Leslie Silko, Joy Harjo, Wendy Rose, Geary Hobson, Gerald Vizenor, Ward Churchill, Russell Means, AIM, the Circle of Elders of the Indigenous Nations of North America, and many others[19] whose voices have joined in identifying and resisting what has been characterized as a new personal "growth industry . . . known as 'American Indian Spiritualism'."[20]

The marketing of North American indigenous cultures is hardly a new phenomenon. Hollywood and highway tourist stops have long trafficked in the sale of "authentic" images and "genuine hand-made" trinkets. Yet the nature and extent of this latest phase of cultural imperialism is startling, for it is spiritual knowledge, spiritual power, and objects that are being commercialized. Indian spirituality—like Indian lands before it—is rapidly being reduced to the status of a commodity. It is seized, made over in the image of its appropriators, and sold. Equally startling, is the fact that the consuming public seems largely to assume not only that it is getting "the real thing" but that it has been gotten in a morally and politically unproblematic way. The literary and scholarly venues for the commodification of indigenous spirituality are extensive. There are the "whiteshaman" poets "who in their poems assume the persona of the shaman, usually in the guise of an American Indian medicine man."[21] Their neo-romanticism is echoed by a chorus of writers posing as Indians and/or Indian "experts," including Carlos Castaneda,[22] Jamake Highwater,[23] Ruth Beebe Hill,[24] and Lynn Andrews,[25] whose books crowd the shelves of New Age stores. Only the most determined and politically naive tunnel vision can regard this literature as a harmless diversion. It is, as M. Annette Jaimes contends:

an insidious political force, disinforming people who might otherwise develop a clearer understanding of the struggles for survival faced by an indigenous population.[26]

There is also what might be described as the do-it/be-there yourself market. Sacred ceremonies and ceremonial objects can be purchased at weekend medicine conferences or via mail order catalogues. How-to books with veritable recipes for conducting traditional rituals are written and dispensed by trade publishers. Assisting in all of this are a succession of born-again spiritual hucksters, known in the Indian community as plastic medicine people, who (with greater or lesser subtlety) present themselves for hire as dispensers of "Native American Spiritual Wisdom."[27] Commenting on this phenomenon, Janet McCloud, activist and elder of the Tulalip Nation, is blunt:

> First they came to take our land and water . . . Now they want our religion as well. All of a sudden, we have a lot of unscrupulous idiots running around saying they're medicine people. And they'll sell you a sweat lodge for fifty bucks. It's not only wrong, it's obscene . . . This is just another in a very long series of thefts from Indian people and, in some ways, this is the worse one yet.[28]

The crassness of this commodification of indigenous spirituality is stunning. Consider the trinkets available from the Berkeley-based GAIA Bookstore and Catalogue Company. Instead of inviting contributions to the many Native-run organizations devoted to enhancing the lives and prospects of Indian people, the *1991 Catalogue* enables the New Agers to support the continued expropriation and exploitation of Native culture by purchasing an array of items marketed as means for enhancing their knowledge of Indian spirituality. For the modest sum of $94.00 they are encouraged to buy their own bit of Native Americana in the form of a "Bear Spirit Mask by Ancient Art." This is advertised as "a powerful animal mask from the Eskimo culture," inspired by the art of our (*sic*) ancestors" and "decorated with bird feathers gathered near the artist's Santa Cruz home."[29] To those whose funds are more limited the catalogue offers, for about half the price, a series of Medicine Cards and Sacred Path Cards that promise "the Discovery of Self through Native Teachings."[30]

Critics of this phenomenon argue that it is a form of cultural imperialism, a coercive exercise of social and political power by the dominant culture that serves simultaneously to extend, as it diverts attention from, the continued oppression of indigenous peoples. Geary Hobson, for example, maintains that cultural imperialists seem to assume that their "interest" in an Indian culture (whether in the name of truth, scholarship, or personal enhancement) makes it okay for them to collect "data" from Indian people. But in effect "this taking of the essentials of cultural lifeways, is as imperialistic as those simpler forms of theft, such as the theft of homeland by treaty."[31] And Simon Ortiz condemns white shamanism as a "process of colonialism," a "usùrping (of) the indigenous power of the people:"

> something takes place that is diversionary . . . symbols are taken and are popularized, diverting attention from real issues about land and resources and Indian peoples' working hours. The real struggle is really what should be prominent, but no, it's much easier to talk about drums and feathers and ceremonies . . . "Real Indians," but "real Indians" only in quotes, stereotypes, and "interesting exotica" . . . So it's a rip-off."[32]

This growing family of Western cultural practices which constitute "American Indian Spiritualism" (henceforth AIS) derives much of its potency from the largely unexamined assumptions on which it rests. I will focus on one of these, a "no-fault" assumption that has a tenacious grip on the assorted practitioners and consumers of AIS; the belief that the literary, artistic, scholarly, and commercial products of AIS are neither epistemologically nor ethically suspect or at fault, that they are cognitively legitimate and morally unproblematic vehicles of spiritual knowledge and power.

It is startling that those who dabble in AIS genuinely take themselves to be learning or conveying "truths" about indigenous spirituality, even as they go about buying or selling products generated by the AIS industry. It is also true that many are genuinely surprised and unsettled by the charges raised against them of arrogance, of hucksterism, of theft, of lack of integrity and respect. Ward Churchill points out the self-deception involved in this. New Age practitioners of AIS, he charges:

> have proven themselves willing to disregard the right of American Indians to any modicum of cultural sanctity or psychological sanctuary. They . . . willingly and consistently disregard the protests and objections of their victims, speaking only of their own "right to know" and to victimize.[33]

Their task is to hang on to what has been stolen while:

> separating themselves from the *way* in which it was stolen. It is a somewhat tricky psychological project of being able to "feel good about themselves" . . . through legitimizing the maintenance of their own colonial privilege.[34]

Psychologically then, the no-fault assumption takes the form of an assiduously crafted self-deception. Renato Rosaldo analyzes the process, suggesting that it is grounded on a courting of nostalgia, wherein the agents of colonialism yearn for what they themselves have altered or transformed. This "imperialist nostalgia" has a paradoxical element to it:

> someone deliberately alters a form of life, and then regrets that things have not remained as they were prior to the intervention. At one remove, people destroy their environment, and then they worship nature. In any of its versions, imperialist nostalgia uses a pose of "innocent yearning" both to capture people's imaginations and to conceal its complicity with often brutal domination.[35]

Such nostalgia is integral to the cultivation of self-deception. It is a "particularly appropriate emotion to invoke in attempting to establish one's innocence and at the same time talk about what one has destroyed."[36]

An illustrative example of self-deception is Gary Snyder's response to indigenous critiques of white shamanism. Snyder has profited as a result of the shaman persona he has cultivated, winning literary awards and selling numerous volumes of poetry. The cultural politics at work here are fundamentally analogous to the attempts of multinational corporations to patent the traditional medicines of the Uru-eu-wau-wau and other indigenous peoples. As a vehicle of cultural imperialism, AIS involves the seizure, repackaging, and profitable sale of highly marketable "spiritual knowledge." Yet Snyder separates himself from this fact, denying any culpability in the appropriation and marketing of indigenous spirituality. Indeed, he maintains it is everyone's duty:

> Spirituality is not something which can be "owned" like a car or a house . . . [it] belongs to all humanity equally . . . we all have not only the right but the obligation to pursue all forms of spiritual insight . . . it seems to me that I have as much right to pursue and articulate the belief systems developed by Native Americans as they do.[37]

In short, the logic of the no-fault assumption seems to be: Indians don't own Indian spirituality, "we" own it, therefore I have a right to do what I want with it. It is the logic of imperialism, whether the subject at hand is land, spiritual knowledge, or genetic resources.

The coercive cultural politics at work in AIS, in the marketing and commercialization of Indian spirituality, seem clear. Whether practiced by white shamans, plastic medicine men and women, opportunistic academics and Indian "experts," or enterprising New Agers, the result is their economic and personal gain[38] at the cost of the exploitation, assimilation, and complete subordination of indigenous cultures. Oneida scholar Pam Colorado makes plain the objections to cultural imperialism, and the ultimate stakes that are involved. By supplanting Indian people even in the area of their own spirituality, it moves beyond physical subordination to effectively secure their absolute ideological/conceptual subordination. If this continues, she states:

> non-Indians will have complete power to define what is and is not Indian, even for Indians . . . When this happens, the last vestiges of real Indian society and Indian rights will disappear. Non-Indians will then "own" our heritage and ideas as thoroughly as they now claim to own our land and resources.[39]

III. Knowledge Systems

To this point my primary concern has been to indicate the nature and extent of the commodification of indigenous spirituality, how this functions as a form of cultural imperialism, and the fierceness with which it is contested by elders, spiritual leaders, scholars, and activists within the Indian community. Part (though only part) of the complex task of ending oppressive cultural practices turns on exposing the untenable assumptions that prop them up. The no-fault assumption sketched above is one such prop. It obscures and mystifies the cultural politics embedded in these practices.

My intent is to undermine the no-fault assumption. I contend that given the oppressive relations of power that structure the interaction between dominant and indigenous cultures and the specific way in which knowledge and value are conceived within the dominant culture, the no-fault assumption emerges as likely. I also consider how this conception of knowledge and value contrasts with that of indigenous cultures.

Before attempting a working characterization of dominant and indigenous knowledge systems, it will help to clarify what is meant by "knowledge system." To speak of a knowledge system is to abandon the idea that a single epistemology is universally shared by, or applicable to, all humans in so far as they are human.[40] Instead, it facilitates a cultural parsing of the concept of epistemology: there are specific epistemologies that belong to culturally distinctive ways of knowing.

Drawing on Stephen Marglin's useful discussion,[41] a knowledge system can be defined in terms of four characteristics: epistemology, a theory of knowledge giving an account of what counts as knowledge and how we know what we know; transmission, dealing with how knowledge is conveyed or acquired, with how it is learned and taught; power, both external (how knowledge communities relate to other knowledge communities) and internal (how members of a given knowledge community relate to one another); and innovation, how what counts as knowledge may be changed or modified. The systemic nature of knowledge is due to the reciprocal influence of these four characteristics upon one another: how we know, how we learn and teach, how we innovate, and how power figures in this are linked. Together they provide valuable conceptual parameters for describing and contrasting dominant and indigenous knowledge systems.[42]

The dominant knowledge system is one that still bears clear traces of positivism. A sprawling and lingering intellectual tradition, positivism has made itself felt in one guise or another for over a century and a half.[43] As one commentator observes, it is, like any other tradition, "a diverse movement, with its dissidents and stalwarts, its ortho- and heterodoxies."[44] There are positivist theories of law, of economics, of literature, of sociology, of religion, of ethics, and of science. There is the Comtean positivism of the 1830s, the neo-Kantian positivism of the last half of the 19th century, and the logical positivism of the early and mid-20th century.[45] While recent developments have significantly undermined its hold on the academic community, the elements of it noted here are part of its thriving legacy.

IV. Value-Neutrality and Fact/Value Duality

How does one know? What counts as knowledge within this knowledge system? And how does one learn and teach it? One of its primary epistemological commitments is to value-neutrality. The process of acquiring and conveying knowledge (paradigmatically, knowledge of the natural world) is held to be value-free.[46] To the degree that a knowledge product may fail in this it is regarded as deviant, an errant departure from the epistemological ideal and from Truth itself which is, of course, also value-free. The natural world is, in Koyré's term "devalorized." As one historian of positivism comments, science is neutral:

> because nature itself is neutral . . . devoid of value . . . [this] ideal of value-neutrality is not a single notion, but has arisen in the course of protracted struggles over the place that science should have in society.[47]

Thus knowledge claims in this tradition are independent of context or perspective, of "personal, social, and cultural values . . . [of] group or individual preferences about what ought to be."[48] Nor are they socially or historically situated. Recent critics describe this as "the view from nowhere" generated by those who can afford the luxury of "the dream from everywhere."[49]

A corollary to value-neutrality is the denial of any significant relations or mutual influences between cognitive and evaluative processes. This is best captured by Poincaré's argument that science is immune to moral critique. Ethics and science have their own domains which "do not interpenetrate . . . they can never conflict since they can never meet. There can no more be immoral science than there can be scientific morals."[50] A fact/value duality is thereby embraced. On the one hand there are facts—claims about what is the case, and on the other, values—claims about what ought to be the case. To attempt to move from one to the other is to commit a logical fallacy. The indigenous view, examined below, that our cognitive rapport with the world is simultaneously a moral one, and that there is an important sense in which knowing and valuing arise together, would be seen to founder on this "is/ought" dichotomy. As Robert Proctor states:

> At one level, value-neutrality is defended as a consequence of an ontological dualism between the true and the good. In the twentieth century formulation, propositions about "what ought to be" can never be derived from propositions about "what is;" facts cannot be derived from values.[51]

Moral and scientific discourse are thus severed.[52]

Coupled with this has been a persistent tendency to reduce all knowledge to propositional knowledge, to only what is expressible in propositions: "all knowledge of objects is knowledge of truths of propositions about these objects."[53] Knowledge is characteristically transmitted in a propositional (usually written) form. In principle, this type of transmission makes knowledge readily accessible, public or open to all. Learning and teaching such knowledge does not require the presence, or mediation, of another person. One learns by comprehending what is asserted in propositions, and for this a book will do. There is a corresponding tendency to reject claims to knowledge that one is unable to express in words. Words thus (as some Native healers have complained) serve as "cages for ideas,"[54] and knowledge, so conceived, is something to which anyone can lay claim as a right or a possession. Knowing is a process of acquiring, of the acquisition of true propositions.[55]

Although Popper[56] takes credit for having "killed" logical positivism,[57] value-neutrality and the broader legacy of positivism persist in a variety of different, sometimes muted or mutated, forms. Within science studies and the philosophy of science for example, one finds it in the debate between internalists and externalists over the role of political, social, and cultural variables in accounts of theory-change. It even emerges among otherwise staunch critics of positivism, such as Barry Barnes and the followers of the influential Edinburgh school's "strong programme" in the sociology of science. As one commentator observes: "Those who announce that science is 'socially constructed' often do so from a neutralist vantage point that rivals the narrowest positivist empiricism of the 1950s."[58] Barnes' principle of the "sociological equivalence of belief systems" embraces a radical relativism according to which no belief is worse, or less worthy, than any other. The evaluations one may find in science, he maintains, are "not of great importance, and . . . [are] eliminable."[59] Consequently, he is prepared to say:

> It would be incongruous to "expose" the writings [of the late 19th century eugenicists] as "racist," since this set of conceptions fitted naturally and securely in the taken for granted world of the time.[60]

The most vigorous defense of value-neutrality has come from economics—a field where questions of value, of why things have the worth that they do, are central. Ironically, the economists most deeply involved in policy-making have most emphatically declared their value neutrality. Milton Friedman, for instance, contends that positive economics is "in principle independent of any particular ethical position or normative judgements."[61] Yet as Proctor observes:

> Something is obviously awry if advocates of conservative, Chicago School economics can portray their work as "value-neutral." How has value-neutrality come to occupy such a special place in economic theory?[62]

Proctor's answer is that it has been an invaluable ideological weapon in debates over distributive justice. The emergence of the new subjective theory of value was central in the rise of modern economics. It allowed value to be seen "as a purely individual phenomenon, dependent on nothing but individual whim or personal preference,"[63] on the pleasure an object brings to the consumer. Challenges raised by Marxists and utilitarians regarding value redistribution could thereby be countered, effectively discouraging "certain structural and ideological questions . . . from becoming the objects of discourse:"[64]

> If preferences are ultimately subjective, then how can anyone really ever know how preferences should be compared? The marginalist principle of subjective value was a brilliant refutation of Mill's argument for redistribution; it also served as a persuasive counterpoint to welfarist arguments that state support for pensions, health care, and so forth would serve the social good.[65]

Knowing and valuing, then, are conceptualized as discreet, autonomous, and closed processes within the dominant system of knowledge. The commitment to value-neutrality and the attendant failure to appreciate the important sense in which epistemology and ethics are implicated in, and by, one another stands in marked contrast to the indigenous view. It also has been instrumental in shaping the diverse practices of cultural imperialism sketched above.

Consider, for example, the archaeologist's portrayal of the desecration of Indian graves as a "real clash" between knowledge and value, between "science and religion"—a concerted effort to shut the science of archaeology down. Are there any moral limits to archaeological inquiry? Are there any ethical and ideological assumptions embedded within it? Does it reflect oppressive relations of power between dominant and indigenous cultures? These questions cannot coherently be formulated across the chasm of the is/ought divide. Yet it is only the sacred sites and burial grounds of Native America that are regularly subjected to archaeological study in the U.S. When the Tennessee Valley Authority caused the excavation of a large number of graves, the remains of over one thousand

Indian graves were stored in boxes for scientific study, while those of persons of other races were reburied with suitable respect for religious beliefs. The scientific value of these materials was the only justification for their excavation.[66] As one tribal leader recently protested in testimony before the U.S. Senate Select Committee on Indian Affairs:

> What other racial group in this country has been forced to endure the sacrilege of watching the remains of . . . relatives ripped from their burial sites and displayed to satisfy a totally unfathomable and morbid sense of scientific curiosity? . . . Archaeological significance [is] the death knell for many sacred sites . . . Initial decisions to dig up and shelve are made by those predisposed to digging and shelving. The propriety of the decision, if questioned, is subjected to peer review by others already predisposed to digging and shelving.[67]

It is also instructive to place the marketing of Native America, the whole collection of profitable cultural practices that constitute AIS, within the context of this value-neutrality and fact/value duality. Such epistemological commitments provide practitioners of AIS with an effective (and as already noted, self-deceptive) means of hanging on to what has been stolen while separating themselves from the way in which it was stolen. It is, after all, just so much value-neutral social scientific knowledge (albeit knowledge of indigenous spirituality) that they are acquiring. That this has been a matter of actual acquisition, of purchase, is significant. When value is regarded as a function of the pleasure an object brings to the person who consumes it (as it is within positive economics), the way is smoothed for the appropriation, remaking, and sale of indigenous spirituality—of sacred objects, ceremonies, and knowledge. Sweat lodges, pipe ceremonies, sun dances, and vision quests all have a price tag attached to them and are placed for sale in the marketplace, their value reduced to and determined by the pleasure they bring to their consumers, to those who, as Donna Haraway so aptly puts it, in the

> cannibalistic western logic that readily constructs other cultural possibilities as resources for western needs and action . . . seek . . . a solution to the forms of alienation built into western scientific and social practice.[68]

V. Anti-pluralism: Knowledge And Power

The dominant knowledge system embraces an anti-pluralism as well, a lack of receptiveness to alternative epistemologies, to other ways of knowing the world. Contributors to a recent volume devoted to the encounter between the dominant knowledge system of the West and the traditional knowledge systems of India, found themselves stymied by a recurrent problem, by:

> the imperialist pretension to universality made on behalf of the Western [knowledge system] . . . and the total inability of its adherents to regard competing systems with anything but contempt, the inability indeed even to contemplate the existence of competing systems.[69]

Knowledge-transmission in indigenous communities traditionally occurs in forms that are, from the dominant perspective, suspect—such as stories and ceremonies. They defy a ready reduction to factual propositions and are seen as "tainted" with a normative and spiritual component. Consequently, other knowledge systems are reduced to "superstition, the very antithesis of knowledge."[70] This encounter:

> is often fatal for indigenous systems because the supreme confidence of Westerners or Westernized elites in their knowledge is coupled to the superior means of political and economic force at their disposal.[71]

Part of what facilitates this closure to alternative epistemologies within the dominant knowledge system is a tendency toward a reductivist scientism—the conviction that science is the best, if not the only, way of knowing,[72] "that we can no longer understand science as one form of possible knowledge but rather must identify knowledge with science."[73] This tendency is apparent in the early Comtean version of positivism, in which the movement of intellectual thought leads from superstition to the triumph of science, the "culminating stage of human knowledge" in which

> one devotes oneself to the search for relationships through observation or experimentation . . . the stage toward which all human history has been advancing.[74]

It emerges at the beginning of this century in Weber's introduction to *The Protestant Ethic and the Spirit of Capitalism*, in which he comments that "Only in the West does science exist at a stage of development which we recognize to-day as valid."[75] And it also surfaces mid-century in a logical positivism committed "to epistemology as the central task of philosophy, to science as the single best way of knowing, and to the unity of science as a goal and methodological principle."[76]

Such scientism aids and abets the kind of cultural practices displayed in Exhibit Four. Appeals to the interests of science, to the advancement of archaeological and biological knowledge, are seen by many to trump the moral objections of indigenous peoples to the desecration of ancestral graves. A key move in the development of scientism is a change in the conception of science. No longer a field of study or a realm of inquiry, it emerges primarily as a method.[77] The assumption that only the West "has" or "does" science is thereby eased. If an indigenous culture is not employing "the scientific method," they cannot be doing science. Nor can their contributions to scientific knowledge be recognized. Those involved with efforts to integrate indigenous and dominant knowledge systems have observed that:

> [a]ll too often it is the Indigenous researcher who is taught the scientific method and forced to adapt his or her cultural reality to that model. Western scientists need the same exposure to TEK (traditional environmental knowledge).[78]

The move to reconceptualize science as a method rather than a field of inquiry effectively facilitates a variety of cultural practices, such as "gene theft." Within the dominant knowledge system, it is doubtful that the Uru-eu-wau-wau can be said to have any "scientific knowledge" regarding the *tiki uba* plant.[79] This cognitive power to determine what constitutes scientific knowledge, conjoined to the economic, political, and legal power of global corporations is a potent combination, enabling violation of the intellectual property rights, and theft of the genetic resources, of indigenous peoples. Small wonder that Daniel Jantzen would bequeath the tropics to himself and his fellow biologists, urging them to buy it and assuming that they alone have the expertise, the right, to determine who will inhabit it.

VI. Sleeptalking: The Dominant Epistemology In Practice

Value-neutrality and anti-pluralism figure prominently in the dominant knowledge system's account of what can be known and how knowledge is to be transmitted. I turn now to a concrete illustration of how these characteristics shape actual practice, and how they are themselves shaped by the existing power relations between dominant and indigenous cultures—an article by Wilcomb E. Washburn, past president of the American Society for Ethnohistory. Its title makes matters very clear, "Distinguishing History from Moral Philosophy and Public Advocacy." Particularly upset about "the process of using history to promote non-historical causes," which he associates with "leftist academics" and "Indian activists," Washburn reacts with consternation to the recent call for historians to:

> form alliances with non-scholarly groups organized for action to solve specified societal problems, with the expectation that historians could function both as moral philosophers and as public advocates.[80]

In doing this, he continues, the enterprise of history:

> is inevitably lost or cheapened. Ideological concepts replace specific facts. Action replaces thought . . . If the obligation to truth is not the first and most overriding obligation of the historian, then he (*sic*) is not a historian.[81]

Washburn offers himself as an example of an historian committed to what one is tempted to call a Great White Truth. Certainly it is a value-neutral Truth, properly cleansed of all traces of the normative—ethical, political, or social:

> all my efforts are guided by, and subject to, the limitations of historical truth . . . I will accept nothing on religious faith, on ethnic tradition, or because of personal belief in the justice of a particular point of view. There is no place in the scholarly profession of history for such distorting lenses. History to me means a commitment to truth . . . however contradictory it may be to our . . . acquired convictions about how the world should be.[82]

Washburn assumes that he has no acquired convictions about how history should be written. Despite the fact that historians have been, and largely still are, strikingly uniform as regards race (white), gender (male), and class (bourgeois), he contends that none of these givens shape historical knowledge. His work and his conception of truth are somehow unburdened by distorting lenses, and remain both value-free and politically innocent. Yet note that this work includes his "recent experiences in writing Indian history, which involve combat with radical theorists on the ideological front," his letters to the *Dartmouth Review* supporting the use of the Indian as a symbol, his efforts abroad to:

> justify United States policy . . . to spike assertions of genocide . . . to disprove the assertion that . . . multinational corporations control the United States Government and seek to exploit the resources of all native peoples against their will.[83]

All this, we are to suppose, is "value-free." And he goes on to claim that some will recognize his "lifelong and quixotic pursuit of the reality of the Indian as 'noble'."[84]

Some curiously nested double standards are at play in historiography such as this. First the goal of historical methodology is held to be a truth attainable only via the production of a certain type of text—namely, ideologically uninformed, value-free, disinterested analyses. Then the work of activist scholars of Indian history is taken to task for violating this commitment, since their "distorting lenses" render their research historiographically unsound. Yet the same charge does not apply when Washburn produces texts that are ideologically committed, value-laden, and (by his own admission) engaged in political battle. Moreover, as he must well be aware, mainstream historiography has itself been engaged for some time in shaking off the vestiges of positivism, and in producing ideologically informed historical analyses specifically intended to expose the embedded assumptions, values, and interests underlying previous historical texts.[85] So Washburn's depiction of his opposition as a radical extremist fringe is disingenuous at best. At worst it evinces yet another double standard—what is methodologically acceptable for mainstream historiography is unacceptable when indigenous peoples are the historical subject.

Washburn is a fine example of what one critic of mainstream philosophical thought has called a "sleeptalker."[86] Sleeptalkers are incapable of discovering how socially regressive tendencies in their culture see through their eyes, speak through their writings, and shape history through their actions. In Vine Deloria's terms, they think "they have corralled the world" in their doctrines, and that "they should be recognized as the only impartial priests of human knowledge."[87] Washburn is clearly convinced that the only people capable of producing knowledge are other sleeptalkers—"impersonal, disinterested, socially anonymous representative(s) of human reason"—who are raceless, genderless, classless.[88] He denies the validity and value of an indigenous perspective. Together with his fellow sleeptalkers, he refuses to recognize as epistemologically powerful the perspective of those whose identities have been devalued by the dominant culture and who are now beginning to take direct control of their own image-making.[89] Those who talk in their sleep deny that the processes of knowing and valuing (or devaluing) proceed in tandem but they do not, cannot, "walk the talk." Their actual practice reveals just how deeply these two processes are interwoven.

A sleeptalking epistemology is an integral part of the dominant culture's knowledge system and is no more value-neutral or immune to evaluative appraisal than the knowledge system itself. Both can be appropriately characterized as oppressive insofar as they serve to "justify and maintain dominant/subordinate relations, or subordination of one group by another."[90] Or, in Joy Harjo's words, insofar as they are committed to "the denial, the incredible denial of anything other than that based on the European soul."[91] Part of what insures such denial and oppressiveness is lack of receptiveness to alternative ways of knowing. In this too, the dominant knowledge system contrasts with, and has much to learn from, that of indigenous cultures.

VII. The Integration of Knowing and Valuing: Respect as A Cognitive Virtue

We have in hand a partial account of the theory of knowledge and knowledge transmission characteristic of the dominant knowledge system. The contrast with an indigenous account is pronounced. Central to the beliefs of many cultures of indigenous North America is the conviction that knowing and valuing are interdependent; they are implicated or embedded in one another. As processes that mutually inform, and are informed by, each other, they constitute a single, integrated system. Nowhere is this clearer than in the fact that respect—one of the prime virtues within indigenous value systems—is appropriately regarded as a cognitive virtue as well as an ethical virtue. It is something we hear emphasized repeatedly in the traditional storytelling of different indigenous cultures, something that many elders and spiritual leaders are ensuring we do not forget. They remind us that if knowledge is not conditioned by respect, it cannot be had, and conversely that there can be no respect where there is no understanding. Here, for example, are the words of Oren Lyons, traditional chief and spiritual leader of the Onondaga Nation, speaking of the seriousness with which the commodification of indigenous spirituality must be approached:

> We have more need for intercultural respect today than at any [other] time . . . and nothing blocks respect and communication faster and more effectively than delusions by one party about another. We've got real problems . . . tremendous problems, problems which threaten the survival of the planet. Indians and non-Indians must confront these problems together, and this means we must have honest dialogue, but this dialogue is impossible so long as non-Indians remain deluded about things as basic as Indian spirituality.[92]

Since the human, natural, and spiritual worlds are tightly interwoven within indigenous cultures, spirituality is a pervasive dimension of natural existence.[93] As Andrew Grey notes, for indigenous peoples:

> knowledge of the environment depends on contacts with the invisible spirit world which plays its own crucial part in ensuring the reproduction of society, culture, and the environment . . . Among many indigenous peoples, particularly of the rain forest, specialists establish a technical prowess in production activities and curing illness from their relationship with the spirit worlds.[94]

Because of this, there is a significant sense in which all knowledge, especially knowledge of the natural world, is to be regarded as spiritual knowledge. Indigenous science has a vital normative, moral, or spiritual, component. "The spiritually based ethic" of the Dene, for example, "governs the interaction between the . . . spiritual, human, and natural worlds and lies in direct contrast to the western scientific explanation of environmental phenomena."[95] One cannot (*pace* Barnes) eliminate or "edit out" this evaluative component and have indigenous science remain.[96]

A striking case of these knowledge systems' diverging approaches to the relation between knowing and valuing is found in the encounter between the Uru-eu-wau-wau's medicinal knowledge and the "gene hunting" corporate scientists. As Simon Brascoupé, a Mohawk/Algonquin professor explains, "'mining' the knowledge of Indigenous people, without considering the cultural context does not provide a sufficient understanding of the knowledge."[97] Such selective extraction of indigenous knowledge is neither new nor without ecological consequence. While indigenous knowledge:

> transformed the world in areas such as food, medicine, politics, and economy, little of the values and culture was understood. However, the Indigenous value base is key to developing a sustainable economy. While Europeans quickly adopted the material benefits of Indigenous foods and knowledge, they did so without respect for Mother Earth.[98]

Brascoupé adds that for the West to adopt and learn from indigenous knowledge, it does not "have to become 'Indigenized'. . . to become just like Indigenous peoples." Rather, "it should listen and learn how to develop sustainable practices from within [its] own history and spirituality."[99]

One characteristic medium for the transmission of indigenous knowledge, for learning and teaching, is storytelling. Stories are rich pedagogical vehicles, well-suited for demonstrating how knowing and valuing are implicated in one another.[100] As William Asikinack suggests, we must:

> listen to and examine our stories and myths, for it is in these stories and myths that . . . our people's values . . . [are] articulated and symbolically expressed. If we continue to ignore or deny the understandings embodied within [them] . . . then we are contributing to the impoverishment of a spiritual legacy left to us.[101]

Consider the traditional Sahaptin legend of the *aiyaiyesh* girl who receives instruction from the Cedar Tree. "*Aiyaiyesh*" means "stupid" or "retarded," and it is clear as the story unfolds that the ignorance from which the girl suffers is a moral ignorance as well. She is neglecting to contribute actively to the well-being of the tribal community:

> While all the other young people of her age helped their elders, the *aiyaiyesh* girl would sit beneath the Cedar Tree, day after day and all day long, watching the world go by. Finally, the Cedar Tree could not stand it any longer and spoke to her.[102]

By showing her how to fashion cedar baskets, the Cedar Tree teaches her the sacredness of circles to her people, and their importance in understanding the cyclical aspects of the natural world and of its human and nonhuman inhabitants. She also learns of the different designs and patterns to be appreciated in nature. The story concludes by showing how she overcomes her moral and intellectual ignorance:

> And when she had learned to put all these designs into her baskets, she returned to her village where she taught her relatives and her friends how to make these baskets. And she wasn't *aiyaiyesh* anymore.[103]

Ernest Benedict, too, indicates that many of the traditional Mohawk stories about various birds and animals were:

> meant to teach children about virtues and faults. The story of how the robin got his red breast, for example, really tells you how to take care of birds and animals, and how you should try to treat them almost as people, as guests.[104]

The centrality of respect within indigenous knowledge systems has already been noted; we need now to explore this concept more fully.[105] Among the Iroquois, it is also referred to as the "wish-to-be-appreciated," the:

> fundamental shared perception—the first principle—of existence. As long as everything is appreciated for what it does and what it shares to sustain the cycles of Creation, the world will be in balance and life will continue.[106]

As an ethical and cognitive virtue, respect mediates not only human, but human/nonhuman relationships; it is readily and regularly extended to the natural world and its nonhuman inhabitants. Since everyone and everything has important functions, they deserve to be respected for what and how they are.[107] Henry Old Coyote comments that:

> We are taught always to respect our surroundings. For example, different clans take different things as their patrons. The one my wife belongs to is known as the Greasy Mouth. [They] take the sun as a patron . . . they respect the sun and address it as Old Man; in

> turn, they are the ones who can communicate with the sun . . . [Other clans] take different animals as patrons . . . as reminders that these animals play a part in our life.[108]

A vital aspect of the indigenous concept of respect is reciprocity, an acknowledgement of the reciprocal relationships that bind human to human, and what is human to what is not.[109] In Winona LaDuke's words, this:

> defines the responsibilities and ways of relating between humans and the ecosystem . . . one cannot take life without a reciprocal offering, usually tobacco . . . There must always be this reciprocity.[110]

There is no question that reciprocity, or relatedness, (what the Lakota call *metakeyasi*) is taken very seriously within indigenous knowledge systems.[111] Vine Deloria argues that it is the central methodological tool of American Indian science: "the major principle of relatedness always remained the critical interpretive method of understanding phenomena."[112] Within indigenous knowledge systems, it can be seen as the primary means of innovation, of gathering and integrating new knowledge. It is not just what is related that is significant, it is the relationships themselves. They are in fact constitutive of what is related, of what is human and what is not. This point is nicely captured by a story, related by Winnebago elder Reuben Snake. In it a grandfather teaches his grandson this important lesson, both spiritual and scientific, about the natural world:

> So they went down the path some more and they came to an open meadow and there were deer feeding on the grass and he said, "Look at those creatures, grandson. One of these days we are going to be obliged to take the life of our brother the deer because we need to eat his flesh, we need his skin to make clothing, to make shelter. We need his bones to make tools, to exist in this creation. Those deer are feeding on your great-grandfather's flesh, the grass that grows is nourished by the flesh of your great-grandfather. So, your great-grandfather is keeping our brother deer alive. In turn, he's going to sacrifice himself for us. Someday, you are going to sacrifice yourself for them.[113]

The indigenous concept of respect diverges from that of the dominant culture not only in that it is both an ethical and a cognitive virtue, but also in its breadth of scope. Generally speaking, within the dominant philosophical tradition, it is possible to respect only what is human or potentially human. In a recent work on the concept of autonomy, this commitment to anthropocentrism is made especially clear:

> to say that autonomy is the ground of respect is to say that autonomous individuals are the "proper" object of respect. This is because autonomy is embodied in people . . . Although the actual ability to function autonomously is the basis of respect, potential or capacity for it (as in infants), may oblige respectful treatment.[114]

To restrict the scope of respect in this way, is to restrict the scope of the intrinsically valuable. Nature is held to lack any intrinsic value, any moral standing of its own. Valued merely instrumentally, as a means to exclusively human ends, its well-being need not be taken into positive account in determining what it is morally permissible to do.[115] As Reuben Snake observes:

> the sacredness goes out of everything. The earth is no longer your mother and all of the things of the Earth become objects and when everything is an object, including your fellow man, you can exploit them to whatever degree you want to and you won't have a guilty conscience.[116]

The instrumental reduction of what is intrinsically valuable lies at the heart of disrespect. Insofar as it structures, and helps to maintain, dominant-subordinate relations, it also lies at the heart of oppressive cultural practices (e.g. the commodification of indigenous spirituality, the theft of indigenous medicines and genetic resources, the archaeologically-justified desecration of burial sites). Moreover, since the land and its nonhuman inhabitants have been devalorized, deprived of significant moral standing, there has been little to check their sustained, systematic abuse. Similar consequences have followed for some of earth's human inhabitants—especially for the indigenous peoples of this continent, whose moral and epistemological standing has been conceptually assimilated to that of the earth. As Winona LaDuke points out:

> the American Indian was rightly, if unwittingly, considered as part and parcel of the natural order, a thing to be profitably surmounted.[117]

She adds:

> as the land suffers, so suffer the people. Whether they are citizens of the natural or the synthetic order, in the end there is no escaping this basic link.[118]

VIII. Epistemological Pluralism and Non-Anthropocentrism

A second feature of indigenous knowledge systems is a commitment to epistemological pluralism. Without glossing over the important differences in indigenous epistemologies (whose full range and richness should be stressed even if it is not here explored), we can note that many indigenous cultures place considerable significance and value on alternative ways of knowing the world, particularly on gaining access to the perspective of the other-than-human. In the story of the *aiyaiyesh* girl, for instance, the Cedar Tree instructs the girl:

> to start walking, keeping her eyes, her ears, and her heart open, and she would discover all sorts of patterns for her basket. And so it was she traveled, and different beings would speak to her . . . the rattlesnake showed her its diamond-shaped designs; the mountain showed her the shape of its triangles; the salmon showed her its gills.[119]

Metakeyasi, the principle of relatedness, comes into play here. Vine Deloria observes that by expanding "our understanding of the sense of being relatives, we discover that plants, birds, and animals often gave specific information to people."[120]

A revealing example of the significance accorded to other-than-human perspectives, and of the full sense in which epistemological pluralism is embraced, can be seen in the language of the Tewa where, of the five verbs that mean "to see," only two relate to physical sight. As children, some tribal members are taught to "see with the eyes of a rock," meaning to perceive as a rock does.[121] Similarly, prior to being trained as Katsina dancers, Hopi and Pueblo children undergo a crucial initiation. The initiate:

> must be able to hold both concepts in his mind simultaneously: a dancer is both human, and while impersonating a Katsina, the Katsina. To believe in only the Katsina is the belief of a child, but to believe in only the human being, is the belief of non-Indians.[122]

The richness of the indigenous commitment to epistemological pluralism lies in the recognition that there are diverse "versions of existence,"[123] diverse ways of being in the natural world, and so diverse experiences to appreciate and respect.[124] Some of these may be shared, though they are not to be appropriated. Access to other ways of knowing is something that must be given, not taken. One cannot lay claim to it, nor demand it as a right. It can only be received, since it is shared by other beings-human and nonhuman.[125] This is reflected in the special status of dreams and visions as vehicles of knowledge. It is in and through such means that humans are typically brought into their most direct, and often transformative, contact with nonhuman beings. "Since everything (trees, rocks, birds, etc.)" is alive and "has a spirit, it is theoretically possible to communicate with the spirit."[126] Vine Deloria underscores the diverse sources of indigenous knowledge: "[t]he Indian understands dreams, visions, and intra-species communications . . . as a natural part of human experience."[127] Yet Western science "discards anything that has a remote relationship with the subjective experiences of human beings and other forms of life."[128]

Intra-species communication occurs often in dreams and visions, where human beings communicate with and learn from nonhuman beings. In "The Woman Who Brought Back the Buffalo," a traditional story of the Blackfoot Nation, a woman and her people learn to communicate with the buffalo through the mediation of the Iniskim, or Buffalo Stone. In a dream, the stone informs the woman:

> I have chosen you to bring me to the camp because you are humble and I know your thoughts are good . . . I will teach you some songs and a ceremony which you must show them. If you do this then I will have my power bring back the buffalo.[129]

It instructs her to tell her people that if they wish to learn to communicate with the buffalo they "should look for one of [their] relatives and bring them home and treat them with respect."[130] Part of what the stone teaches is that humans must not kill the first, solitary buffalo they see, but wait until a whole herd has arrived. It is an ecological lesson repeated by Jake Swamp, a traditional Mohawk sub-chief, in this account of his training in the gathering of medicinal herbs:

> you don't just go out there and pluck it out by its roots and walk away. You have to prepare. You have to know the words that go with it. What I was taught was that when you see that plant, to first see that it's the one you offer thanksgiving to, that plant is still here with us, still performing its duty and that you wish it to continue. You walk past it and you look for the other one, and that one you can pick. For, if you take that first one, who is to know, maybe that's the last one that exists in the world.[131]

Some interesting developments in mainstream science (or more accurately, in certain eddies of it) suggest a belated appreciation of elements of the epistemological pluralism embraced by indigenous science.[132] Recent Japanese primate studies have employed an "anthropomorphic" research method, based on the assumption that "since monkeys have 'minds' of some sort, some kind of empathetic method would be reasonable and likely required to understand simian societies."[133] Indeed the primatologist Masao Kawai advocates an approach called *kyokan*, "the particular method and attitude resulting from feelings of mutual relations, personal attachment, and shared life with the animals," as the foundation of scientific knowledge within the field of primatology.[134] *Kyokan* ("feel-one") refers to the process of "becoming fused with the monkeys' lives where, through an intuitive channel, feelings are mutually exchanged."[135] A number of scientists have also begun to practice "critical anthropomorphism," a term coined by Gordon Burghardt of the University of Tennessee to describe the new discipline, which attempts "to gain insight, through human comparisons, into what an animal might be thinking—while remaining ever cognizant of its life history, biology, and ecology."[136] Harriet Ritvo, an historian at MIT, contends that criticism of anthropocentrism is motivated by the desire to distinguish human beings from the rest of the natural world:

> though the fight against anthropomorphism is usually justified in scientific terms, it can be explained in non-scientific ones . . . one of which is the quasi-religious, quasi-psychological resistance to conflating ourselves as part of the animal kingdom.[137]

A recurrent theme throughout these examples is that an individual must be ready, prepared to receive knowledge. The stone decides to share its knowledge with the Blackfoot woman because she has met certain moral preconditions; she is humble and her thoughts are good. Mohawk medicinal science rests on recognition of the proper plants, as well as of their ecological contingency. It also requires an acknowledgement of limits to one's behavior, and of gratitude for the continuing role of medicinal plants in the natural world. As Phillip Deere, a Muskogee/Creek medicine man, explains:

> If people really lived according to the Indian medicines, the whole world would have to change . . . You don't just take a pill. The medicine demands from you that you approach it with a good frame of mind.[138]

The need for this type of moral and cognitive preparation in knowledge transmission is another distinctive feature of indigenous knowledge systems.

The indigenous account of what can be known and how one comes to know it is immensely generous. The commitment to a non-anthropocentric epistemological pluralism, to coming to know the world through perspectives that are diverse and not restricted to that of humans, runs directly and emphatically counter to the dominant knowledge system's commitment to anti-pluralism. Further, the indigenous integration of the processes of knowing and valuing leads to an account of knowledge transmission that is transformative, rather than acquisitive. To know is not to increase one's holdings of true facts about external reality, but to enhance one's relation to the natural world by learning how to live well within it, in a manner that acknowledges and respects the essential interdependence of the human and the nonhuman. Such knowledge is experientially-based in the fullest sense—integrating and involving all that one is. In this regard, knowledge can be seen as closely allied to, if not grounded upon, integrity or wholeness. Henry Old Coyote, a Crow elder and philosopher, puts it this way:

> The purpose of the Indian's . . . way of knowing, was to keep whole things whole, because only when they are whole is the living presence, the soul or spirit, really there.[139]

Once again, for Native America, the processes of knowing and valuing implicate one another.

IX. Conclusion: Resisting the Politics of Disappearance

Oppressive relations of power continue to characterize dominant and indigenous contact, manifesting themselves not only in social systems, economic systems, and legal systems, but in knowledge systems as well. I have argued that the no-fault assumption, and the array of cultural practices it shields, is the product of a distinctive configuration of knowledge, value, and power within the dominant culture. It has not been my intention to caricature the dominant knowledge system. Despite recent, promising developments that challenge the above epistemological portrait, it does seem fairly to reflect both the prevailing popular understanding of science and aspects of the lingering legacy of positivism in the theory and practice of knowledge. Yet concepts of knowledge and value are cultural artifacts. Like the extant power relations, they are subject to evaluation, comparative critique, and change.

The portrait of indigenous knowledge systems extended here is very much in process and incomplete. However, as Deloria has stressed, it is vital that we begin to accord indigenous knowledge the status it deserves and attempt, from various areas of expertise, to articulate its fundamental features and commitments.[140] Part of this involves taking:

> a careful look at the manner in which the western scientific community receives tribal knowledge and becom[ing] particularly alert to the framework it uses in interpreting and understanding this body of information.[141]

The history of indigenous science and scientific practice (when the existence of this history has been acknowledged), has traditionally been presented as a history of failure—the failure to develop valid (that is, Western) scientific method. As with so much else that is indigenous, it has usually been cast as an unsuccessful effort to win what the West itself has won. Indigenous knowledge of the natural world:

> is thus believed to have been born in a struggle to derive a view of the world that avoided superstitions and spirits and which sought to discover in nature abstract principles that were operative in all places at all times.[142]

The struggle, like the search, was allegedly futile.

In addition to "revisionist" history, two conflicting tendencies in the work of certain scholars and environmentalists further cloud an appreciation of indigenous knowledge systems. On the one hand we find an effort to marginalize the valuable ecological lessons of indigenous science, to denigrate indigenous contributions to understanding the natural world, if not indigenous peoples themselves. This includes claims that: there is no evidence of an American Indian environmental ethic or an indigenous Mother Earth concept; that Indians are miscast as ecologists; that they are responsible for decimating the eagle population, are the first environmental pillagers, and are threats to the habitat.[143] On the other hand, we find a tendency to appropriate and romanticize "Indian environmental wisdom." In classic AIS fashion, what is indigenous is seized and re-cast in the familiar image of those doing the "casting." Often, this takes the form of a "search for an authentic lineage," or an effort "to consolidate the claim that deep ecology is a philosophy of universal significance."[144] Both tendencies reveal how the cultural politics of knowledge have traditionally played themselves out when it comes to native peoples. Both are distorted and distorting. They are also, to paraphrase Ramachandra Guha, monolithic and simplistic. Their characteristic effect, intended or not, is to deny the agency and integrity of indigenous cultures, making them the privileged domain of the dominant intellectual tradition.[145]

Yet the dominant society is currently rethinking its relation to the environment, and groping towards an ecological sustainability that has heretofore eluded it. Increasingly, as it does so, it is turning its gaze on the indigenous cultures it never did succeed in assimilating. Some indigenous people point out that the Seventh Generation prophecy has long predicted this, a time "when the world would come to Indigenous peoples to learn how to develop a sustainable way of life." [146] While others, working to integrate Western and indigenous knowledge systems, express their alarm that the prevailing pattern—even among Western scientists who acknowledge the value of indigenous knowledge—seems to be that of applying Western scientific categories and methods to collect, verify, and validate.[147] Such knowledge "mining" is just another variant of cultural imperialism. As with the commodification of indigenous spirituality, and corporate patenting of indigenous medicines, knowledge that the dominant culture regards as valuable is identified, extracted, culturally decontextualized, then processed to achieve a marketable form. A pattern that began with indigenous land and resources, continues now with indigenous knowledge, spiritual and scientific, of the natural world. The land and resource grabbing has not ended, but a new version of cognitive search-and-seizure has begun. These cultural practices are not mere epiphenomena. They are significant social forces, ideologically legitimating the dominant status and privileged positions of their practitioners, and securing the conceptual subordination of indigenous peoples.

Cultural politics enter into every knowledge transaction. Attempts to ignore them, or self-deceptively will them away, will not make them go away. They may however be buried, hidden from view, by a no-fault assumption that insulates those engaged in knowledge extraction and expropriation from doubts about what they are doing, about whether the practices and products of cultural imperialism—be they generated by the AIS industry or chemical companies—are either cognitively or morally suspect. Such an assumption, I have argued, is facilitated by the way knowledge is conceived within the dominant knowledge system. When knowing and valuing are regarded as discreet, autonomous processes and knowledge itself is conceived as value-free, it should not be surprising that a devotée of the New Age can sit contentedly with Lynn Andrews' latest novel and not ask what might seem otherwise obvious questions about the origins and effects of her commercial venture. Who gained or benefitted (financially and otherwise) from its production and purchase? Who didn't? Do indigenous spiritual leaders recognize its author as spiritually knowledgeable? Does it contribute to or undermine the continued stereotyping of indigenous peoples and cultures? Lastly, does it enhance understanding of the struggles, issues, concerns, and aspirations of the indigenous community?

Since the way in which knowledge is conceived has ethical and political implications, knowledge systems must be critiqued in those terms. Such critiques are vital to the survival of indigenous knowledge systems. In *Monocultures of the Mind*, Vandana Shiva refers to "disappeared" knowledge systems. She observes that in Argentina:

> when the dominant political system faces dissent, it responds by making the dissidents disappear. The *desparacidos* . . . share the fate of local knowledge systems throughout the world, which have been conquered through the politics of disappearance, not the politics of debate and dialogue.[148]

Shiva suggests that the politics of the disappearance of local knowledge systems takes several different forms. One is to simply not see them, to negate their very existence. Another is to deny their cognitive standing, to dismiss their status as systematic knowledge by labelling them primitive or unscientific, superstitious or mystical. Yet another is to destroy the very conditions for diverse knowledge systems to exist, in the way that the introduction of monocultures destroys the conditions needed for species diversity.

All these forms of the politics of disappearance are operative in the cultural practices criticized here. Yet we might add one other. Indigenous knowledge systems can be made to disappear by assimilation. America has historically attempted to address its "Indian problem" by subjecting indigenous peoples to vigorous and varying campaigns of assimilation. As Deloria notes: "Indians were subjected to the most intense pressure to become white. Laws passed by Congress had but one goal—the Anglo-Saxonization of the Indian."[149] Assimilation by the dominant knowledge system leads to the same sort of homogeneity as monoculturization, but it does so in a different way. Rather than having the conditions for their existence destroyed, the distinctiveness and integrity of indigenous knowledge systems themselves are undermined. It is a process more akin to reverse transcription; they are consumed, made over in the image of their assimilator. Such assimilation does not constitute survival in another form. Nor is it inevitable.[150] To suppose that it is to embrace the politics of disappearance as a self-fulfilling prophecy.

**Laurie Anne Whitt is associate professor of philosophy at Michigan Technological University.*

Notes

1. Iris Young, 1992, in "Five Faces of Oppression," (Thomas E. Wartenberg, ed., *Rethinking Power*, Albany, New York: State University of New York Press) points out that oppression tends not to be a central concept in mainstream political theory, where the term "injustice" is instead preferred:

> Speaking the political language in which oppression is a central word involves adopting a whole mode of analyzing and evaluating social structures and practices that is quite incommensurate with the language of liberal individualism that dominates political discourse in the United States. (p. 174)

Part of the intent of this essay is to demonstrate that the discourse of oppression makes sense of much indigenous social and cultural experience. Cultural imperialism is discussed widely by radical theorists and social critics. See, for example, Geary Hobson, 1979, "The Rise of the White Shaman as a New Version of Cultural Imperialism," in G. Hobson, ed., *The Remembered Earth*, Albuquerque: University of New Mexico Press, 1990; Maria C. Lugones and Elizabeth Spelman, 1983, "Have We Got A Theory for You! Feminist Theory, Cultural Imperialism and the Demand for 'The Woman's Voice'," *Women's Studies International Forum*, Vol. 9, No. 6, pp. 573-581; and Iris Marion Young, 1992, *op. cit.* While I agree with Young that it is one of a variety of forms of oppression, my characterization of it differs from hers. For reasons I cannot detail here, I am uncomfortable with construing it (as I take her to do) along predominantly Foucauldian lines. Also, I emphasize how it impacts the cultures subjected to it, in contrast to her emphasis on an individual's experience of it.

2. This was related by Robert Antone in "Education as a Vehicle for Values and Sovereignty," an address given at the Third International Native American Studies Conference at Lake Superior State University in October 1991.

3. José Barreiro, 1992, "The Search For Lessons," *Akwe:kon*, Vol. IX, No. 2, pp. 18-39.

4. Andrew Gray, 1991, "The Impact of Biodiversity Conservation on Indigenous Peoples," in V. Shiva, ed., *Biodiversity: Social and Ecological Perspectives*, New Jersey: Zed Books, p. 68.

5. Vandana Shiva, 1993, *Monocultures of the Mind*, New Jersey: Zed Books Ltd., p. 159.

6. Jack Kloppenburg, 1990, "No Hunting!," *Z Magazine*, September, p. 106.

7. Jason Clay, 1990, "Editorial: Genes, Genius and Genocide," *Cultural Survival Quarterly*, 14, no. 4, p. 1.

8. Andrew Gray, 1991, "The Impact of Biodiversity Conservation on Indigenous People," Vandana Shiva, *supra* note 4.

9. Daniel Jantzen, 1986, "The Future of Tropical Ecology," *Annual Review of Ecology and Systematics*, 17, pp. 305-24.

10. *Ibid.*, at p. 305.

11. *Ibid.*, at p. 306.

12. Cited in Larry Fruhling, 1989, *Gannet News Service*, April 19.

13. *Ibid.*

14. The terminology has been widely adopted. See, for example, Frédérique Apffel Marglin and Stephen Marglin, 1990, *Dominating Knowledge*, Oxford: Clarendon Press and Shiva, 1993, *supra* note 5. While "dominant" knowledge system is an accurate expression that aptly captures the political realities, for various reasons, including the exportation of this knowledge system beyond the geographic confines of the West, "Western" is neither exact nor fully equivalent to it. Yet the wide use of the latter by scholars in various fields makes it difficult to relinquish. And I do not fully do so here. Both terms are exceedingly broad, a fact that may prompt some irritation.

15. References to the "legacy of positivism" abound. For two recent examples see, Dale Jamieson, 1991, "The Poverty of Postmodernism," *University of Colorado Law Review*, Volume 62, Issue 3, pp. 577-595 and Steve Fuller, 1993, *Philosophy, Rhetoric, and the End of Knowledge*, Madison, Wisconsin: University of Wisconsin Press.

16. Barreiro, 1992, *supra* note 3 at pp. 18-39.

17. Batalla, cited in Ward Churchill, 1993, *Struggle for the Land*, Maine: Common Courage Press, p. 408.

18. Barabara Owl, White Earth Anishinabe, in Ward Churchill and M. Annette Jaimes, 1992, *Fantasies of the Master Race*, Monroe, Maine: Common Courage Press, p. 193.

19. A partial listing of these indigenous critiques would include Ward Churchill, 1994, *Indians Are Us: Culture and Genocide in Native North America*, Monroe, Maine: Common Courage Press; Ward Churchill, 1990, "Spiritual Hucksterism," *Z Magazine*, December,

pp. 94-98; Churchill and Jaimes, 1992, *supra* note 16; M. Annette Jaimes, 1993, "Hollywood's Native American Women," *Turtle Quarterly*, Spring/Summer, pp. 40-45; Geary Hobson, 1979, *supra* note 1; Russell Means in M. Annette Jaimes, 1988, "On 'Mother Earth': An Interview With Russell Means," *The Bloomsbury Review*, 8; Wendy Rose, 1980, "For the White Poets Who Would Be Indian" and "The Anthropology Convention," in *Lost Copper*, Banning, California: Malki Museum Press, Morongo Indian Reservation; Wendy Rose, 1984, "Just What's All This Fuss About White-shamanism Anyway?," in Bo Scholer, ed., *Coyote Was Here*, Denmark: Seklos, University of Aarhus Press; Leslie Silko, 1979, "An Old-Time Indian Attack Conducted in Two Parts: Part One: Imitation 'Indian' Poems; Part Two: Gary Snyder's Turtle Island," in Hobson, 1979, *supra* note 1; virtually all of the writers interviewed in Laura Coltelli, 1990, *Winged Words: American Indian Writers Speak*, Lincoln, Nebraska: University of Nebraska Press; Gerald Vizenor, 1987, "Socioacupuncture: Mythic Reversals and the Striptease in Four Scenes" and Michael Dorris, 1987, "Indians on the Shelf," both in Calvin Martin, ed., *The American Indian and the Problem of History*, New York: Oxford University Press; and Young Bear, 1979, "in disgust and response to indian-type poetry written by whites published in a mag which keeps rejecting me," *Winter of the Salamander: The Keeper of Importance*, New York: Harper and Row.

20. Churchill, 1990, *Ibid.*

21. Hobson, 1978, *supra* note 1 at p. 100. These include poets Gary Snyder, 1969, *Turtle Island*, New York: New Directions; David Cloutier, 1980, *Spirit Spirit: Shaman Songs*, Providence, Rhode Island: Copper Beech Press; and Gene Fowler, 1981, *Return of the Shaman*, San Francisco: Second Coming Press. Indigenous identity appropriation in American literature is not confined to poetry. In *American Rhythm*, for example, Mary Austin, 1980, Boston: Houghton Mifflin Co., would have it known that she has, "at times . . . succeeded in being an Indian." (p. 41) Michael Castro, 1983, addresses this issue at length in his *Reinventing the American Indian*, Albuquerque: University of New Mexico Press. See also Ward Churchill's review of Castro in Churchill and Jaimes, 1992, *supra* note 16.

22. Carlos Castaneda, 1972, *The Teachings of Don Juan: A Yaqui Way of Knowledge*, Berkeley: University of California Press.

23. Jamake Highwater, 1981, *Primal Mind*, New York: Harper and Row.

24. Ruth Beebe Hill, 1979, *Hanta Yo*, New York: Doubleday.

25. Lynn Andrews, 1981, *Medicine Woman*, San Francisco: Harper and Row.

26. Churchill and Jaimes, 1992, *supra* note 16 at p. 1.

27. Sun Bear, Wallace Black Elk, Grace Spotted Eagle, Brook Medicine Eagle, Osheana Fast Wolf, Cyfus McDonald, Dyhani Ywahoo, Rolling Thunder, and "Beautiful Painted Arrow:" there is a growing list of individuals who have presented themselves as prepared to sell spiritual knowledge and power to anyone willing and able to meet their price (see, Churchill, 1990, *supra* note 17).

28. Churchill and Jaimes, 1992, *supra* note 16 at p. 217.

29. GAIA, 1991, *1991 Catalogue*, The GAIA Bookstore & Catalogue Company, Berkeley, California.

30. These oracular cards (with titles such as "Medicine Bowl," "Give-Away Ceremony" and "Dreamtime") are presented as "sacred steps of initiation into earth-honoring spirituality . . . practical exercises and adventure tasks for spiritual seekers of the Medicine Way, the path of no-dogma." For more on the theory underlying such practice, GAIA prescribes what can only be regarded as a spiritual stew; two volumes entitled Earth Medicine and The Medicine Way containing a "remarkable system derived from the Medicine Wheel teachings of North American Indians, Taoist teachings of the East, & ancient wisdom of northern European shamanic traditions."

31. Hobson, 1979, *supra* note 1 at p. 101.

32. Simon Ortiz, 1990, interview in Coltelli, 1990, *supra* note 17 at p. 112.

33. Churchill and Jaimes, 1992, *supra* note 16 at p. 210.

34. *Ibid.*, at p. 65.

35. Renato Rosaldo, 1989, *Culture and Truth: The Remaking of Social Analysis*, Boston: Beacon Press, p. 70.

36. *Ibid.*, at p. 70.

37. Cited in Churchill and Jaimes, 1992, *supra* note 16 at p. 192.

38. Though this tends to be true primarily for members of the dominant society. As Vine Deloria, 1991 in "Commentary: Research, Redskins, and Reality," *American Indian Quarterly*, Fall, asks, if the scientific and spiritual knowledge of the Indian community is so valuable, "how can non-Indians receive so much compensation for their small knowledge and Indians receive so little for their extensive knowledge?" (p. 466)

39. Cited in Churchill and Jaimes, 1992, *supra* note 16 at p. 191.

40. I do not defend my adoption of this term here, but note that my use of it is itself at odds with the view of knowledge within the dominant knowledge system. Many who accept that system will insist on an extended defense. I will not attempt that in this essay.

41. Stephen A. Marglin, 1990, "Toward the Decolonization of the Mind" and "Losing Touch" in Marglin and Marglin, 1990, *supra* note 12.

42. *Ibid.*, at pp. 232-233. I develop a preliminary, not an exhaustive, account below. Most of my remarks bear on the links between the first three characteristics.

43. One telling sign of life is the fact that one of the classic texts of emotivism (the ethical manifestation of logical positivism), A. J. Ayer's 1936, *Language, Truth and Logic*, has never been out of print. Indeed, as Robert N. Proctor, 1991, *Value-Free Science?*, Cambridge, Massachusetts: Harvard University Press, points out, by 1986 the text had gone through twenty-seven printings and at least fourteen translations. (p. 203)

44. Proctor, 1991, *Ibid.*, at p. 162.

45. Proctor, 1991, *Ibid.*, provides an invaluable examination of positivism and of the legacy of positivism, to which I am indebted. See also Leszek Kolakowski, 1969, *The Alienation of Reason: A History of Positivist Thought*, Garden City, New York: Doubleday, for an earlier account.

46. This traditional position has been vigorously contested in recent years by researchers from a variety of fields, including science studies, philosophy of science, feminism, environmental ethics, etc. See especially, Helen Longino, 1990, *Science As Social Knowledge*, Princeton: Princeton University Press; Sandra Harding, 1989, "After the End of 'Philosophy'," paper presented to the Philosophy Department of Purdue University; Sandra Harding, 1991, *Whose Science? Whose Knowledge?*, Ithaca, New York: Cornell University Press, Proctor, 1991, *supra* note 41; Joseph Rouse, 1987, *Knowledge and Power: Toward a Political Philosophy of Science*, Ithaca: Cornell University Press; Steve Fuller, 1988, *Social Epistemology*, Bloomington, Indiana: Indiana University Press; Steve Fuller, 1989, *Philosophy of Science and Its Discontents*, Boulder, Colorado: Westview Press; Fuller, 1993, *supra* note 13; and Susan Bordo, 1987, *The Flight to Objectivity*, Albany: State University of New York Press.

47. Proctor, 1991, *supra* note 41 at pp. 262-263.

48. Longino, 1990, *supra* note 44.

49. Harding, 1991, *supra* note 44 and Bordo, 1987, *supra* note 44.

50. Henri Poincaré, [1905], *The Value of Science*, translated by G. B. Halsted, 1958, New York: Dover Publications, p. 12.

51. Proctor, 1991, *supra* note 41 at p. 7.

52. Moreover, within one influential strain of positivist thought—logical positivism—all propositions (including the ethical and political) not susceptible to empirical verification were rendered literally meaningless. This followed from the adoption of a verificationist criterion of meaning.

53. Richard Rorty, 1967, "Intuition," in Paul Edwards, ed., *The Encyclopedia of Philosophy*, IV, New York: MacMillan.

54. Terry Tafoya, 1987, "Circles and Cedar: Native American Epistemology and Clinical Issues," paper presented at the 1987 Native American Studies Conference, Lake Superior State University, Sault Sainte Marie, Michigan.

55. The way in which knowledge is contained, or materially embodied, differs in print and oral cultures:

> In a print culture, to a great extent knowledge is stored in books, in an oral culture, knowledge comes from a person, or in the words of Métis architect Doug Cardinal: "our elders are our books, when we lose one of our elders we lose our books" . . . It is problematic to translate knowledge and wisdom intimately connected with a person's life into the abstractness of the printed word. (Renate Eigenbrod, 1993, "The Oral in the Written: A Literature Between Two Cultures," in T. Schirer and S. Branstner, eds., *Native American Values: Survival and Renewal*, Sault Sainte Marie, Michigan: Lake Superior State University Press, p. 234).

56. Karl Popper, 1982, *Unended Quest*, La Salle, Illinois: Open Court.

57. This followed Passmore's, 1968, *supra* note 48, declaration that logical positivism "is dead, or as dead as any philosophy ever becomes" (p. 56), and the claim of Alan Gewirth, 1974, "The Is-Ought Problem Resolved," *Proceedings and Addresses of the American Philosophical Association*, 47, pp. 34-61, claim that he resolved the is/ought dilemma.

58. Proctor, 1991, *supra* note 41 at p. 223.

59. Barry Barnes, 1974, *Scientific Knowledge and Sociological Theory*, London: Routledge & Kegan Paul.

60. *Ibid.*, at p. 145. Barnes' comment leaves one apoplectic. For whom exactly did such conceptions "fit naturally and securely?" And who was prepared to take a racist world "for granted?" The answer can only be those whose interests were served by theories of eugenics and biological determinism. Then as now that is a minority, though a powerful minority, of humanity.

61. Milton Friedman, 1953, *Essays in Positive Economics*, Chicago: University of Chicago Press, p. 4.

62. Proctor, 1991, *supra* note 41 at p. 183.

63. *Ibid.*, at p. 183.

64. *Ibid.*, at p. 200.

65. *Ibid.*, at p. 187.

66. See, C. Dean Higginbotham, 1982, "Native Americans Versus Archaeologists: The Legal Issues," *American Indian Law Review*, Vol. 10, pp. 91-115.

67. Statement of Pat Lefthand, *Improvement of the American Indian Religious Freedom Act: Hearings Before the Senate Select Committee on Indian Affairs United States Senate on S. 2250*, 100th Congress, 2nd Session 217 (1988), p. 27.

68. Donna Haraway, 1989, *Primate Visions*, London: Routledge, Chapman & Hall, Inc.

69. Marglin, 1990, *supra* note 12 at p. 25.

70. *Ibid.*, at p. 25.

71. *Ibid.*, at p. 25. Marglin, 1990, *supra* note 12, offers the following survivalist argument for rejecting this anti-pluralism, an argument that seems clearly formulated from within the perspective of the dominant knowledge system:

> Cultural diversity may be the key to the survival of the human species. Just as biologists defend exotic species like the snail darter in order to maintain the

> diversity of the genetic pool . . . so should we defend exotic (*sic*) cultures in order to maintain the diversity of forms of understanding, creating, and coping that the human species has managed to generate. (pp. 16-17)

72. Kolakowski, 1968, *supra* note 43, identifies the assumption that science is the best way of knowing as one of six fundamental commitments of positivism.

73. Jurgen Habermas, 1971, *Knowledge and Human Interests*, Boston, Massachusetts: Beacon Press.

74. Proctor, 1991, *supra* note 41 at p. 160.

75. Max Weber, [1930], 1958, *The Protestant Ethic and the Spirit of Capitalism*, New York: Charles Scribner's Sons, p. 13.

76. Proctor, 1991, *supra* note 41 at p. 167.

77. Science thus becomes a matter of procedure rather than content, a function not of what is studied, but of how it is studied. In addition to securing as "science" proper only the Western way of doing science, this move extends the power of the dominant knowledge system in another manner as well. Since the doing of science becomes a matter of adopting a certain methodology, everything can in principle be done "scientifically." Hence the proliferation of "wannabee" sciences. The book titles in any sizeable library reveal the extent and diversity of this aspiration. Cornell's holdings for example, list over four hundred titles that begin with the invocation "The Science of . . ." There are, it would seem, sciences of ethics, of religion, of art, of education, of money, of judicial proof, of mystic lights, of peace, of rights, of revolution, of buffoonery, of fairytales, of housekeeping, of love, of fly fishing, even of scientific method itself.

78. Martha Johnson, 1992, "Documenting Dene Traditional Environmental Knowledge," *Akwe:kon*, Vol. IX, No. 2, p. 77.

79. Partly for this reason I think we should avoid the common juxtaposition of "Western Science" with so-called "TEK" (tradi-

tional environmental knowledge), as though the latter were something other than genuine scientific knowledge.

80. Wilcomb Washburn, 1987, "Distinguishing History from Moral Philosophy and Public Advocacy," in Martin, ed., 1987, *supra* note 17 at p. 95.

81. *Ibid.*, at p. 95.

82. *Ibid.*, at p. 97.

83. *Ibid.*, at p. 94.

84. *Ibid.*, at p. 97.

85. As an illustrative case in point, consider the winner of the Bancroft Prize in American History for 1978—Morton Horwitz's, 1977, *The Transformation of American Law, 1780-1860*, Cambridge, Massachusetts: Harvard University Press. Horwitz sets out to critique certain features of the "'consensus' history that has continued to dominate American historiography since the Second World War" (p. xiii), and has succeeded "in creating the appearance of a neutral, apolitical legal system." (p. xiii) These earlier histories obscure the fact that from 1780 to 1860 "a major transformation of the legal system took place, which reflected a variety of aspects of social struggle . . . [and] enabled emergent entrepreneurial and commercial groups to win a disproportionate share of wealth and power in American society." (p. xvi) Alongside this class analysis of American legal history, one might add its British counterpart—Douglas Hay's, 1987, classic study, *Labor, Law and Crime: An Historical Perspective*, New York: Tavistock.

86. Harding, 1989, *supra* note 44.

87. Vine Deloria, 1980, "American Fantasy," in Gretchen Bataille, *The Pretend Indians*, Ames, Iowa: Iowa State University Press, p. xv.

88. Harding, 1989, *supra* note 44 at p. 7.

89. The hegemony of the sleeptalkers is not absolute. Indigenous peoples have always been subjects, generators of thought, not mere objects of others' thought. And, as Paula Gunn Allen, 1990,

(Interview in Coltelli, 1990, *supra* note 17) observes:

> We're beginning to take control of the image-making again. And that's what must happen, because whatever controls your definition controls your sense of self . . . take it back from Hollywood, take it back from the anthropologists. (p. 18)

The sleep of the sleeptalkers is now a more troubled one.

90. Karen Warren, 1989, "A Philosophical Perspective on the Ethics and Resolution of Cultural Property Issues," in P. M. Messenger, ed., *The Ethics of Collecting Cultural Property*, Albuquerque, New Mexico: University of New Mexico Press, p. 11.

91. Joy Harjo, 1990, interview in Coltelli, 1990, *supra* note 17 at p. 63.

92. Churchill, 1990, *supra* note 17 at p. 94.

93. Johnson, 1992, *supra* note 76 at p. 74.

94. Gray, 1991, *supra* note 4 at p. 66.

95. Johnson, 1992, *supra* note 76 at p. 76.

96. While this is so, it does not rule out some translation, or transculturation, of indigenous thought. Vine Deloria, 1992, "Ethnoscience and Indian Realities," *Winds of Change*, Summer, maintains that if:

> tribal wisdom is to be seen as a valid intellectual discipline, it will be because it can be articulated in a wide variety of expository forms and not simply in the language and concepts which tribal elders have always used to express themselves. (p. 15)

And as Barreiro, 1992, *supra* note 3, contends:

> Nor is Indian society and philosophy so tender or fragile that it ceases to exist at the first instance of *mestizaje* or transculturation. (p. 25)

97. Simon Brascoupé, 1992, "Indigenous Perspectives on International Development," *Akwe:kon*, Vol. IX, No. 2, p. 11.

98. *Ibid.*, at pp. 11 and 14.

99. *Ibid.*, at p. 13.

100. Indigenous authors and literary critics have repeatedly stressed the role of storytelling. Coltelli's, 1990, *supra* note 17, interviews are especially valuable in this regard. See also N. Scott Momaday, 1989, *Ancestral Voices*, Lincoln, Nebraska: University of Nebraska Press; Maria Campbell, ed., 1985, *achimoona*, Saskatoon: Fifth House; and Harry Robinson and Wendy Wickwire, 1989, *Write It On Your Heart*, Vancouver, British Columbia: Talonbooks/Theytus.

101. William Asikinack, 1987, "Anishinabe (Ojibwe) Legends through Anishinabe Eyes," paper presented at the 1987 Native American Studies Conference, Lake Superior State University, Sault Sainte Marie, Michigan, p. 1.

102. Tafoya, 1987, *supra* note 52 at p. 1.

103. *Ibid.*, at p. 1.

104. Cited in M. Morey, and O. Gilliam, 1974, *Respect for Life*, New York: The Myrin Institute, Inc., p. 40.

105. Barbara Owl emphasizes that:

> a lot of things about our spiritual ways may be secret, but the core idea never has been. And you can sum up that idea in one word spelled R-E-S-P-E-C-T. Respect for and balance between all things, that's our most fundamental spiritual concept. (in Churchill and Jaimes 1992, *supra* note 16 at p. 193)

106. Barreiro, 1992, *supra* note 3 at p. 28.

107. See, Jorge Quintana, 1992, "American Indian Systems for Natural Resource Management," *Akwe:kon*, Vol. IX, No. 2, p. 94.

108. Morey, 1974, *supra* note 102 at p. 139.

109. How this respect or wish-to-be-appreciated mediates human and nonhuman relations is well illustrated by a traditional Anishinabe tale called "The Woman Who Married A Beaver," in which the practical knowledge required for successful trapping is held to be unobtainable in the absence of respect:

> Such was what the people truly know. If any one regards a beaver with too much contempt, speaking ill of it, one simply [will] not [be able to] kill it. Just the same as the feelings of one who is disliked, so is the feeling of the beaver. And he who never speaks ill of a beaver is very much loved by it; in the same way as people often love one another, so is one held in the mind of the beaver; particularly lucky then is one at killing beavers. (Thomas Overholt and Baird Callicott, 1982, *Clothed-In-Fur and Other Tales*, Washington, D.C.: University Press of America, p. 75)

110. Winona LaDuke, 1992, "Indigenous Environmental Perspectives: A North American Primer," *Akwe:kon*, Vol. IX, No. 2, p. 54.

111. N. Scott Momaday, 1976, "Native American Attitudes to the Environment," in W. H. Capps, ed., *Seeing With A Native Eye*, New York: Harper and Row, stresses that this isn't widely or fully appreciated:

> I don't think that anyone has clearly understood yet how the Indian conceives of himself in relation to the landscape. We have formulated certain generalities about that relationship . . . but they have been rather too general . . . take the idea that the Indian reveres the earth, thinks of it as his place of origin . . . These statements are true. But they can also be misleading because they don't indicate anything about the nature of the relationship which is, I think, an intricate thing in itself. (p. 79)

112. Vine Deloria, 1992, "Relativity, Relatedness," *Winds of Change*, Autumn, p. 40.

113. Cited in Elizabeth Sackler, 1993, "Living in Harmony With Nature: A Talk by Reuben Snake," *Akwe:kon*, Vol. X, No. 3, p. 12.

114. Joseph Kupfer, 1990, *Autonomy and Social Interaction*, Albany, New York: State University of New York Press, p. 48.

115. The conceptual distancing of the human from the nonhuman in the dominant knowledge system contributes to its dramatically different view of the nature and standing of the nonhuman world. It is a story that can be traced back to the beginnings of Western epistemology, to the Sophists. According to one account of these origins:

> Numerous things which had previously been thought to be part of nature were seen not to be. Thus, a general antithesis was drawn between nature and human convention or custom, and the question of where the line was to be drawn between them arose. (D. W. Hamlyn, 1967, "History of Epistemology," in Paul Edwards, ed., *The Encyclopedia of Philosophy*, III, New York: Macmillan Publishing Company, p. 9).

116. Cited in Sackler, 1993, *supra* note 111 at p. 14.

117. Winona LaDuke, 1983, "From Natural to Synthetic and Back Again," in Ward Churchill, ed., *Marxism and Native Americans*, Boston, Massachusetts: South End Press, p. ii.

118. *Ibid.*, at p. iv.

119. Tafoya, 1987, *supra* note 52 at p. 1.

120. Deloria, 1992, *supra* note 110 at p. 38.

121. Tafoya, 1987, *supra* note 52 at p. 3.

122. *Ibid.*, at p. 3.

123. Yvonne Dion-Buffalo, and John C. Mohawk, 1992, "Thoughts from an Autochthonous Center: Postmodernism and Cultural Studies," *Akwe:kon*, Vol. IX, No. 4, p. 19.

124. My view thus contrasts directly with that of Robin Horton, 1967, "African Traditional Thought and Western Science: Part II," *Africa*, 37, 2:

> in traditional cultures there is no developed awareness of alternatives to the established body of theoretical levels; whereas in scientifically oriented cultures, such an awareness is highly developed. (p. 155)

One does not have to accept Kuhn's view of science to recognize that the description Horton gives of Western science, i.e. that it is "characterized by awareness of alternatives, diminished sacredness of beliefs, and diminished anxiety about threats to them" (p. 156), seems ill-suited to much of the history of Western science. Horton's debt to Popperian philosophy of science is quite apparent. It is also worth pointing out that if Horton is correct that "awareness of alternatives . . . is crucial for the take-off into science" (p. 155), and if I am correct in contrasting the epistemological pluralism of indigenous science with the epistemological anti-pluralism of dominant science, then by this criterion it is indigenous science that emerges as "more scientific," or as "better science."

125. The scope of the indigenous knowledge community is clearly much broader than that of the dominant culture's. Moreover, within indigenous epistemology the process of knowing is constitutive of, and cannot be divorced from, the resulting knowledge. How something comes to be known matters vitally in the determination of what is known. The systemic aspect of Marglin's characterization of knowledge communities is evident here. What can count as knowledge (epistemology), how knowledge may be acquired (transmission), and the relations that govern the interactions of a knowledge community's members (power) are reciprocally linked.

126. Tafoya, 1987, *supra* note 52 at pp. 4-5.

127. Deloria, 1992, *supra* note 94 at p. 16.

128. *Ibid.*, at p. 15.

129. Beverly Hungry Wolf, 1982, *The Ways of My Grandmothers*, New York: William Morrow & Co., p. 164.

130. *Ibid.*, at p. 164.

131. Barreiro, 1992, *supra* note 3 at p. 21.

132. I want here to invert the common tendency "to suggest that when traditional teachings correspond to the findings or present beliefs of western science, then traditional wisdom is validated." (Deloria, 1992, *supra* note 94 at p. 15) The tendency is a prevalent and persistent one, reflecting and reinforcing the power of the dominant knowledge system. As Deloria asks:

> why does that correspondence necessarily validate the tribal insight rather than the other way around? Why do we think that western science is the criterion of truth and accuracy? (p. 15)

133. Haraway, 1989, *supra* note 66 at p. 252.

134. *Ibid.*, at p. 252.

135. Asquith in Haraway, 1989, *supra* note 66 at p. 252.

136. Viva Hardigg, 1993, "All in the Family?," *U.S. News & World Report*, November 1, p. 72.

137. Cited in *Ibid.*, at p. 72.

138. Barreiro, 1992, *supra* note 3 at p. 32.

139. Morey, 1974, *supra* note 102 at p. 197.

140. Deloria, 1992, *supra* note 94 at p. 14.

141. *Ibid.*, at p. 14.

142. *Ibid.*, at p. 13.

143. These claims were advanced by (in order): Tom Regan, 1982, *All That Dwell Therein*, Berkeley, California: University of California Press; Sam Gill, 1987, *Mother Earth*, Chicago: University of Chicago Press; Martin, 1978, ed., *supra* note 17; Ted Williams, 1986, "A Harvest of Eagles," *Audubon*, 88, No. 5; George Wuerthner, 1987, "An Ecological View of the Indian," *Earth First!*, Vol. 7, No. 7.; and David Foreman (cited in Churchill and Jaimes, 1992, *supra* note 16).

144. Ramachandra Guha, 1989, "Radical American Environmentalism and Wilderness Preservation: A Third World Critique," *Environmental Ethics*, Vol. 11, No. 1, pp. 73 and 74.

145. *Ibid.*, at p. 77.

146. Simon Brascoupé, 1992, "Inside the Wall: Pathways of Tradition," *Akwe:kon*, Vol. IX, No. 4, p. 12.

147. Johnson, 1992, *supra* note 76 at p. 76.

148. Vandana Shiva, 1993, *Monocultures of the Mind*, New Jersey: Zed Books, p. 9.

149. Vine Deloria, 1969, *Custer Died For Your Sins*, New York: Macmillan, p. 172.

150. There are some who regard it as inevitable as death:

> Gradual assimilation of distinctive minorities to the culture of the surrounding society over the long term is probably a natural and normal phenomenon. But this does not make forced assimilation permissible, any more that the fact that human death is a natural and normal phenomenon makes murder permissible. (James W. Nickel, 1991, "The Rights of Indigenous Peoples," *Working Paper* 10/91-3, University of Colorado at Boulder: Center for Values and Social Policy, p. 7)

Yet why should we suppose that there is anything "natural and normal" about the death of distinctive cultures? Or that cultural pluralism is no more than a stage en route to some inevitable cultural homogenization? While the dominant culture might welcome their assimilation, historically and currently subordinated cultures have resisted it. And where assimilation is resisted, all assimilation is forced assimilation. Its "gradualness" is simply a matter of tactics. Part of what is so invidious about cultural imperialism is the gradualness of its means.

NATIVE AMERICAN IDENTITY AND SURVIVAL: INDIGENISM AND ENVIRONMENTAL ETHICS

*M. A. Jaimes

I. Environmental Decline and the Marginalization of Native People

The destruction wrought by the technology and the homogenizing tendencies of modern post-industrial society is staggering. The statistical picture in terms of human overpopulation on the planet is bleak. There are presently 5.4 billion people on the planet today. Between 2030 and 2050, 10 billion people will be competing for the Earth's resources. In addition, developed countries, such as the U.S. and Canada, greatly contribute to the destruction of the planet through over-consumption, which itself is a result of overpopulation and over-consumerism. This is illustrated in a sobering trend. With only five percent of the world's people, the U.S. used one-third of the world's flow of non-renewable resources and one-fourth of the gross planetary production of goods and services. The average U.S. citizen uses nearly three hundred times as much energy as the average citizen, for example, in Bangladesh.[1] In 1992, as many as 17,500 plant and animal species will disappear forever. The number of endangered animals on the list maintained by the U.S. Department of Interior has grown from seventy-eight species on the original 1967 list to more that 1,200 which are facing imminent extinction today. On the Hawaiian islands, "more plants and animals . . . are extinct or on the endangered species list than in the rest of the [U.S.]."[2] Although extinction is considered a natural phenomena, what is unnatural is the rapid and alarming rate at which this is occurring in the modern age. Humans are the primary cause of this mass extinction.[3] In the dystopia of modern technology society, there is a tendency to downplay the overall ecological blight of the modern world or to reduce the discussion of the issue to a federal budget problem.[4]

At the same time that this ecological destruction is occurring, Native Peoples are treated as second class citizens and even third world people throughout the Americas. Many, if not most, American Indians in the U.S. and Canada are living under third world conditions in reservation-based tribal communities as well as in ghettoized pockets in urban settings. Indians in South and Central America are struggling for their very existence. A case in point is the Amazonian peoples in the Brazilian Rainforest whose homeland is endangered. This will result in the destruction of the medicinal benefits from that bioregion to humanity and to the ecosystem.

In the past, non-Indians who learned from the ways and views of the Indians did not attribute their inspiration or the knowledge they appropriated from these people to the ones from whom they derived it. Thus, Native people have not only been physically but also culturally marginalized. Thoreau's *Walden* is illustrative of this. This work is a literary classic that made him the 1800s guru of the transcendentalist movement. However, he gave no credit to his local Native guides who, as Eastern Woodland Indians, provided him with information and insight.[5] This tendency toward denigrating the possible and actual contributions of indigenous peoples to new approaches to human problems continues unabated.

In today's discourse on environmental ethics, most current non-Native scholars[6] and activists, such as Earth first, Green Peace, etc., actually play down the role of Native peoples in developing solutions to environmental problems. They tend to ignore the historical contributions of indigenous peoples' current efforts to incorporate their cultural traditions into economic enterprises. These sustainable economies hold to an environmental ethics based on a relationship with Nature and upon lifeways inspired by an indigenous world view. These voices have recognized a Native Wisdom but are cautious in their acknowledgement of what Native peoples and cultures might have to offer as solutions to the present environmental concerns and ecological crisis.

It is the position of this paper that the degradation of the environment and the marginalization of indigenous peoples are not unrelated. The marginalization of Native peoples has involved a suppression of the indigenous world view, and thus has suppressed indigenous traditional practices that create a proper relationship between human beings and their environment. Indeed, civilization has paid a high price for ignoring the indigenous world view, which would provide an alternative that would allow human beings to avoid the environmental decline that the planet is currently experiencing. Sincere traditional indigenous peoples can show the way toward respecting all living creatures, non-humans as well as humans, on what the Iroquois (Haundenasanee) people call "Turtle Island." Hence, this essay will focus on issues and agendas among Native American leaders, activists, and scholars who are concerned with Native peoples' identity and survival within the broader contexts of environmental concerns, economic development, and the international dimensions of human rights for indigenous peoples. As we work our way out of our ecological blight with an identity forged from Indigenism, what emerges is a world view that is similar to the Hopi vision of balance and harmony that leads us to perceive the world in terms of natural rhythms, like a Navajo chant that implores us to always "walk in beauty."

II. Indigenism in Theory

Let's begin by asking, what is Indigenism? Mander develops a list of how the ways of Native peoples and their cultures differ from those of modern, technological society.[7] He identifies general differences in almost all social spheres. In terms of economics, the Native peoples tend to have communal property, subsistence production, barter systems, low-impact technologies, and collective production. In contrast, modern society has private ownership, surplus production, currency systems, high-impact technology, and competitive production. In terms of political relations, Native people have consensual processes, direct "participatory" democracy, and laws embedded in oral traditions. On the other hand, modern society has centralized executive authorities, representative democracy, and written laws. In respect to their social relations, they differ, generally, in terms of matrilineality versus patriarchy, extended versus nuclear families, and low versus high population density. Finally, regarding differences in world view, the Native peoples are polytheistic, derive an understanding of the world from the natural order's rhythms and cycles of life, and include animals and plants as well as other natural features in their conceptions of spirituality, which the cultural anthropologists call animism and totemism. Indeed, from the Native point of view, a river has the natural right to run its course without destructive interference from mankind. Modern societies, on the other hand, are monotheistic, view the environment as something which is mechanically controlled for maximum human labor and the "profit motive" at the expense of health and the general quality of life, and exclude non-humans from any spirituality. There are also overall differences in the time/space/place constructions between the two world views.[8] These differences provide the basis for a conceptualization of Indigenism that counters the negative connotations of its meaning in third world countries, where it has become synonymous with the "primitive," or with backwardness among supersitious peoples.

The pre-Columbian indigenous people of the Americas understood that all living entities exist in a web of intra-dependency and within a finite biotic environment. Natural rules for balance and order needed to be followed, and humans needed to act within the ecosystem so as to maintain the interconnectedness and integrated harmony required for mutual reciprocity. Hence, reciprocity and not sovereignty is the key concept in this respect. This mutual reciprocity is a type of intra-dependency in which the relating members are interacting members *within* a larger whole. Indigenism is a reworking of these concepts which are basic to an American Indian identity on the threshold of the Twenty-first Century. Native American identity, past and present, is linked with a vision of Indigenism that is formed in the context of the land and humanity's natural relationship to it.

One reason that Native values have been undermined in the environmental movement has been presented by Cornell.[9] He points out that early Native peoples were conservationists, who sustained balance, order, and harmony with the natural world. This is in contrast to preservationists, who (because they have let the situation develop into a crisis) must make sacrifices in order to prevent the possible extinction of a part of the natural world. When the indigenous cultures were predominant, the depletion of natural resources and the extinction of plants and animals were not yet critical problems. Today, the environmental movement haggles over pro-intervention versus anti-intervention by humans as approaches to the relationship between humans and the non-human aspects of the environment. The first argues that it is almost always legitimate to impose the human will on nature. The second argues that no such intervention should be undertaken. Instead, one should have the aim of conserving nature. What these points of view do not take into account, then, is the balance of nature from a conservationist stance. Preservationists, on the other hand, are inspired by dichotomies and polarizations derived from Christian dogmatism about good and bad behavior, the sublime versus the profane, and the sacred threatened by the wicked and ultimate evil.

There is also a link between the above concepts and those described by Vandana Shiva.[10] She argues that "monocultures of the mind" are destroying the biodiversity that is essential for the balance, order, and ultimate preservation of our bioregional natural habitats for both human and non-human survival. She asserts that the alternative lies in a Fifth World Stage of human development in which the homocentric and egocentric orientations of Eurocentric ethics are transcended.

Bioregionalism. Bioregionalism, with its emphasis on natural systems as ecosystems, can be identified as a significant attribute of Indian identity and survival. When this is linked to the land and the environment as an indigenous homeland, this is also essential to the Native concept of nationhood predicated on kinship and land-based religions. Bioregions are geographic areas having common characteristics of soil, water-sheds, climate, and native plants and animals that exist within the whole planetary biosphere as unique and intrinsic contributive parts. However, this conceptualization goes beyond the geographical terrain, because it includes a terrain of consciousness as well. Knowledge discovered from the environment, its natural features as well as its plants and animals, provide clues and therefore guidance as to how humans are to relate to the world and to conduct their reciprocal relationship within this particular bioregion. Therefore, bioregionalism:

> differs from a regional politics of place in its emphasis on natural systems. It includes all the interdependent forms and processes of life, along with humans and human consciousness, i.e., as "a place of being."[11]

It is in this physical and mental relation to the environment, then, that "we find the physical truth of our being."[12] This "biological realism" designates an interrelated and more or less self-subsistence whole within which human beings should find their appropriate place. Thus, to attempt to introduce agriculture or a particular agricultural technique into regions not suited for it would not be exhibiting a bioregional form of thought or action. For example, in Africa among the indigenous peoples, the policies of various governments have tried to replace pastoralism with agriculturalism in areas in which the first fits into the environment while the second doesn't. The Euroamericans imposed the same changes on the so-called hunting and gathering Native peoples of the eastern and northeastern bioregions, while Churchill makes the same assessment about parts of middle America.[13] Hence, a bioregional consciousness is 1) contextually-bound but varies within the context, 2) (w)holistic in that it thinks of the world as consisting of unified wholes, but in terms of multiunified wholes among intra-dependent and reciprocal parts, 3) pluralistic and thinks of the world not in terms of one unified whole but in terms of many unified wholes, each of which is capable of existing on its own, and 4) historical in that it thinks of the world in terms of processes by which wholes arise through reciprocal interactions and relations of the parts over long periods of time.[14] Bioregionalism is also linked with *emic* knowledge, as Native wisdom derived from within, in contrast to *etic* knowledge, which is knowledge imposed by others from the outside.[15]

Native American identity is also connected with a bioregional understanding of and relationship with the natural environment that is both respectful and reciprocal in the interdynamics of survival for all active entities. This preservation of a bioregion and of the bioregional consciousness based upon it is what the land/water/resources and cultural/life struggles (including the battles over "sacred sited") among traditional-orientated Native peoples are all about.

Bioregionalism is a state of consciousness that one can take with him/her from one habitat to another. It is an approach to life and existence that requires, indeed mandates, a reciprocal relationship with Nature and its resources, for to have any other relationship to it is to risk death and eventual extinction. Such extinction has occurred in many bioregions in the world, for example, among the plants and animals of the Florida Everglades and the Native fishing societies of the Northwest.

The Native Land Ethic. This concept has been described by Non-Indians as well as by Native scholars.[16] It is a significant element in any discourse about environmental ethics. This is an ethical orientation that puts restraints on the human will, which is motivated by egoism and greed and which is destructive of the natural order. Most notably, Ward Churchill has profoundly articulated this "Native Ethic" in his *Struggle for the Land.* The Native Land Ethic consists of a mutually beneficial and respectful relationship between Native peoples and the land. It requires an ethical relationship to the environment combined with a sustainable economy for self-sufficiency. Churchill writes:

> In simplest terms, the American Indian world view may be this: Human beings are free (indeed encouraged) to develop their innate

> capabilities, but only in ways that do not infringe upon other elements—called "relations," in the fullest dialectical sense of the word—of nature.[17]

Elsewhere he notes the significance of the Native (Great Plains) greeting/blessing, *metakeyasi*, which means "all my relation" and which refers to Native kinship and reciprocity. For example, the Buffalo is considered to be an ancestor to the Great Plains peoples, and even a sacred symbol. In this intra-dependent connection and continuity between the generations, therefore, one does not mistreat or abuse one's relatives or ancestors. There are many blessings, prayers, and rituals offered to honor this special intra-dependent relationship between the two entities and to respect the connection and continuity between the generations. In Native kinship systems, family relations are meant to be ones of mutual aid and support. Just as Nature provides for the aid and support of human beings, so in a reciprocal manner human beings are meant to provide for the aid and support of Nature, as they do for each other in the kinship systems and clan structures of communal societies in land-based cultures.

Winona LaDuke has developed this concept of reciprocal relations with the ecosystem from an Anishinabeg (at White Earth) perspective. She has referred to this as *pimaatisiiwin*, which means "the good life" or "continuous rebirth." This concept of continuous rebirth is based on the "cyclical thinking" found among the Ojibway and Cree peoples of North America.[18] Among these people, reciprocal relationships in kinship are well documented and are manifested in the totemism which is present in the taditional cultures of these Native peoples. This is also what Deloria refers to as "the natural rights of the universe,"[19] which includes non-human species as well as natural features of the environment such as rivers, mountains, etc. Among traditional Native Hawaiians (Kanåka Måoli), Haunani Kay Trask writes that the onset of European explorers to the islands in 1778 "shattered two millennia of Hawaiian civilization characterized by an indigenous way of caring for the land, called *målama 'åina*".[20] These indigenous visions seek balance and harmony in the ecological holism that exists between indigenous peoples and the natural world in a mutually benefitting interdynamic of integration and intra-dependence, as in a living organism. These visions also develop the parasitic consequences of not respecting this symbiosis.

The Natural Order is both communally-based and hierarchical, at the same time, since there is an inherent order and hierarchy in any ecosystem which includes human beings. However, it is not human-centered at the expense of other non-human entities and spheres of "being." In Native Cultures, one finds that age, which transcends gender, is correlated with experience and wisdom and is therefore required for leadership. It therefore behooves humans to follow and respect the dictates of the natural world, for to do otherwise is to increase our chances of extinction by ignoring our reciprocal relations with natural entities that we rely on for our very survival on this planet. In this respect, then, all humans are only meant to be manifestations of their reciprocal relationships within the Natural World. They find human expression, as individuals as well as within a group, within their environment as their natural habitat—rather than shape the natural features to human will for short-term convenience and long-term demise. This is what the individual Native songs, dances, group ceremonies, and rituals were all about. They were an integration of the human spirit with the Great Spirit or the Creator, and all in honor and reverence to Mother Earth and the Cosmos as our spiritual guides.

These Native values have been undermined by Eurocentric ones that promote immature leaders, aggressive power, and monetary greed, with the consequences that a few have too much at the expense of the many! Today the Natural Order and hierarchy has been supplanted by the imposition of the human will upon nature, which arises from attitudes derived from an Euroamerican "modern" society that has placed an abstract value, i.e., a monetary one, on just about everything. This capitalist system that espouses "free enterprise" as the vehicle of this malaise creates disparity and inequality among non-human as well as human populations. Such a delusional system determines the importance of all things significant and necessary for our existence, as well as the natural entities. The order and the hierarchy derived from it create relations of political subordination and domination, which contributes to the present-day entropy, malaise, and dystopia that is destroying culture for technology and pro-development, which in turn is further shrinking our planetary natural resources.

The Fourth World. According to the concept of the Fourth or Host World, indigenous people exist in a "guardianship" relationship with the natural environment—the animals, plants, minerals, and natural features in it. This mutual guardianship involves human respect and honor bestowed on the environment as the natural world, and in turn Mother Nature reciprocates in kind by Her abundance in resources and hopeful benevolence. In this context, since humans are capable of great good as well as wrong, it behooves us to be cognizant of our guardian responsibilities and obligations. This involves sustaining the balance and harmony that needs to exist among humans and their environment. This Fourth World concept is considered in terms of a transitional cycle in human existence. Many Native people have predicted their cultural decline as a result of contacts with outsiders. However, they also predicted that there would be an eventual renewal and restoration of their culture and its ways. This stage will overcome the dominant/subordinate construction that exists in the world today between the First, Second, and Third worlds. Indigenous people, as natural peoples of the Americas, will overcome this oppression of domination and subordination that forces many to live in "third world" conditions, and they will return to their rightful place and relationship to their homelands—what has been called the Host World.[21] Hence, indigenous people will lead the way in restoring balance and harmony in our natural existence with the Earth.

The Fifth World. This world view emphasizes biodiversity that is cultural as well as biological in a particular bioregion in which indigenous groups exist in reciprocal relations with the land and with non-human species. This world view is based on an ecocentric ethics that counters homocentrism and egocentrism. According to Shiva, it is a transcendent stage that will overcome the third world oppression suffered by Native people worldwide.

III. Indigenism in Practice

John Echohawk, Director of the Native American Rights Fund, has identified six major issues important to Native Americans—housing, health care, education, environmental protection, economic development, and sovereignty. As a Native cultural broker, Echohawk is no visionary and, therefore, sees within a limiting Euroamerican paradigm in order to resolve only legal issues. In addition, two other major issues that are facing Native Americans are cultural autonomy and cultural integrity, a problem due to the onslaught of genocide, ethnocide, and ecocide. Native Americans need a context of genuine self-determination and self-sufficiency for their social, cultural, economic, and political survival in the Twenty-First Century. The primary challenge faced by Native Americans in the near future is biological and cultural survival so that indigenism can remain as an approach to human survival.

Social Issues. Most reservation-based tribal communities urgently need to overcome their "third world" conditions. Native peoples are confronted with social problems that rank comparatively high in indices, such as, alcoholism correlated with early death, poor health, disease, family abuse, youth suicides, and low-achievement in mainstream school systems.[22] The Pine Ridge Indian reservation in Shannon County, South Dakota has the most extreme conditions of poverty, which have even worsened. It has moved from the state's eighth poorest in 1970 to the poorest in 1980. In 1990 it had 63 percent of its Native residents living below the federal poverty line, and unemployment was climbing to 85 percent.[23] This is also correlated with more older women with meager incomes heading up families. It has also been reported that the infant mortality rate among American Indians and Native Alaskan tribes, in general, varies from 10.7 to 19.9 per thousand live births.[24] The urban or "ethnic" Indians fair no better under a different set of colonizing circumstances. They have often left their reservation communities due to the deplorable conditions on them, which are themselves caused by coercive government federal policy due to an assimilationist agenda. The urban Indian phenomena developed through several policy periods—Removal and Allotment in the 1800s, Reorganization in the 1930s, Relocation which began in the 1940s and continues to the present, and Termination which was implemented as an "official" policy in the 1950s. All Federal policy has been covertly enforced by "census-taking" and "federal-recognition" regulations. The latter includes the passage of restrictive legislation whose goal is to prevent many Native peoples from "generically" (the way the law reads for federal certification of individuals) identifying as American Indian or Native American. This is so even though U.S. colonization has mandated federal Indian policy and jurisdictional decisions that have broken down tribal structures and affiliations. Such colonizing policies, which are based on assimilationist agendas that subordinate Native individuals as well as groups further, are presently being carried out and are a form of cultural genocide referred to as "statistical extermination."[25]

A critical problem facing modern, technological society is how to stem overpopulation that is causing ecocide without using population control methods that are genocidal toward peoples living in third world conditions. There are documented cases of sterilization of Native women by the federal Indian Health Service clinics in the 1970s. Most notably, a report disseminated by Women of All Red Nations (WARN) presented its research on the subject. They found that there were more cases than the federal Indian Health Services were willing to admit in which Native women did not give their consent before they were subject to permanent birth control by sterilization. In this context, Indian children on the Pine Ridge Reservation and elsewhere have been recently targeted as "quinea pigs" for HIV testing.[26] Such heal and ethical issues are also linked with genetic engineering that is going on among targeted Native groups because of their biological and cultural differences and because of their isolation from mainstream populations.

Cultural Issues. Self-determination and self-sufficiency are required by Native peoples in order to preserve and develop their cultural heritage and integrity. Deward Walker, an anthropologist with both a theoretical and an applied background, has worked with Native peoples in preparing and presenting legal cases for the preservation of traditional cultural practices. He has conceptualized these as cultural and legal rights in what is termed "sacred geography." He has fought for the recognition of specific "sacred sites," among the Great Plains tribal nations who live in South Dakota. In the perception of these natural religions, animism and totemism are strongly developed in the clan moieties. These indicate the bilateral and (w)holistic relations between humans and the animal and plant worlds, which all have "souls."[27] However, the record for winning recognition for the rights of Indians to religious freedom in the U.S. and for the ability of Native people to practice their natural religions and spirituality has not been a successful one. This is more true the higher up the legal ladder a court case finds itself. In recent jurisdictional matters, the Supreme Court decisions on the *Lyng v. Northwest Indian Cemetary Protective Association*[28] and *Employment Division, Department of Human Resources of Oregon v. Smith* cases have blatantly denied Indian religious rights in this arena.[29] Sandra Day O'Connor has been a prime negator of such rights.

In the realm of Indian Art, there is a congressional law (P.L. 101-644-104 *Stat.* 4662; appended to a 1930s Indian Arts and Crafts Act) that prohibits a "non-federally recognized" Native individual from selling his/her art, or for an art gallery from doing so while claiming that the art is Native American. This is backed by a prison sentence as well as by fines that may lead to bankruptcy. This law is implemented by the Bureau of Indian Affairs (BIA), which implements regulations for "BIA certification," and it includes a "quarter blood" standard that operates much like a eugenics code. No other "ethnic" population has currently had such a standard imposed upon it. Even though there has been and continues to be a loud cry of resistance to this genocidal policy, there are neo-conservative Indian spokespersons among the "federally-recognized" Indians who are supporting it. They do so on the duplicitous rationale that the fewer Indians there are, the more federal monies there will be available to serve the interests of themselves and their political constituencies. This is a highly politicized situation that is creating schism, factionalism, and divisiveness in Indian families as well as in tribal communities. There are even cases in which the BIA has certified individuals to be "instant Indians" for political favor. However, a larger number have been conveniently reclassified by the federal government as "ethnic/minorities," which negates their Native heritage and ancestry. This has happened particularly among those of mixed-blood identities, i.e., the mestizos of the southwest and the métis of the northern territories bordering the United States and Canada.

In the area of educational reform, there is a greater need for more genuine multiculturalism that is sensitive to the traditional cultural needs of Native peoples, especially in regards to the preservation of Native languages. There is a need for the deconstruction of the prevailing non-Indian social/moral hegemony in all U.S. institutions. This requires the decolonization of Native Americans in order to free them from American Eurocentrism, which is an oppressive force.[30]

Economic Issues. Self-determination and self-sufficiency are also primary concerns for tribal nations when it comes to issues of economic development and environmental protection. These rights of Native people are based on treaties (approximately four hundred have been ratified) and other agreements, which were like "real estate" transactions between two nations.[31] During the early conquests, Native people gave up their homelands and were relocated in removal campaigns; for example, the Cherokee "Trail of Tears" and the Navajo/Diné people's "The Longest Walk" in the mid-1800s. Both of these resulted in many deaths and was done in order to remove the Native people so that they would be out of the way of "white" settlement and Euroamerican imperialism. These arrangements stipulated treaty appropriations between the Continental government or American Republic and various Indian nations so as to enable them to exist and survive after the conquest—that is at least how the Natives understood them. A Eurocentric mind-set has enabled authorities of the federal government, via the Department of Interior, to assert "eminent domain" under its fraudulent "trust" responsibilities to tribal nations. This has given the federal government the power to seize Indian lands at any time. These unethical scenarios are influenced by pro-development schemes motivated by transnational corporate interests, whose lobbying operations curry political favor from executive cabinet members. Such policies are systematically taken at the expense of traditional positions on anti-development among Native people who still hold to their cultural integrity, in both rural and urban settings.[32]

Yet, there has been a consistent debate among reservation-based Native peoples over pro-development schemes, which pursue the "profit motive" and which include proposals to open gambling operations on tribal land. "Traditionalists" are pitted against "moderate" and "progressive" elements, particularly in regards to mining and the use of other natural resources.[33] Economic scenarios that lead to land erosion have been criticized as "environmental racism,"[34] ecological genocide, and "radioactive colonization."[35] There is systematic evidence that a distinct group of people, their habitat, and their cultural way of life in a community have been labelled as expendable by federal entities and state authorities in conjunction with corporate interests that have destructive pro-development schemes. These schemes involve, for example, uranium mining that leaves radioactive tailings, the use of land as toxic dump sites, chemical contamination from leakages, overall pollution from industry, as well as land erosion from over-grazing. It is often claimed that these resistance groups are, due to their "backwardness," in the way of "progress" and that such development is deemed "for the common good." During the Nixon administration, some Native areas—the Four Corners area among the Navajo, Black Mesa of the Hopi, and the Acoma and Laguna Pueblo—were declared to be "national sacrifice areas." All these locations are in the southwestern states, and designating them sacrifice areas has dire health consequences for the surrounding inhabitants as well as their habitats. Native lands have also been targeted to "host" nuclear sites and other military activity by the U.S. government, as in the Dann dump case among the Western Shoshone of Nevada.[36] Only recently have Indian lands become subjected to "environmental impact statements," which assess the potentially negative consequences of pro-development enterprises affecting the peoples of that area. However, the bureaucracy and corruption (i.e., bribery to tribal leaders and cultural brokers) that abounds in these hazardous schemes are more often than not at the expense of prevention, and ultimately the health and survival of the Native peoples of North America. Peter Matthiessen has grasped acutely the double-bind in which Native peoples have found themselves in controversies over the pros and cons of development.[37] On the one hand, there are the economic needs for survival in the modern pro-development world. On the other, are the potential health hazards to their habitats, as they attempt to establish economic self-sufficiency. Tribal leadership is often torn between more immediate goals, such as reservation employment, and more long-term consequences, such as health hazards and environmental devastation. On the other hand, there are other non-Indian authors, such as Jerry Mander,[38] who have tended to "romanticize" all reservation-based Native peoples as the only "anti-development" pockets among "real" Indians. This is done at the expense of the larger urban-based Indian population located in the U.S., who are somehow "less Indian" because of their urbanization. Actually, traditional Native people and their pro-environment agendas can be sound among the latter as well.

In respect to Native economic self-determination and self-sufficiency, there is the issue of the unique set of human rights that allow for indigenous people, who have a traditional group identity and who desire to maintain their land-based traditions in a communal society, to prosper. There is an urgent need to build communal self-sufficiency by self-rule. This is not what tribal governance is necessarily about, since some tribal leaders are promoting pro-development agendas at the expense of their constituencies' well-being. Based on what can be called internal sovereignty, self-rule requires that Native peoples assert the prerogatives of "first water rights." These are laws that give rights to Native peoples over the source of the water (called the Winter's Doctrine) in their habitat.[39] Asserting such rights is essential to gaining control of tribal land bases and other natural resources so that Native nations can achieve viable economic self-sufficiency. This is part of the "land and life struggles" for the land, the water, and other resources that provide the conditions for the possibility of a cultural restoration, as well as the preservation of important sacred religious sites.

These issues need to be addressed in international arenas and within human rights forums. The rights of all indigenous peoples need to be restored as well as realized in practice. This requires Natives and environmental activists to work in coalitions and alliances for human rights that would affirm the rights of indigenous peoples to exist and to preserve their cultural traditions.[40] This struggle should take place in conjunction with grassroots struggles, ethno-national movements, and bioregional biodiversity. Hence, in regards to the human rights of indigenous peoples, the international arenas need to more effectively address these issues as well as those concerning cross-national boundaries and transnational corporate interests. In this regard, the issues raised by NAFTA, which has been called the "international termination" of indigenous peoples' rights, need to be addressed. These activities demand new constructions of political accountability in world affairs predicated upon confederacy models, as well as decentralization that builds on community needs and cultural rights.[41]

Since the Columbian re-examination of 1992, there is the recognition that pre-conquest Native cultures have been strong hemispheric role models in terms of traditional economic sustainability that involves less-polluting "soft" technologies, decentralized and less human-centered forms of organization, natural living styles that recycle wastes, and labor intensive in contrast to capital intensive economic methods.[42] Currently, there are efforts being made to reclaim and restore Native lands with the express purpose of developing bioregional enterprises for the best interests of the ecosystem instead of for human-centered, pro-development schemes. One such enterprise is called the Buffalo Commons Project, which is focused on the restoration and reinstatement of the Buffalo to the Great Plains region. Non-Indians have also been leading advocates of the proposal. The major goal of this restoration project is to re-establish buffalo ranching on the Great Plains as an economic enterprise.[43] It is also one that has cultural, ecological, and even spiritual significance from a Native American perspective, particularly among those who are descendants of the Great Plains Indians. For them, this is part of a broader vision involving the restoration of their traditional culture in that region. However, land erosion due to overgrazing and other destructive proctices still need to be addressed in this enterprise, as well as others in the context of Native environmental ethics.

In addition, aboriginal approaches to farming should be investigated. These include the use of hybridization in multi-planting for food production, the positive benefits of "slash and burn" techniques in deforestation, the *conuco* and *milpa* systems among earlier Native people, and the remarkable "floating gardens" (called *chinampas*) of the Aztecs (Mexicanos), who had considerable agricultural sophistication.[44] Generally speaking, one of the reasons why Native populations were deliberately kept low within the respective nations was to sustain balance and harmony. If a situation arose whereby a particular area had become overused or eroded due to a too lengthy occupation by human beings, whole groups were moved and encouraged to migrate. There were even some peoples who rotated their seasonal homes, as was the case with the Great Plains cultures, who were denigrated by Euroamericans for not being "civilized" enough to establish more permanent settlements. If a problem arose in respect to a particular plant or animal species or regarding a natural feature of the environment from the overdepletion of resources due to human occupation, then measures were immediately implemented to correct this before it was too late to do so.

Political Issues. In respect to political self-determination and self-rule, one must examine the concept of sovereignty as an Eurocentric concept used to justify empire-building and reassess its validity in the context of the reality of the "global village" today. The crux of the problem is, how can an entity, human or not, be sovereign when each lives in intra-dependency with others? This impacts any human interaction with the natural elements in rapid and even devastating ways. This is evidenced by the extent of endangered species and by the number of people on the planet. One way in which this concept of political sovereignty operates is in dominant/subordinate constructions that are apparent in the overall scheme of Indian/federal government relations.[45] Federal Indian policy and jurisdictional decisions in the courts appear to pit national/domestic "civil rights" against "tribal sovereignty." This distinction is actually inherent in the Eurocentric paradigm wrought by imperialist schemes for empire-building, and it originated in the model of European monarchies.

There are several legal cases that have documented these problems. Most of these affect Native women in both the U.S. and Canada. Among these court cases is *Zarr v. Barlow* in which a Pomo woman in California sued the BIA and won for denying her educational services, since the Bureau did not recognize her even though her tribal community had her on its membership rolls. In cases involving loss of tribal status and housing benefits due to intermarriage, there were two U.S. court cases (not related), *Martinez v. Southern Ute Tribe* and *Martinez v. Santa Clara Pueblo*. Both Martinez women sued their tribes based on their "civil rights," and they both lost their cases. Both federal decisions conveniently used "tribal sovereignty" as a justification for investing power in the predominantly male-dominated tribal councils that arose after the 1934 Indian Reorganization Act. This Act dismantled the traditional tribal governance, which was based on matrilineal descent. In the 1978 case, a Santa Clara woman had married intertribally to a Navajo man who came to live with her at the pueblo, since he came from a traditionally matrilineal society. In these court proceedings, an ethnographer brought to light the fact that the pueblo had been matrilineal prior to its reorganization by the federal government. However, this did not support Martinez' position nor the position of her children, who were plaintiffs as well.

In the Sandra Sappier Lovelace case (1970s to 1980s) on the Togique Reserve in New Brunswick, Canada, a very different outcome occurred than in the two Martinez cases in the U.S., despite similar plaintiff issues. Lovelace and her son also lost their tribal (called reserve in Canada) status when she married a non-Indian and left, even though they still had relatives on the reservation. When she returned with her son after leaving her non-Indian husband, she was not provided adequate housing and was forced to depend on her relatives, as a welfare case. With the support of Native women's groups on the reservation, Lovelace took her case all the way to the United Nations, which then pressured the Canadian government to amend its Indian Rights Act of 1985 so as to prevent male-dominated tribal councils from such corrupt practices against Native women and their offsprings who's rights were violated in the name of tribal sovereignty. The Canadian decision was, of course, condemned by tribal leadership for interfering with "tribal sovereignty." Such cases as these highlight the dire conditions Native peoples can find themselves in since Euroamerican conquest and colonization. This is particularly the case for Native women whose legal histories are documented by these court cases and decisions and whose situational problems are created by this Eurocentric idea of sovereignty.

Sociographic data indicates that there is a high rate of both Indian males and females marrying outside their tribes. About 50 percent of both Native genders marry non-Indians.[46] It has been found that Indian women are more likely to lose their tribal status along with their offspring, when compared to Indian males who, as political leaders, add their non-Indian wives as well as offspring to the rolls. This has been referred to as a kind of "trickle-down patriarchy" wrought by U.S. colonization and interference in internal Indian affairs. This works against the reciprocal relations between genders in traditional kinship and matrilineal societies that can still, although with difficulty, exist among most indigenous cultures and nations.

It is in terms of the cultural traditions of kinship systems that the concept of nationhood among communal societies needs to be explored. This theoretical discourse also needs to address the origins of "democratic" ideals among the indigenous confederacies, such as the Iroquois Confederacy, as it relates to the elements of kinship traditions.[47] These elaborate systems involved social relationships that included exogamy, adoption, and naturalization of "outside" people.[48] These values and ideals allowed for traditional Native societies to be inclusive rather than exclusive. The latter is the case with the federal government and its restrictive criteria for determining who is a member of a tribe. This membership, therefore, was not beholden to biology alone, and race was not a construct used to determine tribal enrollment, as it is today.[49] The Navajo, as traditional Diné, incorporated what were called the Nakai clans. This occurred as a result of Navajo men intermarrying with Mexican Indian women, who followed matrilineal traditions, to illustrate just one traditional kinship system.

Hence, Native nations have not been able to assert their full sovereignty since the European conquest and their colonization. Instead the "treatied" Indians and "federally recognized" groups have had to succumb to a racist paternalism under the so-called trust responsibility imposed upon them by the federal government.[50] The term "sovereign" itself is a Eurocentric political tool that is derived from the European belief in the "divine right of kings." This is a belief that justified monarchies in early Europe and which is manifest in an Euroamerican paradigm for imperialism. The U.S. today may reign militarily supreme, only because it has recently shown it can blow up more people than any other national power at a given time. However, it still needs the support of its allies and the United Nations before it *usually* will act out its aggression on its "enemies," even if it's after the fact in *post hoc* politics. The United States also does not have economic sovereignty, which is what the international "free enterprise" and trade and commerce campaigns as evident in the European Common Market, GATT, and NAFTA agendas. It appears that the aim of these agendas, then, is to Euroamericanize Europe and Mexico as well. In this context, how can one be environmentally sovereign, as a single entity or nation, when the natural world will always have the last word because of the interdynamics of intra-dependency and the essentialness of reciprocity? This is especially so since we have become a "global village" with no buffer zones, and, to use an analogy draw from chaos theory, the flap of a butterfly's wings in Brazil may cause a tidal wave in the Pacific. In these terms, therefore, we are truly all related (*metakeyasi*), connected, and integrated with each other, humans and non-humans alike. Even so, Native peoples need to maintain and even escalate their liberation struggles for decolonization from U.S. domination in their own homelands. The identity and survival of indigenous cultures and lifeways with Native spirituality depend on this outcome.

IV. Getting Beyond *Koyaanisqatsi*, the "Crazy Life"

The Hopi people, dwelling on their ancestral pueblo mesas in Arizona, have a word, derived from their prophecies, which means the "crazy life," *Koyaanisqatsi*. This is a life that is out of balance and harmony with the natural world.[51] There could be no better description of modern pro-technological society. The way out of this environmental entropy and ecological dystopia is to restore balance and harmony and to create circumstances in which humans have a more natural relationship with their environment. The natural world should be considered sacred. Indigenism, as a way of approaching life with a more natural and balanced world, requires one to consider his/her existence as a spiritual quest as well as the socio-cultural creation of identity. This is in contrast to the socio-political division that is characteristic of Indian politics of Native identity today and which was created by U.S. colonialist policy and law which was imposed upon the indigenous people of North America. Hence, the answers for humanity will not be found in an ideology of scientism, genetic engineering, nor nanotechnology, as we come to terms with our alienation from the natural order and the cycle of life and rebirth.

However, Indigenism can only flourish if the Native peoples of the Americas have the cultural, economic, and political self-determination and self-sufficiency to rediscover and sustain not only the theory but the practice of this integrated and intra-dependent sacred relationship with Nature. Indigenous peoples, as natural peoples, have a long tradition of imaging the Earth as "Mother Earth," while environmental and feminist discourses develop a similar concept in the "Gaia" hypothesis, which has been revived from Greek lore. Both conceive of the world as "one organic entity."[52] It is time for humanity to bring together these ecological metaphors in order to develop a shared vision and common ground upon which to confront the environmental dilemma that has been brought on by human activity and to do so with universal humanity, philanthropy, and wisdom. It is time for these views to inspire a symbiosis to replace the parasitic situation so as to engender an environmentally-conscious economics for non-human as well as human survival on our planetary journey.

**Dr. M. Annette Jaimes is Instructor/Lecturer at the Center for Studies of Ethnicity and Race in America at the University of Colorado at Boulder.*

Notes

1. Roy Gallant, 1990, *The Peopling of the Earth*, New York: MacMillan Publishers.

2. Haunani Kay Trask, 1993, *From a Native Daughter: Colonialism and Sovereignty in Hawaii*, Monroe, Maine: Common Courage Press, p. 4. Her book provides for a statistical profile of the shocking impact of corporate tourism on Hawaii. She states:

   > Over thirty years ago, at statehood, Hawaii's residents outnumbered tourists by more than two to one. Today, tourists outnumber residents by six to one; they outnumber Native Hawaiians by thirty to one. (p. 183)

3. Wolf, 1993, *supra* note 1.

4. Nikki Wilkins, 1992, "The Endangered Species Act: A Fight for Survival in 1992," *URSUS: The Cornell Forum for Environmental Issues*, Ithaca, N.Y.: Cornell University, II, 1-2, pp. 4-6.

5. George Cornell, 1992, "Native Americans and Environmental Thought: Thoreau and the Transcendentalists," *Ake:kon Journal*, IX, 3, pp. 6-13.

6. J.B. Callicott, 1989, *In Defense of the Land Ethic*, Albany, New York: SUNY Press, and Carol Merchant, 1992, *Radical Ecology*, New York: Routledge, citing Peter Berg, 1983, "Bioregions," *Resurgence*, Vol. 98, May-June, p. 19. Table 8.1 on ecofeminisms can be found on pp. 184-86; For bioregionalism, see p. 218. In addition, there are various ecological subsets in the overall feminist movement. These include the Liberal, Marxist, Cultural, Socialist, etc. These also complicate the environmental ethics discourse.

7. Jerry Mander, 1991, *In the Absence of the Sacred*, San Francisco, California: Sierra Club Books.

8. Vine Deloria Jr., 1992, *God is Red*, Golden, Colorado: Fulcrum Press. In addition, see Anthony Aveni, 1953/1981, *Empires of Time: Calenders, Clocks, and Cultures*, New York: Basic Books, Inc.

9. Cornell, 1992, *supra* note 5.

10. Vandana Shiva, 1993, *Monocultures of the Mind: Perspectives on Biodiversity and Biotechnology*, New Jersey: Zed Books & Third World Network.

11. Merchant, 1992, *supra* note 6 at p. 218.

12. *Ibid.*, at p. 218.

13. Ward, Churchill, 1993, *Struggle for the Land: Indian Resistance to Genocide Ecocide and Expropriation in Contemporary North America*, Monroe, Maine, Common Courage Press, pp. 15-32.

14. I have Michael K. Green to thank for the further development of my theoretical ideas and concepts here.

15. Pam Colorado, 1988, "Bridging Native and Western Science," *Convergence*, 21, 213, pp. 49-71. Also, refer to Devón Peña's, unpublished paper, "Los Animalitos son Inteligentes: Notes Toward the Bioregional Study of the Indo-Hispano Culture in the Rio Grande Watershed," for a perspective on the Rio Grande Bioregions Project, Colorado College, Sociology Department, Colorado Springs, Colorado.

16. Mander, 1991, *supra* note 7. Also, Callicott, 1989, *supra* note 6.

17. Churchill, 1993, *supra* note 13 at p. 17.

18. Winona LaDuke, 1993, "A Society Based on Conquest Cannot Be Sustained," in Al Gedicks, 1993, *The New Resource Wars: Native Environmental Struggles Against Multinational Corporations*, Boston, Massachusetts: South End Press, pp. ix-xv.

19. Vine Deloria, Jr., 1979, *The Metaphysics of Modern Existence*, New York: Harper & Row.

20. Trask, 1993, *supra* note 2 at p. 4.

21. Winona La Duke, 1993, "Succeeding into Native North America: A Secessionist View," preface to Churchill, 1993, *supra* note 13, pp. 3-6.

22. League of Women Voters, May 1976, *Indian Country*, Washington D.C.: League of Women Voters.

23. Jim Carrier, March, 1992, *Denver Post*, "AIM Action Seared Massacre Into Our Consciousness," 5(c).

24. Women for Racial and Economic Equality (WREE), 1991, "191 Facts About U.S. Women," New York: WREE.

25. M. A. Jaimes, ed., 1992, *The State of Native America: Genocide, Colonization, and Resistance*, Boston, Massachusetts: South End Press.

26. American Indian Anti-Defamation Council Newsletter (AIADC), July 1992, Denver, Colorado: AIADC.

27. Claude Levi-Strauss, 1963, *Totemism*, Boston, Massachusetts: Beacon Press.

28. Deloria, "Trouble in High Places," in Jaimes, ed., *supra* note 25.

29. Ward Churchill and Glenn T. Morris, 1992, "Key Indian Laws and Cases," *Ibid.*, at pp. 13-21.

30. M. A. Jaimes, 1992 "La Raza and Indigenism: Alternatives to Autogenocide in North America," *Global Justice: A Publication of the Center on Rights Development*, University of Denver, Colorado: Center on Rights Development, 3, 2-3, pp. 4-19. Also see Ward Churchill, 1992, "Naming Our Destiny: Towards a Language of Indian Liberation," *Ibid.*, at pp. 22-33.

31. Gedicks, 1993, *supra* note 18.

32. Vine Deloria, Jr. and C. M. Lytle, 1984, *The Nations Within: The Past and Future of American Indian Sovereignty*, New York: Pantheon Books. Also see Churchill, 1993, *supra* note 13.

33. Peter Matthiessen, 1991, *Indian Country*, New York: Penguin Books.

34. Elizabeth Martinez, 1992, "Defending the Earth in '92: A People's Challenge to the Environmental Protection Agency," *Social Justice*, 19, 2, and Craig Kaufman, 1992, "Environmental Racism," *URSUS: The Cornell Forum for Environmental Issues*, Ithaca, New York: Cornell University, II, 1-2, pp. 29-32.

35. Churchill, 1993, *supra* note 13 at pp. 261-328.

36. Glenn T. Morris, 1991, "International Law and Politics: Toward a Right to Self-Determination for Indigenous Peoples, in Jaimes, ed., 1992, *supra* note 25 at pp. 55-86.

37. Matthiessen, 1984, *supra* note 33.

38. Mander, 1991, *supra* note 7.

39. Marianna Guerrero, 1992, "American Indian Water Rights: The Blood of Life in Native North America," in Jaimes, ed., 1992, *supra* note 25 at pp. 189-216 and LaDuke, 1992, *supra* note 18.

40. Glenn T. Morris, 1992, *supra* note 36.

41. Ward Churchill and Eliz. R. Lloyd, 1984, *Culture versus Economism: Essays on Marxism in the Multicultural Arena*, Fourth World Center for the Study of Indigenous Law and Politics, 2nd. ed., Denver, Colorado: University of Colorado at Denver.

42. Mander, 1991, *supra* note 7.

43. Anne Matthews, 1992, *Where the Buffalo Roam*, Wiedenfeld, New York: Grove.

44. M. Anette Jaimes, 1992, "Revisioning Native America: An Indigenist View of Primitivism and Industrialism," *Social Justice*, vol. 19. no. 2, pp. 5-34. Also, Warren Lowes, 1986, *Indian Giver: A Legacy of North American Native Peoples*, Penticton, British Columbia: Theytus Publishers; and Jack Weatherford, 1988, *Indian Givers: How the Indians of the Americas Transformed the World*, New York: Crown Publishers, Inc.

45. Churchill and Morris, 1992, *supra* note 29.

46. Sally Gonzales, 1992, "Intermarriage and Assimilation: The Beginning or the End?," *Wicazo Sa Review,* viii, 2, pp. 48-52. Her data indicates that among American Indians and Alaskan Natives 48 percent of the wife's race compared to 48.3 percent of the husband's marry "whites." It is 46.3 percent of the wife's race compared to 47.6 percent of the husband's who marry other "Natives." (Source: *1980 Census of Population,* Table 5:18 on Marital Characteristics).

47. Donald Grinde, Jr., and B.E. Johansen, 1991, *Exemplar of Liberty: Native American and the Evolution of Democracy,* UCLA: American Indian Studies Center.

48. Mary Shepardson, 1963, "Navajo Ways in Government: A Study in Political Process," *American Anthropologist,* Memoir 96, American Anthropological Association, 65, 3, Pt. 2.

49. Jaimes, ed., 1992, *supra* note 25.

50. This developed from the Marshall decisions in the *Cherokee* Cases of the 1830s—*Cherokee v. Georgia* 1830 and *Worcester v. Georgia* 1832. These declared the Indian groups to be "domestic dependent nations," and therefore holding a kind of "quasi-sovereign" status within the U.S. jurisdiction, if there is in fact such a status.

51. Rex Wyler, 1973, "Hopi Prophecy," in *Blood of the Land,* New York: Everest House.

52. Weatherford, 1988, *supra* note 44. Also, Laurie Ann Whitt, "Biological and Cultural Diversity: Challenges to Environmental Ethics," lecture presented at the Eighteenth Annual Bertram Morris Colloquium on Social Philosophy at the University of Colorado at Boulder, November 1993.

SUBJECT INDEX